JOHN WESLEY
Preacher

BY THE SAME AUTHOR

John Wesley in Lincolnshire
John Wesley: His Conferences and his Preachers
Studies in the Religious Poetry of the Seventeenth Century

JOHN WESLEY
Preacher

by

W. L. DOUGHTY

B.A., B.D.

'Εγένετο ἄνθρωπος ἀπεσταλμένος
παρὰ Θεοῦ, ὄνομα αὐτῷ 'Ιωάνης.
St John 1⁶

WIPF & STOCK · Eugene, Oregon

Wipf and Stock Publishers
199 W 8th Ave, Suite 3
Eugene, OR 97401

John Wesley
Preacher
By Doughty, W. L.
Copyright©1955 Methodist Publishing - Epworth Press
ISBN 13: 978-1-4982-0754-6
Publication date 1/28/2015
Previously published by Epworth Press, 1955

Every effort has been made to trace the current copyright
owner of this publication but without success. If you have any
information or interest in the copyright, please contact the publishers.

TO MY DEAR WIFE

PHYLLIS EILEEN

to whom I owe so much of the happiness of twenty-five years

ABBREVIATIONS

Journal.   *The Journal of the Rev. John Wesley, A.M.* Edited by Nehemiah Curnock. Standard Edition. 8 volumes. (The Epworth Press.)

Letters.   *The Letters of the Rev. John Wesley, A.M.* Edited by John Telford. Standard Edition. 8 volumes. (The Epworth Press.)

M.H.B.   *The Methodist Hymn-book* (1933).

M.H.B. (*1779*).   *A Collection of Hymns for the Use of the People called Methodists.* (The first complete Methodist Hymn-book.)

Mins.   Vol. I of *Minutes of the Methodist Conference.* Edition published in 1862. This volume contains all surviving *Minutes of Conference*, from the first in 1744 to 1798.

P.W.   *The Poetical Works of John and Charles Wesley.* Edited by George Osborn, D.D. (1868–1872). 13 volumes.

W.H.S.   *The Proceedings of the Wesley Historical Society.*

Works.   *The Works of the Rev. John Wesley, A.M.* Edition 1872. 14 vols.

W.M.M.   *The Wesleyan Methodist Magazine.* From 1778, when publication began, to 1797, its title was *The Arminian Magazine.* From 1798 to 1821 it was *The Methodist Magazine.* In 1822 it became *The Wesleyan Methodist Magazine.* When Methodist union took place it reverted to the title of 1798. The letters *W.M.M.* refer to the Magazine, whatever its exact title in the year of reference.

Veterans.   *Wesley's Veterans.* 7 volumes. (The Epworth Press.) These are reprints, newly edited by John Telford, of *Lives of the early Methodist Preachers.*

CONTENTS

	PREFACE	ix
I.	THE ANCESTRAL BACKGROUND	1
II.	PREPARATORY YEARS	9
III.	SHADOWS OF COMING EVENTS	19
IV.	THE VALLEY OF INDECISION	30
V.	THE OPEN ROAD	36
VI.	WESLEY'S APOLOGIA FOR FIELD-PREACHING	45
VII.	WESLEY'S CONGREGATIONS	57
VIII.	MOBS AND HOOLIGANS	74
IX.	JOHN WESLEY'S SUBJECTS	84
X.	A CLOUD OF WITNESSES	107
XI.	SOME EFFECTS OF WESLEY'S PREACHING	128
XII.	SERVICE: SERMON: STYLE	136
XIII.	VOICE AND GESTURE	146
XIV.	ILLUSTRATIONS AND QUOTATIONS	153
XV.	THE PUBLISHED SERMONS	160
XVI.	EARLY MORNING PREACHING	168
XVII.	GOSPEL SERMONS	173
XVIII.	(*a*) LONG SERMONS, (*b*) ITINERANCY, (*c*) FREQUENCY	177
XIX.	OLD SERMONS	181
XX.	THE SERMON REGISTER	185
XXI.	SIDELIGHTS ON WESLEY'S PREACHING	188
XXII.	EVENSONG	195
XXIII.	AVE ATQUE VALE	207
	INDEX OF NAMES	212
	GENERAL INDEX	214

PREFACE

IT MAY well be that more *Lives* have been written of John Wesley than of anyone else, if we include the many books about him and his work. The present volume is not a *Life*, but is concerned to present him in the chief of his many activities, that of a Christian Preacher. A knowledge of the general course of his life is assumed, but that is not essential on the part of the reader nor need the lack of it diminish his interest, for the facts relevant to the subject appear naturally in their proper place.

In the year 1905 the Religious Tract Society published a book with a title similar to that of this volume—*John Wesley: Evangelist*. The writer was the Rev. Richard Green, an eminent authority on Methodist history and the Governor of Didsbury College from 1888 to 1899. In the preface the author states that his book 'is not designed to be in any true sense a Life'. Such was his intention, but he was not wholly successful in carrying it out. What he wrote is a deeply sympathetic and moving account of John Wesley, biographical in character, particularly for the first thirty-eight years of his life, and thereafter a continuation of the biography with special reference to Wesley's evangelistic work. It is regrettable that this beautifully written and valuable book has long been out of print.

The present work, on the other hand, keeps faith with its title; it is a *Study*, not a *Life*, and in no sense a re-presentation of Richard Green's work. There is much more material available for the purpose than could be embodied in a volume of reasonable compass, but what I have selected is representative of the whole.

An adequate treatment of Wesley's regard for and use of the Bible would have added unduly to the size of this book. It is, however, an important and relevant subject, on which I hope to issue a small volume in the near future.

As the book goes to press I have one deep regret. A few years ago I addressed the Birmingham Ministers' Fraternal on this subject, and the late Dr Wilbert F. Howard urged me then, and on several subsequent occasions, to prepare for publication the store of material that I had in hand. My hope was that, when the time came, there would have been a prefatory note by him to this book. That cannot be, but I wish to put on record that I owe much to his friendly encouragement.

I trust that this study of John Wesley as a Preacher will be of help and interest not only to readers generally, but to young Methodists in particular, and especially to those who are either in, or hoping to be in, the ranks of the Ministry or the Local Preachers. May it inspire them to seek a growing acquaintance with and a deeper understanding of the Founder of Methodism! So may their Ministry be enriched and blessed by God!

I am gratefully indebted to the following for permission to quote from published works: Mr Siegfried Sassoon (*Collected Poems*, 1947); Methuen and Co. (*Companion into Oxfordshire*, by E. C. Williams); The Epworth Press (*Samuel Wesley: Musician*, by J. T. Lightwood); A. M. Heath and Co. (*The Structure of Religious Experience*, by J. MacMurray); Dr S. G. Dimond (*The Psychology of Methodism*); Dr J. E. Rattenbury (*The Conversion of the Wesleys*); Dr T. B. Shepherd (*Methodism and the Literature of the Eighteenth Century*).

I am also grateful to the officials of The Epworth Press for their helpful courtesy, and to my wife and my daughters Anne and Judy for assistance in reading proofs.

W.L.D.

LONDON
July 1954

CHAPTER I

THE ANCESTRAL BACKGROUND

ANYONE turning to G. J. Stevenson's *Memorials of the Wesley Family* for information about John Wesley's antecedents is likely to receive a mild shock as he unfolds the vast sheet on which the Wesley pedigree is set forth. It begins in the year A.D. 938, and the erudite Dr Adam Clarke actually traces the name back to the Arabic language, in a root meaning *union* and *conjunction*. Here is ample material upon which the reader may exercise his imagination, for the pedigree includes the names of monks, priests, at least one abbot of a monastery, and a Crusader; at a later date, a chaplain to King Edward the Fourth and others in holy orders. These people are, however, little more than names, until we come to the immediate ancestors of John Wesley, who have been described as 'respectable for learning, conspicuous for piety, and firmly attached to those virtues of Christianity which they had formed from the sacred Scriptures'.[1]

John Wesley's great-grandfather, Bartholomew, was born about the year 1595 and died about 1680. After the Stuart restoration he was ejected from the living of Charmouth, in Dorset, but continued to preach in remote places to those who, like himself, suffered because of loyalty to religious and political convictions.

His only child, John, after a course at Oxford, became, by invitation of the parishioners, the minister of Winterborn-Whitchurch, in Dorset. At that time, episcopal ordination was not a necessary qualification for the ministry of the English Church, but candidates had to be approved locally and also to satisfy Cromwell's 'Triers'[2] as to their fitness for the office. After securing this approval and being appointed to the living in May 1658, John Wesley appears to have offended certain local and influential people because, acting entirely within his rights, he had discarded the Liturgy and used presbyterian or Independent forms of worship. In 1661 he was summoned to wait upon

---

[1] Adam Clarke, *The Wesley Family* (Edit. 1836), I.21.
[2] See Richard Baxter's *Autobiography*, I.vi.

Dr Gilbert Ironside, the Bishop of Bristol, and he made a careful transcript of the conversation which took place between them. The main point at issue was *episcopal ordination*, which the Bishop maintained was necessary in order to regularize Wesley's preaching, but which the latter refused to receive, mainly because it carried with it obligation to perform certain clerical functions beside those of the preacher and the pastor. Wesley held that he was called to the *work* of the Ministry, though not to the *office*, adding, 'there is, as we believe, *vocatio ad opus, et ad munus*'. For proof of the validity of a separate call to preach, he challenged the Bishop:

If it please your lordship to lay down any evidence of godliness agreeing with the Scriptures, and if they be not found in those persons intended (viz., to whom he had ministered), I am content to be discharged from my ministry. I will stand or fall by the issue thereof.[3]

Here was a man who had the indubitable call to preach; a direct spiritual descendant of St Paul and the Apostles. He had received no 'call' to the work of an ordinary incumbent, and his own people recognized this. He was what they wanted him to be— an evangelist, with no 'priestly' pretensions. So long as he be allowed to preach, it mattered to him not a jot whether he were regarded as a layman or as a cleric. He lived in an atmosphere where such distinctions are very thin. Not only was he an itinerant preacher, going where he was moved or invited, to proclaim 'Christ Crucified', but he gathered religious societies together in several places and called himself a 'son of the prophets'. He laid great stress on the three credentials of a preaching ministry: Grace, Gifts, and Fruit—all of which he possessed in a marked degree. Every student of Methodism who meditates upon the life of this humble, godly, and competent man, will agree with Adam Clarke's comment: 'He was in conduct a kind of *epitome of Methodism*, in mode of preaching, matter, manner, and success.'[4]

Soon after his interview with the Bishop of Bristol he was deprived of his living and he and his family suffered grievously under the wicked acts of the Stuart restoration. Poverty, concealment, imprisonment, and social ostracism marked his closing years, and he died in 1678 at the age of forty-two.

His wife had intimate Church connexions, her father being

[3] Adam Clarke, *supra*, pp. 37ff. [4] ibid., p. 49.

the Rev. John White, who, after his university course, preached in and around Oxford—another itinerant preacher! In 1606 he was appointed to the living of Trinity Church, Dorchester. It is interesting to notice that in 1630, at the instigation of Archbishop Laud, he was prosecuted for preaching against Arminianism, a 'crime' for which his great-grandsons, John and Charles Wesley, made ample atonement.

Our information about the family of John Wesley of Winterborn-Whitchurch is confined to two sons: Matthew, who became a physician and lived mainly in London, and Samuel, who became the Rector of Epworth and the father of John and Charles Wesley of the Methodist Revival. In Samuel's life there is little of that adventurous element which characterized the lives of his father and grandfather. The more settled times in which he lived afforded less opportunity, but that he was of similar metal is beyond doubt. He was a man of sturdy, reasoned, and independent opinions, who discovered that his spiritual and ecclesiastical needs were better met in the Establishment than in Dissent. It may well have been that the trials and tribulations of his father, which he was bound in some degree to share and which must have deprived him of a large measure of that youthful joy and ease of circumstance which a child in a Christian country has a right to expect, were factors in determining his future spiritual allegiance. Honourable his motives must have been, but it was no primrose path that lay before him. He was relegated to comparative obscurity, his lot being cast among people with whom, culturally, he had nothing in common, and who went out of their way to do him ferocious harm; relegated, too, to a remote part of the country that afforded next to no scope for the healthy exercise of his abilities, which, in consequence, suffered at times from inhibitions or sought expression in such futile occupations as the compilation of his ponderous *Dissertations on the Book of Job*. His 'call' was to the full ministerial office; he made no such distinction as that of his father, between the *vocatio ad opus* and the *vocatio ad munus*. He was what some people would call today a 'faithful parish priest'. We know that he preached *sound doctrine*, and failed not to point out to his congregation the sins and failings of their lives. He confined his activities to his own two parishes of Epworth and Wroot and there is no indication that he ever became restive under those parochial restraints which impelled his forebears to exercise an itinerant ministry and his son to claim the world as his parish. As a preacher, we are told that 'with invincible power he confirmed the wavering and confuted heretics. . . . His style was sweet and manly, soft without satiety, and learned without pedantry.'[5] When he was lodged in Lincoln jail for debt, against which he had struggled for years in vain, he wrote to Archbishop Sharpe, of York:

> I do not despair of doing some good here, and it may be I shall do more in this new parish than in my old one; for I have leave to read prayers every morning and afternoon in the prison, and to preach once on Sunday, which I choose to do in the afternoon, when there is no sermon at the minster.[6]

Fortunately we have a letter of advice which Samuel Wesley wrote to a young ordinand. The directions about preaching exhibit the author's own views and are exceptionally revealing, amounting here and there to self-confession. He points out that Preaching is

> not, indeed, the whole of a Minister's office, but a great part of it: for to this very thing we are ordained, 'Take thou authority to preach the word of God'.
>
> *A general method for sermons.* Your best that I can think on, is to begin a course as accurate as you can make them, on all the principles of religion, so as to comprise, as near as may be, the whole body of divinity. . . . These sermons may be best written, or rather copied . . . on one side of a large quarto and the other blank, for additions and alterations; as you will see great occasion for both, as you increase in knowledge and judgement; and that perhaps to the last moment of your life.

Subject and text having been determined upon,

> you should humbly and earnestly pray unto God to assist you . . . and then *fall to in the name of God*. And the first thing I would set about should be the short plan or outline of the sermon: the explication of the text and context should not be over short, but of a just length. . . . The propositions or doctrines, which would not be too long or too many, and the clearer the better, include and open the main drift of the design. The illustrations should be proper and lively; the proofs close and home; the motives strong and cogent; the inferences and application natural, and yet laboured with all the force of sacred eloquence. . . .
> If you would be popular, you must get your sermons without

[5] Luke Tyerman, *The Life and Times of Samuel Wesley*, p. 139.
[6] ibid., p. 301.

book . . . which less than a twelvemonth's practice would make much more easy than you can now imagine.

When John Wesley was preparing for ordination his father sent him a copy of this letter. So thoroughly did the former approve of the advice given that years later he published the letter with a commendatory preface by himself.[7]

The reverence with which Samuel Wesley regarded the preaching office is further exemplified in a letter which he wrote in 1706 to his eldest son, also Samuel, who was contemplating offering for the Christian ministry.

You are to be very attentive to the sermon, because you know in whose name and by whose commission it is delivered; and faith and obedience, too, come by hearing: this being God's ordinance for the conversion of mankind, and the Church's edification, or increase in charity and knowledge.[8]

Quite the most important and far-reaching event in the life of Samuel Wesley was his marriage, in 1688, to Susanna, the youngest daughter of Dr Samuel Annesley, one of the best-known, most highly honoured and erudite Nonconformist divines of his day. He had been driven out of the National Church by the same harsh measures that had operated against the Wesleys, chiefly the Act of Uniformity. We know that his preaching was thoroughly evangelical and he had many seals to his ministry.

Susanna must have been one of the most extraordinary women of her time. By the early age of fourteen she had *reasoned* herself into an attachment to the Established Church, her loyalty to and affection for which never wavered. She was eminently fitted to be the mother of outstanding preachers. In these days she would have had opportunities of proving her own fitness for the preaching office, which did not exist for women in the eighteenth century. There was at least one occasion when she showed clearly what powers she possessed.

In November 1710 Samuel Wesley went to London, leaving his curate, Inman, in charge of the parish. The preaching of this young man was far from giving satisfaction, being chiefly concerned with the paying of debts and acting the part of good neighbour. Attendance at the Parish Church declined, and Susanna Wesley decided to make up, as far as possible, for this

[7] Thomas Jackson, *Life of Charles Wesley*, II.525. See also Richard Green's *Bibliography*, No. 4.
[8] G. J. Stevenson, *Memorials of the Wesley Family*, p. 99.

deplorable lack of religious instruction and edification. She therefore instituted a Sunday-evening service for her own family and domestic staff in the kitchen of the rectory. Others, hearing of it, sought permission to attend, and Mrs Wesley though dubious at first about the wisdom of such an innovation, felt she could not, as a Christian, refuse. By the end of January the number attending was about two hundred. It was an informal kind of gathering, at which Mrs Wesley read a sermon. The disgruntled curate wrote to the Rector, complaining that she had turned the rectory into a conventicle. Thereupon Samuel Wesley wrote to his wife, suggesting that someone else should read the sermon. Her rejoinders were effective and unanswerable. In face of the spiritual needs of the men and women of the parish, the objections that her husband had advanced (such as the oddness of the proceedings, her sex, his own official position), are of little weight. As for the sermon: 'I do not think one man among them could read a sermon without spelling a good part of it.' She explains how the gatherings began and the numbers increased, and adds:

I never durst positively presume to hope that God would make use of me as an instrument in doing good; the farthest I ever durst go was, 'It may be: who can tell? With God all things are possible. I will resign myself to Him'; or, as Herbert better expresses it—

> Only, since God doth often make
> Of *lowly matter*, for *high uses meet*,
>   I throw me at His feet;
> There will I lie until my Maker seek
> For some *mean stuff* whereon to show His skill;
>   Then is *my* time.

And thus I rested, without passing any reflection on myself, or forming any judgement about the success or event of this undertaking.

Inman wrote a second letter to the Rector, in which he asked him to *command* the discontinuance of the services, and Samuel Wesley appears to have suggested this course to his wife without actually ordering it. Her reply is a masterpiece of cogent reasoning and heart-felt pleading and she concludes:

If you do, after all, think fit to dissolve this assembly, do not tell me that you *desire* me to do it, for that will not satisfy my conscience; but *send me your positive command, in such full and express terms as may absolve me from all guilt and punishment, for neglecting this opportunity of doing good, when you and I shall appear before the great and awful tribunal of our Lord Jesus Christ.*[9]

Before such a challenge the Rector's luke-warm opposition gave way and the services continued. The impression is inescapable that Susanna Wesley had gifts of self-expression beyond the ordinary and it is certain that she had very positive and enlightened ideas about preaching and the call to preach. Years later, when, as a widow, she was living at the Foundery house in London with her son John, she heard Thomas Maxfield preach. He was one of the first-fruits of John Wesley's ministry in Bristol, and Wesley had appointed him to meet the Society in London, to pray with the members and give them needful advice during his absence. Presently it was reported to Wesley that Maxfield was *preaching*. Disturbed, as his father had been years before, at such irregularity, he hastily returned to London determined to put a stop to such presumptuous proceedings, and burst in upon his mother, exclaiming: 'Thomas Maxfield has turned preacher, I find.' She looked at him attentively and replied:

John, you know what my sentiments have been. You cannot suspect me of favouring readily anything of this kind. But take care what you do with respect to that young man, for he is as surely called of God to preach as you are. Examine what have been the fruits of his preaching and hear him yourself.

John took her advice. Hitherto he had regarded preaching as permissible only to those episcopally ordained, but 'his prejudice bowed before the force of truth, and he could only say, *It is the Lord, let him do what seemeth him good*'.[10]

So Susanna had much to do with founding the race of Methodist Preachers, for from that moment her son perceived that here lay ready to his hand a mighty instrument for the accomplishment of his purposes, and one without which his work would soon have become impossible nor could Methodism ever have been born.

As we should expect, in her wonderful letters to her sons Susanna touched occasionally upon the subject of preaching. She wrote to John, in 1727:

Suffer now a word of advice. However curious you may be in searching into the nature, or in distinguishing the properties of the passions or virtues of human kind for your own private satisfaction, be very

[9] Adam Clarke, *supra*, II.88 and following.
[10] Henry Moore, *Life of John Wesley*, I.505.

cautious in giving nice distinctions in public assemblies; for it does not answer the true end of preaching, which is to mend men's lives, and not fill their heads with unprofitable speculations. And after all that can be said, every affection of the soul is better known by experience than any description that can be given of it. An honest man will more easily apprehend what is meant by being zealous for God and against sin, when he hears what are the properties and effects of true zeal, than the most accurate definition of its essence.[11]

Eight years later and two months before the death of his father she wrote an impressive letter to John, chiefly on the universal need for a Redeemer, remarking:

Here, surely, you may give scope to your spirits: here you may freely use your Christian liberty, and discourse without reserve of the excellency of the knowledge and love of Christ, as His Spirit gives you utterance. . . . Let us speak boldly, without fear. These truths ought to be frequently inculcated and pressed home upon the consciences of men; and when once men are affected with a sense of redeeming love, that sense will powerfully convince them of the vanity of the world, and make them esteem the honour, wealth and pleasures of it as dross or dung, so that they may win Christ.[12]

We cannot wonder that this great Christian woman should bear such children as those who, under God, brought the Methodist Church into existence. We feel that, given the opportunity and encouragement which her age denied to her, Susanna Wesley could have proclaimed the Gospel that her life adorned as powerfully and persuasively from the pulpit as she set it forth with urgency and lucidity in her letters to her sons. After her death John Wesley justly remarked of her: 'I cannot but further observe that even she (as well as her father and grandfather, her husband, and her three sons) had been, in her measure and degree, a preacher of righteousness.'[13]

[11] Adam Clarke, *supra*, II.25.   [12] ibid., p. 29.   [13] *Journal*, III.32.

CHAPTER II

PREPARATORY YEARS

FROM THE previous chapter we learn that there were strong, hereditary forces helping to shape the career of John Wesley, with 'ancestral voices prophesying war' against the Kingdom of Darkness; voices of medieval churchmen, of the Reformed Church of England, and of the finer elements among the Puritan sectaries.

Our approach to Wesley as a preacher would be both simplified and vivified had the gramophone invaded our civilization two hundred years earlier. What a thrill would be ours could we listen to his recorded voice addressing the crowds in Gwennap Pit or on Tyneside! As it is, we are largely dependent for our knowledge of him as a preacher upon his own scattered references in his *Journal*, *Diaries*, and *Letters*, with a few supplementary comments by contemporaries who heard him. There is, however, another indirect, valuable and reliable source of information: Wesley's advice and instructions to others on the art of preaching. These are abundant, and we may be sure that, for the most part, he spoke out of his own experience and gave advice which he himself had beneficially followed.

Wesley received deacon's orders in the Church of England on 19th September 1725 and preached his first sermon at South Lye, or Leigh, near Witney, on the following Sunday, 26th September. Arriving at the church on horseback he presented his credentials, signed by Bishop Potter, and preached from 'an exquisitely neat little manuscript'.[1] Ethel Carleton Williams, in her book, *Companion into Oxfordshire*, enables her readers to join in imagination in the service of that day. We enter the village church, where

an inscription on the pulpit recalls a mid-September day in the year 1725, when a young deacon entered the pulpit to preach his first sermon. The congregation saw a short, slim figure with rosy cheeks and hair falling in long locks to his shoulders, and bright, piercing eyes. What manner of sermon was it, one wonders, that those farm-labourers

[1] *Journal*, I.60.

and their wives heard? ... Little though they guessed it, they were listening to one whose sermons were soon to resound throughout the length and breadth of England. For the preacher was none other than John Wesley, whose dauntless courage and tireless energy were to awaken the country from the religious apathy into which it had fallen.

Seemingly the writer was unaware that the manuscript of the sermon still exists and has been published *in facsimile*. The text is St Matthew 6^{33}, on seeking first the Kingdom of God. It is a pleasant, neat, compact and ingenuous little discourse, to which exception could hardly be taken, and one calculated to make such of Wesley's hearers as understood him feel happy and comfortable; a sermon couched in Scripture language, containing many Scripture quotations and adaptations and full of good advice, but lacking that pungent exposition of the central doctrines of the Christian Faith that was presently to characterize his preaching and, metaphorically, to 'shake the gates of hell'.

Thereafter his *Diary* records services conducted and sermons preached in various churches. The references are very meagre. He 'writ' a sermon and 'preached', with no note of any distinguishing feature of the service or any comment on his own feelings about the sermon or the effects it may have produced. He appears either to have read his sermons or memorized them for delivery.... We know that he preached occasionally in certain Cotswold villages, especially at Broadway, Buckland and Stanton, in whose vicarages he was always a welcome guest. The first record of a 'preaching Sunday' in his *Diary* is under date 3rd October 1725: 'Preached and read prayers at Fleet Marston.' On 15th February 1727 he conducted service in Broadway Parish Church and preached a funeral sermon for 'Robin' Griffiths, who had died suddenly, early in the year—one of his own particular friends and the son of the Rector.[2] During the period of his diaconate Wesley courageously preached a sermon in Wroot Parish Church, of which his father was the incumbent, implicitly denouncing Samuel Wesley's merciless treatment of his daughter Hetty. By its Christian charity it amply atoned for any lack of filial respect on the part of the preacher.[3]

On 22nd September 1728 Wesley was ordained by Dr Potter, Bishop of Oxford, to the full ministry of the Established Church. He remained in the city about three months, but, apart from that,

---

[2] See Elsie Harrison, *Son to Susanna*, Chap. 9. Also *W.M.M.* (1797), p. 425.
[3] See A. Quiller Couch, *Hetty Wesley*, Bk. III, Ch. 14.

from August 1727 to November 1729, he served his father as the curate at Wroot, this being his only experience of parish work in England.

During this period he preached a sermon on *Corrupting the Word of God* (2 Cor. 2¹⁷). It is valuable for our purpose, as establishing certain principles of expository preaching which Wesley observed to the end of his life. Luke Tyerman thus indicates the main points:

Among corrupters:
1. Those who introduce into it 'human mixtures, and blend with the oracles of God impure dreams, fit only for the mouth of the devil'.
2. Those who mix it with false interpretations.
3. Those who do not add to it, but take from it, 'washing their hands of stubborn texts, that will not bend to their purposes, or that too plainly touch upon the reigning vices of the places where they live'.

Those who do not corrupt the Word of God 'preach it genuine and unmixed', unimpaired and in all its fullness. 'They speak with plainness and boldness, and are not concerned to palliate their doctrine to reconcile it to the tastes of men. They will not, they dare not, soften a threatening so as to prejudice its strength; neither represent sin in such mild colours as to impair its native blackness.'[4]

When, in 1746, the Wesley of the 'warmed heart' looked back upon this period of his life, he passed this judgement:

From the year 1725 to 1729 I preached much, but saw no fruit of my labour. Indeed, it could not be that I should; for I neither laid the foundation of repentance, nor of believing the gospel; taking it for granted, that all to whom I preached were believers, and that many of them 'needed no repentance'.[5]

The years 1729 to 1734 were devoted to tutorial work at Oxford, during which he sought to make his students genuine, practising Christians. On his return from Lincolnshire to the University he had found that little company gathered around his brother Charles which we know as the Holy Club, and naturally, inevitably, John assumed the leadership. The story of how the members spared not themselves in good works, devotional exercises, Bible study and religious instruction is well known, and yet John Wesley, reviewing these years in 1746, comments:

Laying a deeper foundation of repentance I saw a little fruit. But it was only a little, and no wonder: for I did not preach faith in the covenant.[6]

[4] *Life and Times of John Wesley*, I.56. [5] *Works*, VIII.468. [6] ibid.

Richard Green records the description given by someone who examined a number of unpublished sermons, written by Wesley during the ten years that followed his ordination. It states that

> in not one of them is there any view whatever, any glimpse afforded of Christ in any of his offices. His name occurs in the benediction. That is about all. Frequent communion is insisted on as a source of spiritual quickening; regeneration by baptism is assumed as the true doctrine of the Church; but Christ is nowhere, either in his life, his death or his intercession. Church formalism and strict morality, ceremonies and ethics, are all in all.[7]

The years 1734 to 1738 are vitally important in Wesley's life. In 1735 he met George Whitefield. On 25th April of that year his father died. Earlier in the same year circumstances had compelled him to attempt extemporary preaching. He had attended Allhallows Church in Lombard Street, to hear Dr Heylyn preach. As the Doctor failed to appear, 'I preached ... at the earnest request of the churchwardens, to a numerous congregation. ... This was the first time that, having no notes about me, I preached extempore.'[8] On Sunday 28th January 1776 he preached again in this church, and, whilst putting on his gown in the vestry, said to Mr Thomas Letts:

> It is fifty years, sir, since I first preached in this church. I remember it from a peculiar circumstance that occurred at that time. I came without a sermon, and going up the pulpit steps I hesitated, and returned into the vestry under much mental confusion and agitation. A woman who was there noticed that I was deeply agitated, and she inquired, 'Pray, sir, what is the matter with you?' I replied, 'I have not brought a sermon with me.' Putting her hand upon my shoulder she said, 'Is that all? Cannot you trust God for a sermon?' That question had such an effect upon me that I ascended the pulpit and preached extempore, with great freedom to myself and acceptance to the people, and I have never since taken a written sermon into the pulpit.[9]

On 14th October 1735 John and Charles Wesley and their companions embarked for Georgia, but weather conditions were such that they did not finally leave English harbours until 10th December. During this long waiting period they were actively regardful of the spiritual welfare of those on board. John wrote in his *Journal* for 19th October: 'I now first preached extempore

---

[7] Richard Green, *John Wesley: Evangelist*, p. 134.
[8] *Journal*, VI.96.   [9] *W.M.M.* (1825), pp. 105–6.

(evidently as a regular practice) to a numerous and, as it then seemed, serious congregation.' Some people presently objected to 'so much expounding', and Wesley says: 'We proposed to them fairly to leave it off. This they utterly protested against, and desired us to go on as we began, which I did till we came out to sea.' This was on 10th December, when they sailed from Cowes and encountered heavy seas in the Bay of Biscay. For a great part of the voyage thereafter storms prevented regular worship, but when the opportunity arose Wesley preached, one occasion being on Christmas Day.

During the outward journey Wesley also wrote sermons, many of which are included in the Standard Volumes. From one of his companions, Ingham, we learn that 'during the voyage Wesley went over our Saviour's Sermon on the Mount', which he later expounded in thirteen discourses.

Looking back upon his spiritual state during the voyage to America, Wesley wrote in his *Journal*, immediately before the account of his 'conversion' on 24th May 1738:

On shipboard, however, I was again active in outward works; where it pleased God of his free mercy to give me twenty-six of the Moravian brethren for companions, who endeavoured to show me 'a more excellent way'. But I understood it not at first. I was too learned and too wise. So that it seemed foolishness unto me. And I continued preaching, and following after, and trusting in, that righteousness whereby no flesh can be justified.

On 5th February 1736, the long voyage ended and on Sunday 7th March Wesley wrote:

I entered upon my ministry at Savannah by preaching on the Epistle for the day, being the 13th of the first of Corinthians. In the second lesson (Luke 18) was our Lord's prediction of the treatment which He Himself (and consequently His followers) was to meet with from the world; and His gracious promise to those who are content, *nudi nudum Christum sequi*: 'Verily I say unto you, There is no man that hath left houses, or friends, or brethren, or wife, or children for the kingdom of God's sake, who shall not receive manifold more in this present time, and in the world to come life everlasting.'

Yet, notwithstanding these plain declarations of our Lord, notwithstanding my own repeated experience, notwithstanding the experience of all the sincere followers of Christ whom I have ever talked with, or read or heard of; nay, and the reason of the thing evincing to a demonstration that all who love not the light must hate Him who is continually labouring to pour it in upon them; I do here bear witness against myself, that when I saw the number of people crowding into the church, the deep attention with which they received the word, and the seriousness that afterwards sat on all their faces, I could scarce refrain from giving the lie to experience and reason and Scripture all together. I could hardly believe that the greater part of this attentive, serious people would hereafter trample underfoot that word, and say all manner of evil falsely of him that spake it. (viz. John Wesley.)

From the outset of his ministry in Georgia Wesley comported himself as the model 'parish priest', with immediate and disastrous consequences. Being now his own master in ecclesiastical affairs he set his face sternly against the abuses, irregularities and negligences that had offended him at home, by enforcing the rubrics in every particular. We know that he carefully prepared his sermons. The *Journal* for 11th April 1736 records:

I preached at the new storehouse (Frederica) on the first verse of the Gospel for the day, 'Which of you convinceth me of sin? and if I say the truth, why do ye not believe me?' There was a large congregation whom I endeavoured to convince of unbelief, by simply proposing the conditions of salvation as they are laid down in Scripture, and appealing to their hearts whether they believed they could be saved on no other terms.

This is probably generally descriptive of his preaching in America. He assumed, with an ease and feasibility that are impossible today, that he and his congregation shared a common belief in the final and supreme authority of all Scripture. Therefore, having selected a suitable text, he expounded it to them; challenged them to instant, personal decision, fixing the onus of choice or rejection upon them. He was 'clear of their blood'. It was the method of the logician, lacking the warm and winning appeal that only emotional conviction can give.

Shortly before Wesley sailed for Georgia he received a long letter of instruction and advice from Dr Burton, a distinguished scholar and an old friend. As one of the trustees of the colony he had introduced Wesley to General Oglethorpe, the Governor, and had been eager in promoting his appointment. It is the letter of a wise, far-sighted Christian gentleman, and one can only wonder that John Wesley failed to take it thoroughly to heart. On Wesley's duties as a Christian minister and preacher he wrote:

The apostolic manner of preaching from house to house will, through God's grace, be effectual to turn many to righteousness. You come to a people, some ignorant and most disposed to licentiousness. . . . The generality of the people are babes in the progress of their Christian life, to be fed with milk instead of strong meat. The wise householder will bring out of his stores food proportioned to the necessities of his family. The circumstances of your present Christian pilgrimage will furnish the most affecting subjects of discourse, and what arises *pro re nata* will have greater influence than a laboured discourse on a subject in which men think themselves not so immediately concerned. . . . It is to be observed that historical narratives gain attention more than other sorts of discourses, and insensibly convey with them the good moral which often miscarries under other sorts of conveyance. Of this kind was our Saviour's preaching in parables to the people.

With regard to the behaviour and manner of address, that must be determined according to the different circumstances of persons, etc.; but you will always in the use of means consider the greatest end, and therefore your applications will, of course, vary. You will keep in view the pattern of the gospel preacher, St Paul, who became all things to all men, that he might gain some. Here is a nice trial of Christian prudence. Accordingly, in every case you would distinguish between what is essential and what is merely circumstantial to Christianity; between what is indispensable and what is variable; between what is divine and what is of human authority.[10]

Wesley endorsed this letter, 'Mr. Burton. Sept. 28. 1735. Advice concerning Georgia.' Had he but taken it, how different the story of Georgia might have been! His reply was written on 10th October, in the course of which he remarks:

My chief motive, to which all the rest are subordinate, is the hope of saving my own soul. I hope to learn the true sense of the gospel of Christ, by preaching it to the heathen. They have no comments to construe away the text, no vain philosophy to corrupt it, no luxurious, sensual, covetous, ambitious expounders to soften its unpleasing truth, to reconcile earthly-mindedness and faith, the Spirit of Christ and the spirit of the world. They have no duty, no interest to serve, and are therefore fit to receive the gospel in its simplicity. They are as little children, humble, willing to learn and eager to do the will of God, and consequently they shall know of every doctrine I preach whether it be of God. By these therefore I hope to learn the purity of that faith which was once delivered to the saints; the genuine sense and full extent of those laws which none can understand who mind earthly things.[11]

[10] *Journal*, VIII.287.   [11] ibid., pp. 288–9.

The day was at hand when Wesley was to discover how far this idealistic dream was from reality. It is likely that he had Dr Burton's letter in mind when, on 24th January 1738, while on the homeward voyage, he wrote in his *Journal* a kind of review of his Georgia ministry, and it seemed to him that some of his mistakes had been:

1. Making antiquity a co-ordinate rather than subordinate rule with Scripture. 2. Admitting several doubtful writings as undoubted evidences of antiquity. 3. Extending antiquity too far, even to the middle or end of the fourth century. 4. Believing more practices to have been universal in the ancient Church than ever were so.

He was still moving in shallow waters and concerned with comparative trivialities from which acceptance of Dr Burton's advice would have helped to deliver him.

As the *Journal* continues we become increasingly aware of public opposition. The outspoken directness and disciplinary measures of their spiritual leader had aroused resentment in certain influential quarters. Thus, Wesley tells how on Sunday 19th June 1736, 'I summed up what I had seen or heard of at Frederica inconsistent with Christianity, and, consequently, with the prosperity of the place. The event was as it ought: some of the hearers were profited and the rest deeply offended.' The old accusation was made, that Wesley was attacking individuals: sure sign that some of his shafts were striking home!

A year later, in spite of the gathering clouds, Wesley's outlook upon his work was distinctly optimistic. On 29th March 1737, he wrote to a Mrs Chapman:

I feed my brethren in Christ, as he giveth me power, with the pure, unmixed milk of his Word; and those who are as little children receive it, not as the word of man, but as the word of God. Some grow thereby, and advance apace in peace and holiness: they grieve, it is true, for those who did run well but are now turned back; and they fear for themselves, lest they also be tempted; yet, through the mercy of God, they despair not, but have still a good hope that they will endure to the end.

On 16th June he wrote to James Hutton:

I think our Lord is beginning to lift up his standard against the flood of iniquity which hath long covered the earth. Even in this place it hath pleased him in some measure to stir up his might and come and help us. There is a strange *motus animorum*, as it seems, continually increasing. Those 'who fear the Lord speak often together', and many of them are not ashamed of the gospel of Christ in the midst of an adulterous and sinful generation. The enemy hath great wrath and rageth much. May it be a sign that his time is short! One or two whom he has long seemed to lead captive at his will are just now recovering out of his snare, and declare openly without fear or shame that they will not serve him but the living God.

But the end of Wesley's Georgia ministry was at hand, with whose distressing details we are not concerned. On 30th September 1737, he wrote:

Having ended the *Homilies*, I began reading Dr Rogers's eight sermons to the congregation, hoping they might be a timely antidote against the poison of infidelity which was now with great industry propagated among us.

It may well be that the mental turmoil of these weeks made pulpit preparation impossible, so unlike the authentic John Wesley is the preaching of other people's sermons.

Life in Georgia had been to Wesley a season of profit and loss, and amongst the gains Nehemiah Curnock notes that 'he wrote with the utmost care many of his finest sermons, not a few of which are studied today'. In a review of Wesley's ministry in Georgia the same writer gives his own impressions of him as a preacher at this time.

It was a ministry partly settled and parochial, partly itinerant and episcopal. It was a ministry of lofty purposes and great conceptions of duty; a ministry that gathered its ideals from the earliest centuries of church history; a ministry priestly and dominant, yet severely controlled by law, usage, and by a remorseless pursuit of duty—always remorseless save when, in spite of himself, the priest became a man, and the pathway was traversed by affection and human weakness. Underneath the steel-bound system there throbbed a heart that craved to give and receive sympathy. The gentleness that eventually made him great became his weakness. Blinded by tears, eyes that ordinarily could read men through and through failed. He could not discern spirits. He misread the simplest facts. A shrewd observer, for a while he became the sport of fools and hypocrites. But this also was training, painful to a proud man, but salutary, for by the things he suffered was he perfected for the ministry of the future.[12]

Caelum non animum mutant, qui trans mare currunt. 'Those who go voyaging across the sea change the sky above them but not the

[12] *Journal*, I.174.

spirit within.'¹³ So it was with John Wesley, in certain important respects. There had been for him no re-birth of the human spirit under those tropic skies, but that re-fashioning was not far away. A re-orientation of his spiritual understanding was already taking place. Nearly forty years later he wrote:

In the beginning of the year 1738, as I was returning from Georgia, the cry of my heart was,

> O, grant that nothing in my soul
> May dwell, but thy pure love alone!
> O, may thy love possess me whole,
> My joy, my treasure and my crown!
> Strange fires far from my heart remove;
> My every act, word, thought, be love!¹⁴

'I took my leave of America', wrote Wesley on Thursday 22nd December 1737, 'though, if it please God, not for ever, going on board the *Samuel*.' But it *was* 'for ever'. Two days later 'we sailed over Charlestown bar, and about noon lost sight of land.' So he crossed those wintry, tempest-stricken seas, returning to an England that was in dire need of him, there, in God's good time, to answer his brother's prayer:

> Open their mouth, and utterance give;
> Give them a trumpet-voice to call
> On all mankind to turn and live,
> Through faith in Him who died for all.¹⁵

Geographically, John Wesley was returning to the 'Old World', but on the chart of his spirit's voyaging was marked a 'New World', which he was about to enter and possess.

---

[13] Horace, *Epistles*, I.xi.27. [14] *Works*, XI.369. [15] *M.H.B.*, No. 791.

CHAPTER III

SHADOWS OF COMING EVENTS

WESLEY landed at Deal at five o'clock in the morning of Wednesday 1st February 1738, and on that day he commenced his English *Journal* with these words:

After reading prayers and explaining a portion of Scripture to a large company at the inn, I left Deal, and came in the evening to Faversham. I here read prayers and explained the Second Lesson to a few of those who are called Christians, but were indeed more savage in their behaviour than the wildest Indians I have yet met with.

It is significant and prophetic that, upon reaching England after a long and perilous voyage, his first action was to preach the Gospel. It is a revelation of the man; of his steadfastness of purpose and loyalty to an ideal in a moment when their brightness was eclipsed by a sense of failure, unworthiness and physical exhaustion, and evidence of his iron ruling of body and spirit.

On the Friday he reached London and the *Journal* records how he preached in one church after another. The invitations were probably due, in the main, to the fact that he had just returned from Georgia, a colony in which there was widespread public interest, and it is likely that the desire to see, as well as to hear John Wesley, helped to swell his congregations. The first of these services took place in the afternoon of Sunday 5th February, in the Church of St John the Evangelist, at Millbank, Westminster, when he preached on 'those strong words, *If any man be in Christ he is a new creature*'. The sermon was substantially that which he published later entitled *Sin in Believers*, and the entry closes with the words ominous for the future and whose iteration, in slightly varied phrase, soon becomes almost monotonous: 'I was afterwards informed, many of the best in the parish were so offended that I was not to preach there any more.' Already there was an arousing note in his sermons which was resented by complacent hearers. The following Sunday he preached at St Andrew's, Holborn, and 'here too, it seems, I am to preach no more'.

There is nothing in the *Journal* to indicate that Wesley was, at this time, depressed by such treatment, or that he faltered for a moment in his belief that he was called to the Christian ministry. That confidence was presently to be shaken, but for an entirely different reason. It was fortunate that in such a trying moment he enjoyed the friendship and support of Peter Böhler, a Moravian who was passing through England on his way to missionary work in South Carolina, and with whom, a few days later, he travelled to Oxford. There Wesley preached on the Sunday at the Castle, 'to a numerous and serious congregation'. Returning to London the next day, he preached on the Tuesday at Gt. St Helen's, in Bishopsgate, on *If any man will come after me, let him deny himself and take up his cross daily and follow me*. One can well believe that a sermon on such a text would be emotionally enriched by his own recent experiences.

On Saturday 4th March, Wesley was in Oxford again, where he found his brother Charles recovering from an attack of pleurisy and attended by Peter Böhler. This was a momentous occasion in Wesley's life, for he records that, on the Sunday, he had a conversation with Böhler and 'was clearly convinced of unbelief, of the want of that faith whereby alone we are saved.' There is an explanatory note in Thomas Jackson's edition of the *Journal*, which is probably an insertion by Wesley himself at a later date:—*with the full Christian salvation*. The *Journal* continues:

Immediately it struck into my mind, 'Leave off preaching. How can you preach to others, who have not faith yourself?' I asked Böhler if he thought I should leave it off or not. He answered, 'By no means'. I asked, 'But what can I preach?' He said, 'Preach faith *till* you have it; and then, *because* you have it, you *will* preach faith.'

Böhler's advice has not passed without criticism, especially by those who maintain that there can be no effective or honest preaching other than that which springs spontaneously and warm-heartedly from a man's own experience, and that without it the congregation is likely to form a false conception of the preacher's own spiritual state. But there is more to be said than that. Every teacher knows that teaching is one of the best ways of learning. John Wesley, guided by Peter Böhler, was coming to see more clearly the nature of *saving faith*, and was increasingly anxious to experience its grace and power for himself. Therefore he would preach it as a spiritual treasure to be sought and ultimately found by his hearers and himself alike. Such preaching would inevitably clarify his own mind and strengthen his desire and determination. J. E. Rattenbury's comment upon this is:

Sometimes this saying is quoted as if he (Böhler) meant, 'Preach what you don't believe till you believe it.' What he really meant was, 'Preach your new doctrine, the truth which your mind accepts, until it becomes your spiritual conviction.'[1]

On Tuesday 14th March, Wesley set out for Manchester with Mr Kinchin, Rector of Dummer, in Hampshire, and one of the early members of the Holy Club, preaching on the way in inns where they rested. On their return journey to Oxford he displayed his aptitude for taking advantage of emotional opportunities created by unusual and impressive occurrences, for at Hednesford they heard of a young woman who had dropped dead the day before and Wesley says: 'This gave us a fair occasion to exhort all that were present, so to number their days that they might apply their hearts unto wisdom.'

At Oxford they found Peter Böhler and the conversations between the two men were resumed. One day Wesley preached at the Castle from *It is appointed unto men once to die*, having condemned prisoners specially in mind, one of whom experienced 'the peace and joy of faith'. With this man Wesley had a private interview and entered in his *Journal*: 'We prayed with the condemned man, first in several forms of prayer, and then *in such words as were given us in that hour.*' Wesley had moved an important stage nearer to the day when he could sing,

> My chains fell off, my heart was free.

On the morning of Easter Day (2nd April) he had a more august congregation than usual, for he preached in Lincoln College Chapel on 'the hour cometh, and now is, when the dead shall hear the voice of the Son of God, and they that hear shall live'. He preached the sermon again at the Castle in the afternoon and at Carfax in the evening. His comment on the day is: 'I see the promise; but it is afar off.'

The reference is to *saving faith*, which he now saw to be promised to him on Scripture authority, but it was not nearly so 'far off' as he imagined. He decided to 'wait for the accomplishment of it in silence and retirement', so on Easter Monday he

[1] *Conversion of the Wesleys*, p. 71.

went to stay with Mr Kinchin at Dummer. A fortnight later he returned to London and the *Journal* becomes heavy with the sense of impending great events. On Saturday 22nd April, there was a momentous meeting with Peter Böhler. Wesley had already accepted the Moravian's account of *saving faith*, as (according to the Church of England definition) 'a sure trust and confidence which a man hath in God, that through the merits of Christ his sins are forgiven and he reconciled to the favour of God'. His difficulty was *instantaneous conversion*. Wesley could not conceive such a faith being given in a moment, but found to his astonishment that almost all the New Testament examples of conversion were instantaneous, and that Paul's conversion, at the end of three days, was one of those longest delayed. His only retreat, he says, was to assume that such happenings were possible in the earliest ages of Christianity, but that 'the times are changed'. That such a mind as Wesley's could rest in so faulty and make-shift a conclusion is inconceivable.

The *Diary* records that at five on the following day Wesley was 'at home with Böhler and others and was convinced . . . at once'. The corresponding *Journal* entry records how he was 'beat out of this retreat too'; viz., the assumption that instantaneous conversion was confined to apostolic days. Peter Böhler gives his own account of how this happened.

I took four of my English brethren to John Wesley . . . that they might relate their experience to him, how the Saviour so soon and so mightily has compassion and accepts the sinner. . . . John Wesley and those that were with him were as if thunderstruck at these narrations. . . . He took me alone into his own room and declared that he was now satisfied of what I said of faith, and that he would not question any more about it; but how could he help himself, and how could he obtain such faith? . . . He wept heartily and bitterly as I spoke to him on this matter, and insisted that I must pray with him. I can say of him, he is truly a poor sinner and has a contrite heart, hungering after a better righteousness than that he has till now possessed.

Wesley gives his own testimony to 'the concurring evidence of several living witnesses' and adds: 'Here ended my disputing. I could now only cry out, *Lord, help Thou my unbelief!*' Again the doubt about his fitness to preach assailed him, but when he suggested that he should refrain Böhler urged him not to hide in the earth the talent God had given him. Böhler then tells us what neither *Diary* nor *Journal* records.

In the evening he (Wesley) preached from 1 Corinthians 1[23]: *But we preach Christ crucified, etc.* He had above four thousand hearers, and spoke upon this subject until the congregation was astonished, because no one had ever heard such things from him. His first words were, 'I hold myself from my very heart unworthy to preach the crucified Jesus.'[2]

Böhler's account seems to imply that this service took place on the evening of the same Sunday. There are several obvious difficulties. Why does neither *Diary* nor *Journal* nor Charles Wesley's *Journal* notice so tremendous an occasion? The *Diary* reads: '6. Tea, singing, the Cross. 7. Conversed to Böhler, prayer; 7.30. Mr Hutton's, the Cross. 8. Singing, prayer. 9. Conversed with Metcalf. 9.30. supper. 10.30. at home.' Where and at what hour did Wesley conduct this extraordinary service? What church in London was capable of holding 4,000 people? What induced 4,000 people to attend on that occasion? Were there so many people accustomed to hearing Wesley preach, at this stage of his ministry, as to justify the statement that 'the congregation was astonished, because no one had ever heard such things from him before'? It is all rather mystifying.

On Wednesday 26th April, Wesley again set out for Oxford, Böhler walking a few miles with him and exhorting him 'not to stop short of the grace of God'. He wrote to James Hutton on the Friday:

This thing I do: I still follow after, if haply I may attain faith. *I preach it to all, that at length I may feel it.* Only may I never be content with any other portion!

He returned to London on Monday 1st May, and that evening 'our little society began, which afterwards met in Fetter Lane'. The following Thursday Böhler left London for Carolina and Wesley then began a round of what mainly proved to be 'farewell' visits to London churches. On Sunday 7th May, he was again at St Lawrence's and St Katherine Cree's and notes:

I was enabled to speak strong words at both, and was therefore the less surprised at being informed I was not to preach any more in either of those churches.

On Tuesday 9th May:

I preached at Gt. St Helen's to a numerous congregation on *He that spared not His own Son, but delivered Him up for us all, how shall He not*

---

[2] J. P. Lockwood, *Memorials of the Life of Peter Böhler*, pp. 76–80.

with Him freely give us all things? My heart was now so enlarged to declare the love of God to all that were oppressed by the devil, that I did not wonder in the least when I was afterwards told, 'Sir, you must preach here no more.'

It is not surprising to read, the next day:

From this time to Saturday, the 13th, I was sorrowful and very heavy; being neither able to read, nor meditate, nor sing, nor pray, nor do anything.

Yet he was 'a little refreshed' by a letter from Peter Böhler. On the Sunday morning, 14th May, he preached at St Ann's, Aldersgate, and in the afternoon at the Savoy, on 'free salvation by faith in the blood of Christ'. He adds: 'I was quickly apprised that at St. Ann's likewise I am to preach no more.'

On that same Sunday, obviously moved by these distressing experiences, Wesley wrote to William Law. Whilst acknowledging his debt to him, Wesley was now convinced that Law's teaching was not fully consonant with New Testament doctrine, and at one point he describes how this had adversely affected his preaching.

For two years (more especially) I have been preaching after the model of your two practical treatises; and all that heard have allowed that the law is great, wonderful and holy. But no sooner did they attempt to fulfil it but they found that it is too high for man, and that by doing 'the works of the law shall no flesh living be justified'.

To remedy this, I exhorted them, and stirred up myself, to pray earnestly for the grace of God, and to use all the other means of obtaining that grace which the all-wise God hath appointed. But still both they and I were more and more convinced that this is a law by which a man cannot live; the law in our members continually warring against it, and bringing us into deeper captivity to the law of sin.[3]

With the details of this controversy we are not concerned. Wesley wished to express his feelings about these exclusions from the pulpits of London churches and quotes for that purpose a letter which John Gambold had written to Charles Wesley on 23rd January. Gambold had been a member of the Club at Oxford and was later ordained to the ministry of the English Church. He had resigned this office to join the Moravians and in time became one of their bishops. We will let John Wesley express his own thoughts in Gambold's words.

[3] *Letters*, I.239.

I have seen . . . how intolerable the doctrine of faith is to the mind of man, and how peculiarly intolerable even to most *religious* men. . . . If you speak of faith in such a manner as makes Christ a Saviour to the utmost, a most universal help and refuge; in such a manner as takes away glorying, but adds happiness to wretched man; as discovers a greater pollution in the best of us than we could before acknowledge, but brings a greater deliverance from it than we could before expect,—if any one offers to talk at this rate, he shall be heard with the same abhorrence as if he was going to rob mankind of their salvation, their Mediator or their hopes of forgiveness. . . .[4]

There are harsh words and judgements in this letter, which should be read, but they sprang from harsh experiences and bitter disappointments, and we must make allowance for them accordingly. Wesley, at that moment, could enter into his friend's feelings, for he, too, knew what it was to proclaim the truth in love and to offer God's gift of salvation to all, only to have his message scorned and himself reviled and cast out.

The closing doors now profoundly distressed him. 'I had', he writes, 'continual sorrow and heaviness in my heart', and he enlarges upon it by transcribing part of a letter which he wrote to a friend. It is very revealing.

Oh, why is it that so wise, so holy a God will use such an instrument as I! Lord, 'let the dead bury their dead', but wilt Thou send the dead to raise the dead? Yea, Thou sendest whom Thou *wilt* send, and showest mercy by whom Thou *wilt* show mercy. Amen! Be it then according to Thy will!

. . . I see that the whole law of God is holy, just and good. I know every thought, every temper of my soul, ought to bear God's image and superscription. But how am I fallen from the glory of God! . . .

The whole letter is a cry from the heart, poignant in its sincerity; the prayer of a soul intellectually convinced but spiritually frustrated. Wesley then outlines his spiritual pilgrimage by way of preface to his account of how 'the change which God works in the heart through faith in Christ' warmed his own heart. His experiences of that momentous day, 24th May 1738, are so well known that we will only quote the familiar passage from Charles Wesley's *Journal*: 'Towards ten, my brother was brought in triumph by a troop of our friends, and declared, "I believe". We sang the hymn with great joy and parted with prayer.'

Reaction followed; doubts, fears, and temptations, but God

---

[4] Tyerman, *The Oxford Methodists*, p. 169.

sent him 'help from His holy place', and he was 'always conqueror'. Interpret these yearnings and experiences as we will, they were the spiritual birth-throes of a new John Wesley and nothing was ever quite the same again. This was for him a day of apocalypse, and he began to discern 'a new heaven and a new earth'. The former things had passed away and the divine word had come even unto him.

On Sunday afternoon, 11th June, he preached in St Mary's Church, Oxford. The discourse, on *Salvation by Faith* (No. 1 in the *Standard Sermons*), was obviously born out of his recent experiences and should be consulted at this point. As we read it we can enter, in some degree, into the emotional life of Wesley during those days that were so critical and vital for his future ministry. Heart and mind were now at one, and nothing less than that could give peace and confidence to such a man as he. He stated his case, or God's case, with that ease, clarity and grace of diction of which he was a pastmaster, and we are left wondering what were its effects upon an assembly that represented the national culture of the day.

On the Monday he went to London, and the next day, in the company of Benjamin Ingham, another old friend of the Oxford 'Club' days, he set sail for the Moravian Settlement at Herrnhut, arriving there on Tuesday 1st August 1738. In the *Journal* he gives an enthusiastic description of what he saw, heard and experienced. His 'new faith' found ample confirmation. He had long conversations with nearly a dozen of the Brethren, who related to him their spiritual histories, and these he duly records. His letters to his mother, his brothers and James Hutton are all in the same strain of joyful enthusiasm. On the return journey he was delayed at Rotterdam, where he had time 'to exhort several English whom we met with at our inn to pursue inward religion, the renewal of their souls in righteousness and true holiness'. He went on board ship on Saturday 9th September, and that afternoon 'read prayers and preached in the great cabin'. Owing to unfavourable winds the ship did not sail till Wednesday, and the following Saturday night Wesley reached London.

We have lingered somewhat over the details of Wesley's life between his landing in England from Georgia and from Herrnhut, because, taken together, they give us one of the most intimate accounts of the fashioning of a great preacher in the annals of the Christian Church. What kind of a man and a preacher was the John Wesley who arrived at Deal in the dark hours of a February morning? The answer lies implicit in the opening words of that revealing bit of spiritual autobiography which he wrote during his return voyage from Georgia to England.

I went to America to convert the Indians; but oh, who shall convert me? Who, what is he that will deliver me from this evil heart of unbelief? I have a fair summer religion. I can talk well; nay, and *believe myself*, while no danger is near. But let death look me in the face, and my spirit is troubled. Nor can I say, 'To die is gain!'

He then quotes from John Donne, the poet-preacher in whose succession Wesley himself was one day worthily to stand:

> I have a sin of fear, that when I've spun
> My last thread I shall perish on the shore.

Here is unflinching honesty. Whatever else Wesley may have learned or failed to learn in Georgia, he had come very near to that self-knowledge which some have held to be the *summum bonum* of human wisdom, and he was appalled to the point of despair. He had practised the Christian virtues almost to perfection and excelled in deeds of kindness and charity. He had played the part of the model parish priest, rigorously self-exacting in the performance of every duty and expecting complete co-operation from his parishioners. Now all appeared as play-acting. He had kept the *priest* in the lime-light and only occasionally allowed the *prophet* a minor part upon the stage. All had ended in confusion, heart-burnings, hatred and—*flight*. His natural pride had been wounded; his self-confidence severely shaken; and the demon of despair was seated at his elbow. Atlantic storms were raging around him, but there was a more devastating storm within.

Wesley's despair sprang, in part, from a consciousness of *defeat*. He had suffered defeat in the sphere of his *opinions*, both theological and ecclesiastical; in that of his *intentions*, to Christianize and turn into 'good churchmen' the colonists and Indians of Georgia; on the field of his own *good deeds*, which were many and outstandingly praiseworthy; and in the sphere of his *affections*, through mistrust of his natural, human instincts;—a phase of his life in Georgia which does not fall to be considered here, but which contributed more than any other factor to his final decision to return to England.

On the other hand, Wesley's contacts with the Moravians and the influence of their teaching had lightened his despair with a gleam of hope. In their insistence on *Salvation by Faith* Wesley felt that they were right, but he had hitherto been unable to give that intellectual assent to the doctrine that was so essential to the peace of his logical mind. It was, for a time, a tentative acceptance and he forced himself to preach it. That seems to be the explanation of the fact that, though Wesley returned to England in despair and defeat, he yet preached with such vigour that churches were closed against him. He faced his London congregations with their own neglected or forgotten doctrine of *Salvation by Faith* and the impotence of Good Works alone, and left them to make a personal decision in the matter. Then it was that the opposition appeared. They resented this disconcerting mode of preaching. Wesley's attitude at this time has a Socratic touch about it. He seems to have assumed that he had only to state the truth and his hearers, being reasonable creatures, would be bound to accept and act upon it. He was soon to learn that raw human nature does not ordinarily react in that way, unless the truth in question be a palatable one. His hearers were not prepared to be honest with themselves as Wesley was honest with himself.

The change from despair to 'optimistic despair' became more marked when Wesley renewed his association with the Moravians by meeting Peter Böhler and conversing long and deeply with him; we see hope and confidence strengthening. The solution of his problem becomes clear to his mind, but he lacks the means to make it spiritually effective. In his wholesome honesty he preached the truth about Salvation as his mind accepted it; preached, not out of his experience but out of what he wanted that experience to be. It was *imaginative* preaching: as he pleaded with others he was pleading with and for himself, and such preaching is bound to be emotional, charged with the turbulence within. As we have seen, there were moments when his confidence in a divine call to the ministry wavered, but it was soon restored. In this certainty of his call lay a great measure of his hope about himself, for if God had summoned him to the Christian ministry and he himself had wholly consented, as he had, it was in the sure providence of God that one day he would be fitted for the office.

So he came by degrees to triumph over that initial sense of defeat. It was on that historic 24th of May that all this tumult reached its climax in a sudden calm. Wesley had been changing almost from day to day, but the change of that day had a finality and determination about it that the passage of the years confirmed.

Looking back, in 1746, upon this period of his life which ended with his 'conversion', he wrote:

Speaking more of faith in Christ, I saw more fruit of my preaching and visiting from house to house than ever I had done before; though I know not if any of those who were outwardly reformed were inwardly and thoroughly converted to God.[5]

In his third Conference, held in Bristol in 1746, the question was asked:

Wherein does our doctrine now differ from that we preached when at Oxford?

The answer sums up, in Wesley's own way and words, the change that had come to him, revolutionizing both his life and his preaching.

Chiefly in the two points: 1. We then knew nothing of the righteousness of faith in justification; nor, 2. of the nature of faith itself as implying consciousness of pardon.

Wesley returned from Georgia *a Mourner Convinced of Sin.*

> In the wilderness I stray,
>   My foolish heart is blind;
> Nothing do I know; the way
>   Of peace I cannot find.[6]

Then, in the providence of God, he passed to the Earthly Paradise of *Believers Rejoicing*, assured that

> Thy mighty name salvation is,
>   And keeps my happy soul above;
> Comfort it brings, and power, and peace,
>   And joy, and everlasting love;
> To me, with Thy dear name, are given
>   Pardon, and holiness, and heaven.[7]

So, rejoicing in spirit, John Wesley went to share the fellowship and friendship of the Moravian Brethren at Herrnhut, to whom, under God, he owed so much.

[5] *Works*, VIII.468.   [6] *M.H.B.* (1779), No. 105; *P.W.*, II.93.
[7] *M.H.B.*, No. 98; *P.W.*, V.50.

CHAPTER IV

THE VALLEY OF INDECISION

JOHN WESLEY was absent from England exactly three months. The change from life with the Moravian Brethren to life in London exceeds our powers of imagination. In Herrnhut the simplest, most ordinary duties were carried out as a part of man's service to God. The thought of God was ever present and every person was a professing, practising Christian, partaking regularly and devoutly in Christian worship and fellowship. Every hour of the twenty-four was permeated with the atmosphere of religion, for, writes Wesley,

Two men keep watch every night in the street, as do two women in the women's apartment, that they may pour out their souls for those that sleep, and by their hymns raise the hearts of any who are awake to God.[1]

On 7th July he wrote to his brother Samuel:

God has given me at length the desire of my heart. I am with a Church whose conversation is in heaven, in whom is the mind that was in Christ, and who so walk as He walked.[2]

Coming at such a time, these experiences had a profound effect upon John Wesley. Now he was back in Hogarth's England: a transition from the Gate of Heaven to the purlieus of Hell. The contrast that greeted him would have depressed and daunted many men, but

> Not all the powers of hell can fright
> A soul that walks with Christ in light,

and we note the moving and magnificent opening words of his new English *Journal*:

1738. September 17, Sun. I began again to declare in my own country the glad tidings of salvation, preaching three times, and afterwards expounding the Holy Scriptures to a large company in the Minories.

So, to the eager, rejoicing spirit of Wesley, the spectacle that his country presented was a spur to renewed endeavour and, as it proved, the gateway to a new sphere of service.

[1] *Journal*, II.56.   [2] *Letters*, I.251.

It was a strange period that followed Wesley's return. There is a feeling of 'drift' in it all. The *Journal* is very scanty, but the *Diary*, in its staccato way, very full. In the main his time was occupied with visits to Religious Societies and the private houses of religious people. In the former he 'read prayers and expounded':—usually the 'new' doctrines; and on occasion there was discussion and even a measure of opposition, but this sprang from genuine religious interest and fervour, and the desire of pious souls for 'true doctrine', and not from resentment such as Wesley had aroused in people whose religion was purely formal. In the houses, where several of his friends and his brother Charles often met him, there was conversation with singing and prayer and an occasional administration of the Sacrament of the Lord's Supper. In the Societies and private houses alike, Wesley was concerned to justify and clarify those doctrines of experimental religion which eventually became distinctive of Methodism. There were also interviews with persons who sought his advice in their spiritual difficulties, and from time to time he preached in Newgate, especially to condemned felons.

In a letter to Benjamin Ingham he refers to his activities at this time.

God hath been wonderfully gracious to us ever since our return to England. Though there are many adversaries, yet a great door and effectual is opened; and we continue through evil report and good report, to preach the gospel of Christ to all people, and earnestly to contend for the faith once delivered to the saints. Indeed, He hath given unto us many of our fiercest opposers, who now receive with meekness the engrafted word.[3]

Whenever opportunities arose, and they were frequent, he preached in London churches. True, pulpit doors still banged behind him, unceremoniously and disapprovingly; and the attitude of many of the clergy was like that of the vicar of Pensford, on whose behalf a note was delivered to Wesley: 'Sir, our minister, being informed you are beside yourself, does not care you should preach in any of his churches.'[4] This kind of treatment now scarcely disconcerted him at all. The exclusions were not quite so persistent and inevitable as they had been a little earlier, and in several churches, such as St Antholin's, he ministered with fair regularity.

[3] *Letters*, I.258.   [4] ibid., p. 310.

Wesley visited Oxford during these weeks and lived among old friends and acquaintances, exercising much the same kind of ministry as in London. Some ill-disposed person had complained to the Bishop of London, Dr Gibson, that the Wesleys were preaching 'an absolute assurance of salvation', and the two brothers therefore waited upon him on 21st October 1738. Charles gives a full account of the conversation, which includes this reference to preaching:

Bishop. If by 'assurance' you mean an inward persuasion, whereby a man is conscious in himself, after examining his life by the law of God, and weighing his own sincerity, that he is in a state of salvation, and acceptable to God, I don't see how any good Christian can be without such an assurance.
The Wesleys. This is what we contend for; but we have been charged as Antinomians for preaching justification by faith only.
Bishop. Can any one preach otherwise who agrees to our Church and Scriptures?

The following February the brothers had another interview with him and on the same day one with the Archbishop of Canterbury, Dr John Potter, of which Charles Wesley tells us:

He (the Archbishop) showed us great affection . . . (and) cautioned us to give no more umbrage than was necessary for our own defence; to forbear exceptional phrases; to keep to the doctrines of the Church. We told him we expected persecution; would abide by the Church till her Articles and Homilies were repealed. He assured us he knew of no design in the governors of the Church to innovate, and neither should there be any innovation while he lived; avowed justification by faith only; and his joy to see us as often as we pleased. From him we went to the Bishop of London, who denied his having condemned or even heard much of us.

We gather that both brothers were anxious not to arouse official opposition to their preaching. As ordained ministers of the Church of England they held in due respect those who exercised authority over them in spiritual things. If their preaching commended itself to those who were the appointed guardians of the purity of the Church's doctrine, then they had the less to fear from their opponents, and were the more emboldened to continue their campaign for the souls of men. Having conversed with the Wesleys, Archbishop and Bishop alike could find no fault in them.

In three letters written during this period Wesley refers to himself as a preacher. On 14th October he wrote to *The Church at Herrnhut*:

Though my brother and I are not permitted to preach in most of the churches in London, yet (thanks be to God) there are others left wherein we have liberty to speak the truth as it is in Jesus. Likewise every evening ... we publish the word of reconciliation, sometimes to twenty or thirty, sometimes to fifty or sixty, sometimes to three or four hundred persons, met together to hear it.

The same day he wrote to a Dr Koker, whom he had met in Rotterdam:

(God's) blessed Spirit has wrought so powerfully, both in London and Oxford, that there is a general awakening, and multitudes are crying out, 'What must we do to be saved?'

To George Whitefield he wrote during the following February:

Our Lord's hand is not shortened amongst us. Yesterday I preached at St Katherine's and at Islington. ... I think I never was so much strengthened before. The fields after service were white with people praising God.

As we read and ponder we ask, 'What is this restless, eager man of thirty-five going to *do* with his life? It cannot, surely, continue for him in this rather purposeless, haphazard way!' The *Diary* shows how fully occupied his time was, but he lacked clear intention in the realm of action. It was a day-to-day existence, unrelated to any central purpose; the life of a disturbed, anxious man, groping amidst half-achievements, nor yet sure of the Divine will for him; a man whose imperfectly defined ideals and tethered impulses outran the circumscribed area of his opportunities.

Then an event occurred which was to have the profoundest effect upon John Wesley's life and ultimately to unravel all this tangled skein of good works: George Whitefield returned to England from Georgia. Debarred from the churches of Bristol, he had resort to a pulpit from which none could exclude him, roofed by the blue sky and bounded by the everlasting hills; a pulpit before which his congregations could gather in their thousands and there would yet be room for more, and in their thousands they came. But Whitefield's time was drawing short and Georgia was calling him to return. Deeply concerned about this new and promising work in the open-air, and especially that amongst the miners of Kingswood, he decided to appeal to John

Wesley, as the man above all others fitted to continue the work so triumphantly begun. So he wrote to him:

Bristol, March 22, 1739.

Reverend Sir,

... If the brethren, after prayer for direction, think proper, I wish you would be here the latter end of next week. ... I go away, God willing, next Monday sennight. If you were here before my departure, it might be best. Many are ripe for bands. I leave that entirely to you. I am but a novice; you are acquainted with the great things of God. Come, I beseech you; come quickly. I have promised not to leave this people till you or somebody come to supply my place.

He adds in a postscript: 'I beseech you come next week; it is advertised in this day's journal. I pray for a blessing on your journey, and in our meetings. The people expect you much. Though you come *after*, I heartily wish you may be preferred *before* me. Even so, Lord Jesus. Amen!'[5]

Wesley and his friends had heard, with some misgivings, of these unconventional doings in the West of England, and now they had to determine and declare their attitude toward them. Wesley refers in his *Journal* to the receipt of this letter, 'entreating me in the most pressing manner to come to Bristol without delay. This I was not at all forward to do.' On 28th March the matter was laid before the Society in Fetter Lane. Charles 'would scarcely bear the mention of it'. Opinion was so divided that lots were cast, 'and by this it was determined I should go'. Charles wrote in his *Journal*:

We dissuaded my brother from going to Bristol, from an unaccountable fear that it would prove fatal to him. A great power was among us. He offered himself willingly to whatsoever the Lord should appoint. The next day he set out, commended by us to the grace of God. He left a blessing behind. I desired to die with him.

It reads like an extract from *The Acts of the Apostles*, and such it proved to be. John Wesley left London on Thursday 29th March, and reached Bristol on the Saturday. There he met Whitefield, who wrote: 'I was much refreshed with the sight of my honoured friend, Mr John Wesley, whom God's providence has sent to Bristol. "Lord, now lettest Thou Thy servant depart in peace!" ' On Monday 2nd April Wesley closed a letter to his friends at Fetter Lane with these words:

[5] Tyerman, *Life of George Whitefield*, I.193.

Our dear brother Whitefield expounded . . . on Sunday morning to six or seven thousand at the Bowling Green; at noon to much the same number at Hanham Mount; and at five to, I believe, thirty thousand from a little mount on Rose Green. At one today he left Bristol. I am straitened for time. Pray ye, my dear brethren, that some portion of his spirit may be given to your poor, weak brother,

John Wesley.

With that letter an epoch in the life of John Wesley was brought to an end and a new one was begun.

CHAPTER V

THE OPEN ROAD

Monday, 2nd April, 1739. At four in the afternoon I submitted to be more vile, and proclaimed in the highways the glad tidings of salvation, speaking from a little eminence in a ground adjoining to the city (Bristol), to about three thousand people. The scripture on which I spoke was this (is it possible any one should be ignorant that it is fulfilled in every true minister of Christ?), 'The Spirit of the Lord is upon Me, because He hath anointed Me to preach the gospel to the poor. He hath sent Me to heal the broken-hearted; to preach deliverance to the captives, and recovery of sight to the blind; to set at liberty them that are bruised, to proclaim the acceptable year of the Lord.'

HARD OF heart and dull of imagination must he be who can read these words without emotion. *2nd April 1739!* One of the momentous dates in the spiritual history not only of this country, but of the world! One of the finest hours in the life of a great spiritual leader of men, comparable with and complementary to 24th May 1738, for without the former the latter would have had little more than personal and ephemeral interest!

Seeing we are compassed about with so great a cloud of witnesses, we can imagine celestial beings gazing with wonder and joy upon what was happening in Bristol on that day. They had seen this same John Wesley preaching in the open-air on board ship, lying off Gravesend, but *this was different*; it called for more incisive qualities, and a clear-eyed courage. A certain Paul, a 'bond slave of Jesus Christ', who once preached from an 'eminence' in the city of Athens would be of their company; Augustine and Paulinus; Aidan and Cuthbert; Dominican Friars of the black robe, not, perhaps, quite so approving as their grey-robed brethren of the Franciscan Order, of whose Founder Augustus Jessop so justly observes, 'St Francis was the John Wesley of the thirteenth century, whom the Church did not cast out';[1] Wycliffe and his Lollards, those travelling preachers whom John Wesley, as a member of Lincoln College, was supposed to denounce, as

---

[1] *The Coming of the Friars*, p. 47.

he had opportunity, throughout the diocese of Lincoln;[2] John Donne, one-time Dean of St Paul's, and all who, in their life upon earth, had responded *Vae si non* to the voice of God. There, also, would be Bartholomew Wesley and his son John; and, probably the most interested and observant of all, Samuel Wesley, one-time incumbent of Epworth and Wroot in the County of Lincoln, who, had he still been in the flesh, almost certainly would have regarded such unconventional procedure on the part of his son John with some misgiving, but who must have rejoiced with his fellows in the light of that clearer understanding of the things of earth which we believe to be the portion of the emancipated spirits of the righteous. On this day his son might have written, as he did fourteen years later, 'If those in Paradise know what passes on earth, I doubt not but my father is rejoicing and praising God.'[3]

Wesley had been quite candid about himself when he met George Whitefield in Bristol and wrote in his *Journal*:

I could scarce reconcile myself at first to this strange way of preaching in the fields. . . . Having been all my life (till very lately) so tenacious of every point relating to decency and order, that I should have thought the saving of souls almost a sin if it had not been done in a church.

So—*I submitted to be more vile*. The more we ponder these words the more closely do we draw to the John Wesley of that moment; the more moving do they become. The old props upon which he had relied were falling around him, and no man can endure that sight and sensation with entire equanimity. There is a note of pathos in the words, as though he had stooped to something of which one part of him was ashamed. The Oxford scholar and don, with his inherited aristocratic instincts and ingrained respect for what was regular and constitutional, had become a 'field preacher', a man beyond the pale of the regular ministry, knowing that the hand of authority would be increasingly heavy against him; that he would forfeit the regard and friendship of many of his own order; that he was making himself 'a fool for Christ's sake'.

But, standing on that 'eminence', a new world opened up to John Wesley, whose far horizons were as yet hidden from him. We feel how possessed he was by a new and hitherto unimagined

---

[2] See J. H. Overton, *John Wesley*, p. 16; Fuller's *Church History of Britain*, Book IV. Section II, pp. 41–2.
[3] *Journal*, IV.67.

exaltation of spirit. It was a moment of amazing, thrilling discovery; he found that he had the power to hold crowds and to make his voice as the voice of God. His *Journal* and *Letters* of these days vibrate with excitement. They are no mere chronicle of astonishing events; the very words and phrases are charged with the ecstasy of mind of the man who wrote them, and we sense the emotional atmosphere of these things which were not done in a corner. Having once begun, there was no turning back. Here was a new weapon against the powers of darkness, which had lain too long, unsuspected, in his well-stocked armoury, and its exercise gave fresh meaning and purpose to his life. Henceforward, all that hitherto had been erratic, uncentralized, unrelated to some clearly-defined purpose and manner of life, was rapidly to disappear. The way was opening before him and he knew, exultantly, that he had power to tread it. Closed pulpits! How absurdly ineffective these now appeared! His love for the souls of men had now such opportunity of expression that he could laugh at pulpit locksmiths. He had found a pulpit that some of his forebears had occupied and their spirit was alive within him, as was that of his intrepid mother when she wrote to her husband:

Send me your positive command, in such full and express terms as may absolve me from all guilt and punishment, for neglecting this opportunity of doing good, when you and I shall appear before the great and awful tribunal of our Lord Jesus Christ.

Above all, there was that precedent which none could gainsay, set by Him who preached on the hillsides of Judaea and by the Sea of Galilee. That alone was sufficient. There was, too, a word of His which admitted of no refusal: *Behold, I send you forth as sheep in the midst of wolves.* The 'wolves' were there, obvious enough in King George II's England. But there was another word for John Wesley from those same lips: *Lo, I am with you all the days, even unto the end of the world.* No man proved the truth of that promise more assuredly than Wesley, and when the last of those 'days' on earth came for him, he sang Isaac Watts's hymn,

> I'll praise my Maker while I've breath.

The promise had been fulfilled.

So there opened in John Wesley's life a new chapter, the last and the longest, covering more than half a century, and marked by no such violent changes as Epworth to Charterhouse, Charterhouse to Oxford, Oxford to Georgia and Georgia to London. The significant events of the subsequent years were corollaries of that Sermon on a Bristol Mount, being linked each to each in an almost inevitable sequence. If ever there has been a religious organization of natural growth, it is John Wesley's Methodism. The story from 1739 to 1791 is an indivisible whole. For that reason we shall not regard it in detail, but content ourselves with a description of Wesley as a Preacher, which finds illustration at almost any and every point within that period.

We notice how rapidly field-preaching became central in his ministry. He remained in Bristol for ten weeks and a typical *Journal* entry is:

Sunday, 8th April. At seven in the morning I preached to about a thousand persons at Bristol, and afterwards to about fifteen hundred on the top of Hanham Mount in Kingswood. I called on them in the words of the Evangelical Prophet, 'Ho! every one that thirsteth, come ye to the waters; come and buy wine and milk, without money and without price.' About five thousand were in the afternoon at Rose Green (on the other side of Kingswood); among whom I stood and cried, in the name of the Lord, 'If any man thirst, let him come unto me and drink. He that believeth on me, as the Scripture hath said, out of his belly shall flow rivers of living water.'

Gradually the pattern of the future unfolded itself, as presently the Bristol ministry was extended to Bath, where, on 5th June, occurred the famous encounter with Beau Nash. It is in Wesley's letters of this period that we are most conscious of his emotional reactions. During those ten weeks he wrote twelve to his friends at Fetter Lane, directing them to James Hutton. For a full appreciation of that Bristol ministry they should be read at this point, so vividly and feelingly do they supplement the outline story of the *Journal*.

The John Wesley who returned to London on 13th June 1739, was a very different man from the John Wesley who had left it on 29th March. He had gone forth with fears and misgivings; he returned in triumph and confidence, to begin in London a ministry parallel in every respect to that of Bristol. Soon he became a familiar and, in the main, a welcome figure in such places as Moorfields, Blackheath, and Kennington Common. During the following months he divided his time between London and Bristol, continuing and consolidating his work, and gradually pushing further afield from both these centres, particularly from Bristol, visiting, amongst other places, Thornbury, Gloucester, Wells, Reading, and Wycombe. On 15th October 1739, he went to Wales, having received a pressing invitation, and the *Journal* account of his itinerary is full of interest.

During one of his visits to Bristol, Wesley had interviews with the Bishop; or, to use his own words, he *conversed* with him. It is specially interesting to note that the Bishop was Joseph Butler, the distinguished author of the *Analogy of Religion*, which had been published three years earlier. Wesley made a transcript of what passed between them and the part relevant to our subject is as follows.

Bishop. Well, Sir, since you ask my advice, I will give it you very freely. You have no business here. You are not commissioned to preach in this diocese. Therefore, I advise you to go hence.
Wesley. My Lord, my business on earth is to do what good I can. Wherever, therefore, I think I can do most good, there must I stay, so long as I think so. At present I think I can do most good here; therefore, here I stay. As to my preaching here, a dispensation of the Gospel is committed to me, and woe is me if I preach not the Gospel, wherever I am in the habitable world. Your Lordship knows, being ordained a Priest, by the commission I then received, I am a Priest of the church universal: and being ordained as Fellow of a College, I was not limited to any particular cure, but have an indeterminate commission to preach the word of God in any part of the Church of England. I do not therefore conceive that, in preaching here by this commission, I break any human law. When I am convinced I do, then it will be time to ask, 'Shall I obey God or man?' But if I should be convinced in the meanwhile, that I should advance the glory of God and the salvation of souls in any other place, more than in Bristol, in that hour, by God's help, I will go hence; which till then I may not do.[4]

John Wesley was now a man with a sense of *vocation*, and thereby the outstanding ethical problems of his life, some of them concerned with ecclesiastical procedure, were henceforward to find their solution. All were to be viewed in their relation, not to a John Wesley for whom John Anybody-Else might be substituted, but to this specific John Wesley who had been called of God to be a preacher of the Gospel of the Grace of God through Jesus Christ, in an age that had largely forgotten, if it ever knew, that Gospel's real meaning. That was the significant fact that was to

[4] Henry Moore, *Life of Wesley*, I.463–5. See Overton and Relton, *History of the English Church*, VII.111, for account of Butler.

lead him straight to the answers to many questions of conduct presently to arise in his ministry.

But more was needed. The answers might be plain beyond all possibility of denial; there remained the problem of their implementation. The weak, fearful soul, doubtful of its own powers of achievement and constancy, may play traitor to the certainty within.

> Our doubts are traitors,
> And make us lose the good we oft might win,
> By fearing to attempt.[5]

Is there any good man who has never cried with St Paul, *The good which I would I do not*? Given, then, this sense of vocation, with its directive voice in the ethical decisions of life, how is it to be made effective in a largely hostile world?

The answer is plain. It is by *Courage*; the natural courage that men possess in varying degrees, but strengthened in the case of men like Wesley by the consciousness of vocation and the Grace of God. We see it in Wesley on many occasions; every student of his life is impressed by it, as Isaac Taylor was when he wrote:

The men (John and Charles Wesley) who commenced and achieved this arduous service (rousing the country from spiritual slumber) and were scholars and gentlemen, displayed a courage far surpassing that which carries the soldier through the hail-storm of the battle field. Ten thousand might more easily be found who would confront a battery, than two who, with the sensitiveness of education about them, could mount a table by the road side, give out a psalm and gather a mob.[6]

He might have added, 'and who would beard a Bishop in his palace'. Wesley found that 'courage mounteth with occasion', and he was to have frequent opportunities of putting it to the test. He knew, roughly, what the future entailed, should he persist in being true to the call of God and in becoming the kind of preacher that his heart and his conscience prompted him to be, but he went forward unafraid. He knew a little of that forward way—but his Master knew all. It was as if his brother Charles were singing to him:

> Courage, your Captain cries,
> Who all your toil foreknew;
> Toil ye shall have: yet all despise,
> I have o'ercome for you.

[5] Shakespeare, *Measure for Measure*, I.iv.77.   [6] *Wesley and Methodism*, p. 34.

We look back at him and his companions, from an age when much that he did and taught has become familiar and even commonplace—perhaps too much so. We see him standing in public places, on tables, on walls, preaching a Gospel that to most of his hearers was strange and to some unacceptable, and we cry with Matthew Arnold:

> Hail to the courage which gave
> Voice to its creed, ere the creed
> Won consecration from time.[7]

With field-preaching in London and Bristol the pace of religious revival began to quicken. Individuals from a distance, who heard Wesley and responded to his appeal, returned home to tell what great things the Lord had done for them. Strongly desirous that the members of their own household, their friends and fellow-townsmen should share these blessings, they prepared the way for Wesley and urgently requested him to visit their neighbourhood. Thus it came about that Methodist Societies were springing into existence in localities where Wesley had never been. This *preparatio evangelica* immensely increased the effectiveness of his ministry, but at the same time added to its exactions. There was, for example, John Nelson, to whom later reference will be made, who, having heard Wesley preach in Moorfields to the great comfort of his soul, returned to his native place of Birstal, in Yorkshire, and preached in the neighbourhood with considerable success. Wesley complied with Nelson's invitation to visit that area, and recorded how he

went to Birstal and found his (Nelson's) labour had not been in vain. Many of the greatest profligates in all the country were now changed. Their blasphemies were turned to praise. Many of the most atrocious drunkards were now sober; many Sabbath-breakers remembered the Sabbath to keep it holy. The whole town wore a new face. Such a change did God work by the artless testimony of one plain man. And from thence his word sounded forth to Leeds, Wakefield, Halifax and all the West Riding of Yorkshire.[8]

This may be taken as generally descriptive of an important feature of the Methodist Revival; that people who had received with joy the Gospel message as delivered by Wesley or one of his preachers, returned home

> *to publish abroad His wonderful name*;

---

[7] *Haworth Churchyard.*   [8] *Works*, XIII.310.

and when Wesley followed later, it was to find a Methodist Society already established.

The day after leaving Birstal Wesley arrived in Newcastle, where he stands out more clearly than ever in the distinguished succession of Him of Whom it is recorded that 'the common people heard Him gladly';—'the common people', ὁ πολὺς ὄχλος; *the great crowd*. Of this visit Christopher Hopper, later to become one of Wesley's preachers, tells how

in May, 1742, we heard a strange report of one Wesley, a Church clergyman, that had been at Newcastle-upon-Tyne and had preached in Sandgate to many thousands, who heard him with astonishment. This new thing made a huge noise. The populace entertained various conjectures about him; but few, if any, could tell the motive in which he came or the end he had in view. He made a short blaze, soon disappeared, and left us in a great consternation.[9]

Probably that is how Wesley's first visits appeared to many and is also descriptive of their reactions;—'he left us in great consternation'. But it was a healthy consternation, and Hopper goes on to describe the later visits of both John and Charles Wesley; how presently 'all mouths were filled with Wesley and his followers; some for and many against them'. The 'short blaze' became a steady flame and a cleansing fire in one of the strongholds of Ignorance and Evil.

Wesley had now secured three key points, London, Bristol and Newcastle. Two yet remained for possession: Leeds, won mainly through the instrumentality of William Shent, and Manchester, through the initial efforts of John Nelson and John Bennet. In one of these five centres Wesley held his annual Conferences, where he preached to his preachers and the thousands who gathered to hear him. Far-away Cornwall has its own romantic story, which began when two lay preachers were sent there from Bristol and Charles Wesley followed them in July 1743. John Wesley paid his first visit the following month and stayed three weeks. In the summer of 1747 Thomas Williams went to Dublin, the first Methodist preacher to visit Ireland, and in August of the same year Wesley began the first of his twenty-one tours of that country, to which Tyerman estimates that he gave six years of his life. Scotland has its own deeply interesting story. John Wesley visited it twenty-two times, the first occasion being

[9] *Veterans*, I.114.

in April 1751, George Whitefield having preceded him by ten years.[10]

When, in 1746, Wesley reviewed his ministerial career, he thus referred to the period during which he became a field-preacher:

> From 1738 to this time (1746), speaking continually of Jesus Christ, laying Him only for the foundation of the whole building, making Him all in all, the first and the last: preaching only on this plan, 'The Kingdom of God is at hand; repent ye and believe the Gospel', it was glorified more and more: multitudes crying out, 'What must we do to be saved?', and afterwards witnessing, 'By grace are we saved through faith.'[11]

So we find John Wesley at last in the true Apostolical Succession, in which the grace of ordination is an undoubted gift of God, conferred by no *ex opere operato* sleight of hand; confident to the end that the *Woe!* of St Paul and John Donne and every truly-called preacher of the Word rested upon him. As late as 1781 he published to the world:

> I must go on: for a dispensation of the gospel is committed to me; and woe is me, if I preach not the gospel.[12]

---

[10] For fuller detail, see Wesley F. Swift, *Methodism in Scotland, The First Hundred Years.*
[11] *Works*, VIII.468.
[12] ibid., XIII.301.

CHAPTER VI

WESLEY'S APOLOGIA FOR FIELD-PREACHING

WE HAVE noticed how, in spite of excellent precedents in Christian history, field-preaching in the eighteenth century had fallen into desuetude and, with many of the regular clergy, into contempt. Readers of Samuel Butler's *The Way of All Flesh* will remember how Ernest Pontifex was attracted to open-air preaching as a means of reaching the people in general, about whose spiritual welfare he was at that time gravely concerned. He discussed the matter with his fellow-curate, Pryer, referring to the success of John Wesley and George Whitefield. Pryer

> treated it as something too outrageous to be thought of. Nothing, he said, could more tend to lower the dignity of the clergy and bring the Church into contempt. . . .
> You cannot and must not hawk Christ about in the streets, as though you were in a heathen country whose inhabitants had never heard of Him. The people here in London have had ample warning. Every church they pass is a protest to them against their lives, and a call to them to repent. Every church-bell they hear is a witness against them; everyone of those whom they meet going to or coming from church on Sundays is a warning voice from God. If these countless influences produce no effect upon them, neither will the few transient words which they would hear from you. You are like Dives, and think that if one rose from the dead they would hear him. Perhaps they might; but then you cannot pretend that you have risen from the dead.[1]

Thus did this modern descendant of the Apostles seek to salve whatever conscience remained to him with specious words that many a parson of Wesley's day would gladly have made his own.

There were several people with whom, at the outset, John Wesley had to come to an understanding in this matter, and one of the first was his brother Charles, who was profoundly disturbed at the thought of John embarking on such a course and 'would scarcely bear the mention of it'. The deeply interesting story of how Charles's scruples were overcome should be read.[2]

---
[1] op. cit., LVI.   [2] Charles Wesley's *Journal*, 29th May 1739, etc.

Against every opponent, and they were many, Wesley hastened to defend his action by most cogent arguments. Men needed to have clear minds and accurate premisses before engaging him in controversy. In 1743 he published a kind of *Apologia pro Sua Vita*, which he called *An Earnest Appeal to Men of Reason and Religion*. This was followed in 1745 by a *Farther Appeal*, in which Wesley deals with various attacks made upon him and his Methodists, and field-preaching is one indictment of his critics. He tells briefly how he came to engage in this work and comments:

Be pleased to observe: (1). That I was forbidden, as by a general consent, to preach in any church, (though not by any judicial sentence), 'for preaching such doctrine'. This was the open, avowed cause; there was at that time no other, either real or pretended, except that the people crowded so. (2). That I had no leisure or design to preach in the open air, till after this prohibition. (3). That when I did, as it was no matter of choice, so neither of premeditation. There was no scheme at all previously formed, which was to be supported thereby; nor had I any other end in view than this—to save as many souls as I could. (4). Field-preaching was therefore a sudden expedient, a thing submitted to, rather than chosen; and therefore submitted to, because I thought preaching even thus, better than not preaching at all: First, in regard to my own soul, because 'a dispensation of the gospel being committed to me', I did not dare 'not to preach the gospel': Secondly, in regard to the souls of others, whom I everywhere saw 'seeking death in the error of their life'.[3]

Wesley then goes on to rebut the accusation that field-preaching is contrary to the laws of the land. He always took great care to acquaint himself with what the laws were, as they affected him in his capacity of a Christian minister of an unusual type.

In *Part III* of the *Farther Appeal*, published a few months later, Wesley returns to the subject and cites objections that have been raised: 'What need is there of this preaching in fields and streets? Are there not enough churches to preach in?' He then goes on:

No, my friend, there are not; not for us to preach in. You forget; we are not suffered to preach there, else we should prefer them to any places whatever. 'Well, there are ministers enough without you.' *Ministers enough and churches enough!* For what? To reclaim all the sinners within the four seas? If there were, they would all be reclaimed. But they are not all reclaimed: Therefore it is evident that there are not churches enough. And one plain reason why, notwithstanding all

[3] *Works*, VIII.112ff.

WESLEY'S APOLOGIA FOR FIELD-PREACHING 47

these churches, they are no nearer being reclaimed, is this—they never come into a church, perhaps not once in a twelve-month, perhaps not for many years together. Will you say, (as I have known some tender-hearted Christians), 'then it is their own fault; let them die and be damned'? I grant it is their own fault; and so it was my fault and yours when we went astray like sheep that were lost. Yet the Shepherd of souls sought after us, and went after us into the wilderness. And 'oughtest not thou to have compassion on thy fellow-servants, as He had pity on thee?' Ought not we also 'to seek', as far as in us lies, 'and to save that which is lost'?

Wesley then points out that the people he has in mind, 'the outcasts of men', have, in their folly, no regard for the ordinary means of grace, and so they become the devil's prey. But God has so great regard for them that He has gone out of the usual way and commanded a voice to cry in the wilderness, 'Prepare ye the way of the Lord. The time is fulfilled. The Kingdom of Heaven is at hand. Repent ye, and believe the gospel.' He describes these people as he himself has seen them, who

week after week spent the Lord's day either in the ale-house or in idle diversions, and never troubled themselves about going to church or to any public worship at all.

He asks:

Now, would you really have desired that these poor wretches should have sinned on till they dropped into hell? Surely you would not. But by what other means was it possible they should have been plucked out of the fire? Had the Minister of the parish preached like an angel, it had profited them nothing; for they heard him not. But when one came and said, 'Yonder is a man preaching on the top of the mountain', they ran in droves to hear what he would say; and God spoke to their hearts. It is hard to conceive anything else which could have reached them. Had it not been for field-preaching, the uncommonness of which was the very circumstance which recommended it, they must have run on in the error of their way and perished in their blood.

Then, in words glowing with the white heat of his own passion, he flings his challenge to these cynical shepherds of souls:

But suppose field-preaching to be, in a case of this kind, ever so expedient or even necessary, yet who will contest with us for this province? May we not enjoy this quiet and unmolested? Unmolested, I mean, by any competitors: for who is there among you, brethren, that is willing (examine your own hearts) even to save souls from death at this price? Would not you let a thousand souls perish, rather than you would be the instruments of rescuing them thus? I do not speak now with regard to conscience, but to the inconveniences that must accompany it. Can you sustain them, if you would? Can you bear the summer sun to beat upon your naked head? Can you suffer the wintry rain or wind, from whatever quarter it blows? Are you able to stand in the open air without any covering or defence when God casteth abroad his snow like wool, or scattereth his hoar-frost like ashes? And yet these are some of the smallest inconveniences which accompany field-preaching. Far above all these, are the contradiction of sinners, the scoffs both of the great vulgar and the small; contempt and reproach of every kind; often more than verbal affronts, stupid, brutal violence, sometimes to the hazard of health or limbs or life. Brethren, do you envy us this honour? What, I pray, would buy you to be a field-preacher? Or what, think you, could induce any man of common sense to continue therein one year, unless he had a full conviction in himself that it was the will of God concerning him?

He then goes on to plead with these men that, if they will not help, they will at least decline to hinder.

Do not increase the difficulties which are already so great, that, without the mighty power of God, we must sink under them. Do not assist in trampling down a little handful of men who, for the present, stand in the gap between ten thousand poor wretches and destruction, till you find some others to take their places.[4]

It is a noble passage; and, as we read, we feel the heart-throbs of a compassionate, courageous lover of the souls of men. Incidentally, Wesley here graphically describes physical conditions in which field-preaching and travelling frequently took place.

In a famous letter to his old friend and one-time supporter, James Hervey, Wesley defends his practice of field-preaching.

God, in Scripture, commands me, according to my power, to instruct the ignorant, reform the wicked, confirm the virtuous. Man forbids me to do this in another's parish: that is, in effect, to do it at all; seeing I have now no parish of my own, nor probably ever shall. Whom, then, shall I hear, God or man? ...

Suffer me now to tell you my principles in this matter. I look upon all the world as my parish; thus far, I mean, that in whatever part of it I am, I judge it meet, right and my bounden duty to declare, unto all that are willing to hear, the glad tidings of salvation. This is the work which I know God had called me to; and sure I am that His blessing attends it. Great encouragement have I, therefore, to be

[4] *Works*, VIII.229ff.

faithful in fulfilling the work He hath given me to do. His servant I am; and, as such, am employed according to the plain direction of His word—'as I have opportunity, doing good unto all men'. And His providence clearly concurs with His word, which has disengaged me from all things else, that I might singly attend on this very thing, 'and go about doing good'.[5]

On 6th June 1755, Wesley noted in his *Journal* that he had been reading certain 'elaborate tracts on the *Rubrics and Canons*', by Dr Sharp, Archdeacon of Northumberland, in which the old charges against Methodism had been given a fresh airing in public. He comments thus:

He (the Archdeacon) observes with regard to all these (viz., rubrics and canons): (1). That our governors have power to dispense with our observance of them. (2) That a *tacit* dispensation is of the same force with an *explicit* dispensation. (3). That their continued connivance at what they cannot but know, is a tacit dispensation. I think this is true; but, if it be, he has himself answered his own charge against the Methodists (so called). For, suppose the Canons did forbid field-preaching, as expressly as playing at cards and frequenting taverns, yet we have the very same plea for the former as any clergyman has for the latter. All our governors, the King, the archbishop and bishops connive at the one as well as the other.

Here was a new line of defence of his field-preaching and a neat rejoinder to his clerical opponents, derived directly from one of themselves. The King, as the temporal head of the Church and the whole Anglican hierarchy had tacitly condoned, if not actually approved it.

The subject of field-preaching engaged the attention of the first Conference, which assembled at the Foundery on 25th June 1744. It was attended by John and Charles Wesley, four other clergymen and four lay preachers. The question was asked: 'Is field-preaching lawful?'

Answer. We do not conceive that it is contrary to any law, either of God or man. Yet (to avoid giving any needless offence) we never preach without doors, when we can with any conveniency preach within.

There is an almost apologetic tone in this reply; but these were early days and fuller experience was to come. No building could, in time, contain the crowds that gathered, nor would an inside

[5] *Letters*, I.285-6.

service attract many passers-by. So this apologetic tone does not recur. The subject was not raised again until the fourth Conference met, also in the Foundery, in June 1747. Meanwhile the work had continued, in spite of much fierce opposition. Nearly four years had passed since the savages of Darlaston and Walsall had fought for the possession of Wesley's body that they might have the honour and privilege of knocking out his brains. There had been terrible scenes in Cornwall in 1745. Early in 1747 Charles Wesley had narrowly escaped death at the hands of a murderous mob in Devizes. There had been many minor incidents of a like nature, but nevertheless the Conference of 1747 faced the astonishing question:

Have we not limited field-preaching too much?
Answer. It seems we have. (1). Because our calling is to save that which is lost. Now we cannot expect the wanderers from God to seek us; it is our part to go and seek them. (2). Because we are more peculiarly called, by going out into the highways and hedges (which none will do if we do not) to compel them to come in. (3). Because that reason against it is not good, 'The house will hold all that come'. The house may hold all that will come to the house, but not all that will come into the field. (4). Because we have always found a greater blessing in field-preaching than in any other preaching whatever.

So these amazing men, who could in truthful simplicity sing,

> We have through fire and water gone,

actually felt that they had fallen short and were called to do greater things. More than once, in his verse, Charles Wesley displayed their unconquerable and trusting spirit, as when he wrote:

> If Thou preserve our souls in peace,
>   Our brethren shall afflict in vain:
> Most patient, when they most oppress,
>   We all their cruel wrongs sustain,
> And strengthened by Thy meekening power,
> The more they hate, we love the more.[6]

And to the simple truth of this the story of those days bears eloquent testimony.

From his letter to 'John Smith' on 24th March 1747, we gather that Wesley's open-air preaching did not, at that time, evoke any immediate and widespread response in personal surrender to

[6] *P.W.*, VI.105.

the call of Jesus Christ, for to the charge that the impression made on men's minds by his irregular way of preaching was chiefly due to 'the force of novelty', he replies:

> I believe it was to obviate this very supposition that my preaching so rarely made any impression at all till the novelty of it was over. When I had preached more than six score times at this town (Newcastle), I found scarce any effect; only that abundance of people heard and gaped and stared and went away much as they came. And it was one evening, while I was in doubt if I had not laboured in vain, that such a blessing of God was given as has continued ever since, and I trust will be remembered unto many generations.

There was one obvious temptation to excuse himself from further field-preaching which Wesley vigorously resisted, and which presented itself when the civil authorities forbad the practice or put obstacles in his way. It appears to have been within the province of a magistrate to decide whether any particular gathering was or was not a 'lawful assembly'. For the law and those who administered it Wesley had great reverence, but was always ready to argue against what seemed to him to be an unjust judgement, when it affected him and his people. Instead of accepting an adverse decision in this matter, in meek submission, and flinging the responsibility before God upon the magistrates and invoking the blood of the masses upon their heads, as he might have done, he reasoned and pleaded his cause, that there might be no stigma of lawlessness on his open-air work, and that it might continue.

Any temptation Wesley may have experienced to discontinue field-preaching would be strengthened by a natural disinclination to which he more than once refers. Having 'preached abroad' in the north of England, he wrote (26th June 1759):

> I preached . . . to twice the people we should have had at the house. What marvel the devil does not love field-preaching! Neither do I: I love a commodious room, a soft cushion, a handsome pulpit. But where is my zeal, if I do not trample all these underfoot in order to save one more soul?

As late as 6th September 1772, he wrote in his *Journal*:

> I preached on the Quay at Kingswood, and near King Square. To this day field-preaching is a cross to me. But I know my commission and see no other way of 'preaching the gospel to every creature'.

Throughout the *Journal* occur such testimonies to the value of field-preaching as these:

A vast majority of the immense congregation in Moorfields were deeply serious. One such hour might convince any impartial man of the expedience of field-preaching. What building, except St. Paul's Church, would contain such a congregation? And if it would, what human voice could have reached them there? By repeated observations I find I can command thrice the number in the open air that I can under a roof. And who can say the time for field-preaching is over while (1) greater numbers than ever attend; (2) the convicting, as well as convincing power of God is eminently present with them? (27th September 1759.)

I preached to a large and very serious congregation on Redcliff Hill (Bristol). This is the way to overturn Satan's kingdom. In field-preaching, more than any other means, God is found of them that sought Him not. By this, death, heaven and hell come to the ears, if not the hearts, of them that 'care for none of these things'. (30th September 1767.)

From time to time the subject so near to his heart creeps into Wesley's letters, as when he wrote to James Rea, one of his preachers in Ireland:

Preach abroad ... if ever you would do good. It is the cooping yourselves up in rooms that has damped the work of God, which never was and never will be carried on to any purpose without going out into the highways and hedges and compelling poor sinners to come in. ... Preach abroad in every place. Mind not lazy or cowardly Methodists. 'Tis a shame to preach in a house before October, unless in a morning.[7]

There was one outstanding feature of an ordinary church which Wesley required in his field-preaching—a pulpit. Very much would have been lost had he stood on a level with his congregation. He needed to see the faces before him and himself to be seen and heard. A table or chair, a wall, an open, upper window, a market cross, the steps of a building, a horse block, a tombstone: all these served him in turn, and some are preserved with reverence to this day because Wesley preached from them.

Some of these pulpits are of special interest. At Seaton, near

[7] *Letters*, V.23.

Whitehaven, 'the poor people had prepared a kind of pulpit for me, covered at the top and on both sides, and had placed a cushion to kneel upon of the greenest turf in the country'. (2nd June 1752.) In Glasgow, 'a tent, as they term it, was prepared: a kind of moving pulpit, covered with canvas at the top, behind and on the sides. In this I preached.' (19th April 1753.) At Haworth 'the church would not near contain the people who came from all sides; however, Mr Grimshaw had provided for this by fixing a scaffold on the outside of one of the windows, through which I went after prayers, and the people likewise all went out into the churchyard'. (12th July 1761.)

Even when he ministered within doors Wesley found himself, from time to time, in buildings so strange that they would have daunted the enthusiasm of many preachers. The time came when Methodists built their own preaching-houses or purchased and adapted some existing building, but he still had occasional unpleasant experiences. He was peculiarly sensitive to cleanliness, which was far from being a characteristic feature of all the Anglican churches which he either visited as a worshipper or in which he was permitted to preach. He relates how (24th April 1774) he preached in Llanddwy church, near Brecknock, and 'such a church I never saw before. There was not a glass window belonging to it: but only boards, with holes bored here and there, through which a dim light glimmered in. Yet even here may the light of God's countenance shine. And it has shone on many hearts.'

However plain the Methodist preaching-houses might be—and their plainness bespoke the poverty of their devoted builders—they were almost invariably clean. In a letter to a friend, Wesley remarks upon this:

The longer I am absent from London, and the more I attend the service of the Church in other places, the more I am convinced of the unspeakable advantage which the people called Methodists enjoy: I mean even with regard to public worship, particularly on the Lord's Day. The church where they assemble is not gay or splendid, which might be a hindrance on the one hand; nor sordid or dirty, which might give distaste on the other; but plain as well as clean.[8]

We note, in passing, that Wesley refers to the preaching-house as a 'church'.

[8] *Letters*, III.226.

Where there was no preaching-house such as they favoured, his Methodists were not always able to secure for him a place that was clean and suitable, but they did their best. At Bedford (23rd November 1759), he had a peculiarly trying experience: 'We had a pretty large congregation, but the stench from the swine under the room was scarce supportable. Was ever a preaching-place over a hog-sty before? Surely they love the gospel, who come to hear it in such a place!'

The *Journal* is not remarkable for descriptions of natural beauty. But occasionally Wesley sketches a charming little word picture that helps to re-create for us the scene of his preaching. At Penryn (20th September 1757):

It was an extremely pleasant place on the side of a hill, commanding a fruitful vale, the opposite hills, and Falmouth Harbour. Tall trees hung over me, and surrounded a bowling-green which was behind me.

At Brough (Westmorland. 2nd June 1768):

I preached, at noon, at a farmer's house. . . . The sun was hot enough, but some shady trees covered both me and the congregation. A little bird perched on one of them and sang without interruption, from the beginning of the service to the end.

Near Dewsbury (5th July 1770):

I preached at six at Dawgreen. . . . All things contributed to make it a refreshing season: the gently declining sun, the beauty of the meadows and fields, through which

> The smooth, clear river drew its sinuous train;

the opposite hills and woods, and the earnestness of the people, covering the top of the hill on which we stood; and, above all, the day-spring from on high, the consolation of the Holy One!

At Tanderagee (Ireland. 23rd June 1778), on 'a fair calm evening',

I took my place under a tall, spreading tree, in the midst of a numerous congregation, who were still as night. There could not be devised a more pleasing scene: the clear sky, the setting sun, the surrounding woods, the plain, unaffected people, were just suitable to the subject, 'My yoke is easy and my burden is light'.

There was probably no open-air preaching-place which Wesley loved more than Gwennap, in Cornwall. He was seventy-two when he wrote (3rd September 1775):

I preached ... at five in the evening in the amphitheatre at Gwennap. I think this is the most magnificent spectacle which is to be seen on this side heaven. And no music is to be heard upon earth comparable to the sound of many thousand voices, when they are all harmoniously joined together, singing praises to God and the Lamb.

It is pleasing to recall these scenes. Wesley's field-preaching was not all, or even mainly, in the cobbled streets and grimy, open spaces of the industrial centres; there were places where people flocked to hear him other than Moorfields, Kennington Common and the streets of Midland and Northern towns. To stand in the open spaces of 'England's green and pleasant land', with blue skies above and Nature in all her loveliness and variety around him; with crowds, breathless and deeply moved, listening to his message, must have been ample compensation for every harsh criticism and every rejection on the part of those who should have been standing side by side with him, but who knew not the day of their visitation.

Wesley preaching on a hill-side or beneath the spreading branches of a tree, brings us very near to the Gospel story. Under his ministry England became a Galilee, where the Master walked and taught again in the person of His latest disciple, and the common people heard him gladly. There were seasons when Nature herself seemed to be wholly in harmony with him and his message, and to give her benediction to the Divine word. Sometimes, with excellent Scriptural precedent, the gathered crowds called upon Nature to rejoice with them in their joy, as at Builth (21st February 1748), when

more than all the town were gathered together in that pleasant vale, and made the woods and mountains echo while they sang,

> Ye mountains and vales, in praises abound;
> Ye hills and ye dales, continue the sound;
> Break forth into singing, ye trees of the wood,
> For Jesus is bring lost sinners to God.

So the preaching went on, in spite of all the bishops on the episcopal bench, the parsons in their parishes, the magistrates on their seats of jurisdiction, the squires in their mansions and the mobs swarming from their hovels and gin-palaces, while Charles Wesley flung out both the defiance and the unconquerable resolution of Methodism, in such words as:

Forth in Thy strength, O Lord, we go,
   Forth in Thy steps and loving mind,
To pay the gospel-debt we owe,
   The word of grace for all mankind,
To sow th'incorruptible seed,
And find the lost, and wake the dead.[9]

As troubles arose Wesley maintained his difficult but dutiful course without wavering, believing that 'you muste not forsake the shippe in a tempeste, because you can not rule and kepe downs the wyndes'.[10] The compensations were there and the Lord was 'omnipotently near'. Out on the open fields of their warfare, Wesley and his men knew that

   From Sion's top the breezes blow,
   And cheer us in the vale below.[11]

In 1781, ten years before his death, Wesley published his *Short History of the People called Methodists*. It is a retrospective survey over a long stretch of years, and looking back to the time of his return from Herrnhut he wrote:

Being thus excluded from the churches, and not daring to be silent, it remained only to preach in the open-air; which I did at first, not out of choice, but necessity; but I have since seen abundant reason to adore the wise providence of God herein, making a way for myriads of people who never troubled any church, nor were likely to do so, to hear that word which they soon found to be the power of God unto salvation.[12]

[9] *P.W.*, VI.100. [10] Thomas More, *Utopia*, Book I.
[11] *P.W.*, IV.263. [12] *Works*, XIII.307–8.

CHAPTER VII

WESLEY'S CONGREGATIONS

WESLEY'S congregations are one of the most interesting studies that the *Journal* affords. We see them as cross-sections of the populace of Gt. Britain in the eighteenth century, almost every class of the community being represented. He himself took a deep interest in them, regarding them, not as conglomerate masses of human beings, but as individual men and women with souls to be saved. He wanted to know them as such; to call them by their Christian names, and to few has it been given to enter into so many and varied personal relationships and friendships. From the outset he realized the comparative futility of merely preaching to a miscellaneous crowd of people and leaving the matter there. Individuals needed to be befriended, shepherded, instructed and encouraged, and hence arose the Societies which became the nuclei of the Methodist Church. This is one respect in which he differed from George Whitefield, who was content to preach and hope for the best. Wesley insisted on following up his initial work and, as a rule, declined to preach where continuity and consolidation seemed to be impossible. For example, at Mullingar (Ireland. 10th July 1750), whose inhabitants were predominantly Roman Catholic, 'the sovereign of the town' urged him to preach, but 'I had little hopes of doing good in a place where I could preach but once, and where none but me could be suffered to preach at all'. Apparently he declined. When at Haverfordwest (25th August 1763) he noted: 'I was more convinced than ever that the preaching like an apostle, without joining together those that are awakened and training them up in the ways of God, is only begetting children for the murderer.' (viz., the Evil One.) Whitefield ultimately realized that, in this respect, Wesley had been wiser than he, and said, towards the end of his life, 'My brother Wesley acted wisely. The souls that were awakened under his ministry he joined in class, and thus preserved the fruit of his labour. This I neglected, and my people are a rope of sand.'[1]

Gradually the miscellaneous, haphazard complexion which his

[1] Quoted by K. L. Carrick Smith, *The Church and the Churches*, p. 140.

congregations had at first, diminished. By the grace of God he was making *Methodists*, and these became the permanent and reliable elements of the crowds wherever he went. As preaching-houses were established throughout the country these Methodists became a yet stronger and more consolidated body of hearers, and their manner of life made so favourable an impression locally, that many people were drawn even into the preaching-houses when Wesley went their way.

He thus came to have, in an increasing number of places, two congregations, one within doors and one without. In both he had the support of his own Methodists, and it frequently happened that so great a number pressed to enter the house that Wesley had, in all kinds of weather, to adjourn to the open-air. He thus established contacts both with those who needed guidance and encouragement in their newly-experienced Christian life, and with those who needed to be spiritually awakened.

Hogarth assists us as, in imagination, we take our stand with John Wesley in the open-air and look out, with him, over the assembled multitudes. We can picture the faces upraised to his, many bearing the marks of brutality, debauchery, ignorance, hatred and poverty; faces savage, sullen, soulless, even to the point of idiocy. We can sense some of the emotions that must have moved him: repulsion, horror, bewilderment, a sense of his own utter helplessness: pity, yearning and a righteous wrath against all elements in the national life conducive to evil and misery, and against the privileged persons, lay and clerical, who supinely tolerated their continued existence. Wesley knew that, in spite of all his plainness of speech and choice of simple words, there were people in his congregations of understanding so dull and brutish that his message, at first hearing, would have no meaning for them. The middle class was also represented: tradesmen, professional men and some manual workers, and, in the country, yeomen or farmers, with agricultural workers. Also, on many occasions, there were local 'gentry', generally on the far edge of the crowd and often seated in their carriages, some of them cynically amused, others half-convinced. But here and there amongst the rest, increasing in numbers as time went on, were faces lighted by grace and beautified by peace, and then Wesley knew that he had allies in the great crowd, a knowledge that always lightens a preacher's task and gives him inspiration and courage to press his message home.

Wesley was quick to sum up the temper of his hearers, in terse and often caustic speech. Some audiences appeared to be largely composed of uncomprehending people, as at Abingdon (July 1741), when 'so stupid, senseless a people, both in a spiritual and natural sense, I scarce ever saw before'. In Halifax (May 1747), he preached 'to a civil, senseless congregation', and a little later to a 'stupid one' at Berwick. At Whitby (June 1779) the people 'were deeply attentive; but no more affected than the stones they stood upon'. At 7 o'clock on a November morning, 1768, he preached in Bedford on *Awake thou that sleepest*, and comments: 'never was more need: for a more sleepy audience I have not often seen'. In November 1776, he 'preached at Beccles. A duller place I have seldom seen. The people of the town were neither pleased nor vexed.'

Such congregations did not, apparently, depress John Wesley, and they certainly did not deter him; a dead wall of indifference often strengthened his determination. Sometimes he refused to speak in an atmosphere of tepid interest, as at Ulverston, in June 1752, where 'few people had any desire to hear, so I went quietly back to my inn'. His doubtfulness of results at times induced a pessimistic outlook, as at Athlone, in April 1748, where he had conducted a strenuous preaching campaign throughout the area, addressing large and enthusiastic gatherings. Surveying his work, he wrote:

I preached once more at 5. Great part of the congregation were in tears. So loving a people have I scarce ever seen, nor so strong and general drawings from above. Almost the whole town seems to be greatly moved, full of goodwill and desires of salvation. But the waters spread too wide to be deep; I find not one under sound conviction, much less had anyone received remission of sins under 30 or 40 sermons. So that as yet no judgment can be formed whether there will be any considerable work of God here or no; although all the people are now willing, were it possible, to pluck out their own eyes, and give them unto us.

Similar doubts about the permanence of his work assailed him at Morvah (Cornwall. September 1743): 'I could not find the way into the hearts of the hearers, although they were earnest to hear what they understood not.' Wesley had entered upon the last year of his life when he wrote of a Liverpool congregation: 'They seemed utterly amazed when I explained, *Now faith is the evidence of things not seen*. I believe many were convinced; but, alas, how soon will that conviction die away!' At Chatham (6th December 1771): 'The huge congregation here devoured the word; yet I hope they digested it too.'

Sometimes, as Wesley was aware, his congregations contained people who did not even try to understand what he was saying, as at Deptford (February 1740), where he 'explained . . . the nature of Christian faith and salvation. Many seemed to receive the word with joy. Others complained, "Thou bringest certain strange things to our ears"; though some of them had not patience to hear what this new doctrine was.'

As a rule Wesley's estimate of the mental and spiritual qualities of his hearers was very discerning, but occasionally he was mistaken. Such was the case at Leicester (19th June 1777), of whose people he entertained, on the whole, a rather poor opinion. He had, however, the kind of surprise that sends a preacher rejoicing on his way and expectant of further blessings, and which demonstrates the fallibility of human judgements. 'I did not reach Leicester', he wrote, 'till the congregation had waited some time; so I began immediately to enforce, *Believe on the Lord Jesus Christ and thou shalt be saved.* I had designed not to call here at all, supposing it would be lost labour. But the behaviour of the whole congregation convinced me that I had judged wrong. They filled the house at five in the morning, and seemed determined to stir up the gift of God which was in them.'

Wesley's scorn was sometimes aroused by the irreverent behaviour of people who should have known better and on occasion he publicly rebuked them, or they were rebuked by others in the audience. He had several encounters with 'pretty butterflies', as at St Ives (Cornwall. September 1762), when 'two or three pretty butterflies came and looked and smiled and went away'; and at Liverpool (April 1768), where 'some pretty, gay, fluttering things did not behave with so much good manners as the mob ('wild as wild might be') at Wigan'. Wesley believed that vanity moved some of these young women to laughter. When he was preaching in Ireland, in May 1769, 'all behaved well but one young gentlewoman, who laughed almost incessantly. She knew there was nothing to laugh at; but she thought she laughed prettily.'

Nor was it the ladies alone who were guilty of indecorous conduct; men were more obtrusive in their disrespect. At Heptonstall (June 1752), an attorney who happened to be in the town, endeavoured to interrupt, relating some low, threadbare stories, with a very audible voice. But some of the people cut him short in the midst, by carrying him quietly away.

One can imagine the lawyer's surprise and the delightful comedy of his exit. In the open-air, in Newcastle (March 1775), 'one buffoon laboured much to interrupt; but, as he was bawling with his mouth wide open, some arch boys gave him such a mouthful of dirt as quite satisfied him'. At Burnley (July 1782) there was an equally ludicrous incident, where

all were eager to hear, except one man, who was the town-crier. He began to bawl amain, till his wife ran to him and literally stopped his noise; she seized him with one hand and clapped the other upon his mouth, so that he could not get out one word. God then began a work which I am persuaded will not soon come to an end.

Wesley recounts these and similar stories with evident relish.

Irreverence always jarred upon him. He was at Stourport in March 1790, where the people 'seemed to be all serious and attentive as long as I was speaking; but the moment I ceased, fourscore or one hundred began talking all at once. I do not remember ever to have been present at such a scene before. This must be amended; otherwise (if I should live) I will see Stourport no more.'

In some congregations varied religious opinions were represented. Wesley shunned doctrinal controversy, not because of difficulty in maintaining his own position, but because he knew how futile, in the main, such discussion is. For those who loved this kind of disputing he had little patience and less time. At Portsmouth, in 1753, he found it difficult to preach, because his hearers were too deeply engrossed in theological controversy. He describes them as 'people who disputed themselves out of the power and wellnigh the form of religion'. 'However', he continues, 'I laboured (and not altogether in vain) to soften and compose their jarring spirits.' When in Liverpool (April 1755), he learned that many of the people 'were dear lovers of controversy; *but I had better work. I pressed upon them all repentance toward God and faith in our Lord Jesus Christ.*' In July of the following year, during his tour in Ireland, he noted with profound misgivings the many varieties of religious belief represented in his congregation at Lisburn. He spoke 'very plain' to them, but 'between Seceders, old self-conceited Presbyterians, New-Light men, Moravians, Cameronians and formal Churchmen, it is a miracle of miracles if any here bring forth fruit to perfection'. Wesley, of course, did not decry theological discussion, but he was acutely aware of its dangers, especially among the lesser educated. He observed of his hearers in Manchester, in April 1772, that 'the speculative knowledge of the truth has ascended here from the least to the greatest. But how far short is this of experimental knowledge! Yet it is a step toward it not to be despised.'

Wesley's Scottish congregations deserve special mention. We cannot fail to notice inconsistencies between some of his expressed opinions about them. Often he seems to have yielded to the mood of the moment, without referring his latest judgements to his earlier ones. They vary between condemnation and praise. At times he makes the all-too-common mistake of generalizing upon a particular case. The attentiveness of his Scottish hearers always impressed him, as did their decorous conduct and their susceptibility to reason. 'Only show them the *reasonableness* of it in Scotland, and they will conform to anything', is a not wholly complimentary comment in the *Minutes* of 1766, which only John Wesley could have made. When visiting the country during the summer of 1764 he remarked: 'There is seldom fear of wanting a congregation in Scotland. But the misfortune is, they know everything; so they learn nothing.' A fortnight later, after preaching at Nairn, he made amends to his Scottish audiences in these words: 'Oh, what a difference is there between South and North Britain! Everyone here (N) at least loves to hear the word of God; and none takes it into his head to speak one uncivil word to any for endeavouring to save their souls.' In June 1779, he paid the Aberdeen people the compliment of describing them as 'a people that can feel as well as hear'. Edinburgh seems to have been, on the whole, one of Wesley's disappointments. He was there on Sunday 25th of April 1784, and wrote: 'I am amazed at this people; use the most cutting words and apply them in the most pointed manner, still they *hear*, but *feel* no more than the seats they sit upon.' He returned four days later, when 'the house was well filled. So that we must not say the people of Edinburgh love the word of God only on the Lord's Day.' Four years later, in Dumfries, so attentive was the congregation, that he declared, 'Surely the Scots are the best hearers in Europe!'

On Glasgow congregations he made one of his very caustic

observations. This was during his fourteenth visit to Scotland, when he reached the city on 12th May 1774. He 'preached on the Old Green to a people, the greatest part of whom hear much, know everything and feel nothing'. During the last year of his life, in May 1790, he preached in the city one Friday, when 'the congregation was miserably small; verifying what I had often heard before, that the Scots dearly love the Word of the Lord—on the Lord's Day. If I live to come again, I will take care only to spend the Lord's Day at Glasgow.' On at least one occasion the people of Perth impressed him with their air of 'omniscience', for in May 1774, he wrote:

I returned to Perth and preached in the evening to a large congregation; but I could not find the way to their hearts. The generality of the people here are so wise that they need no more knowledge: and so good that they need no more religion! Who can warn them that are brim-full of wisdom and goodness to flee from the wrath to come?

In Wesley's contacts with Scottish audiences he experienced both sunshine and shadow, as elsewhere, but, on the whole, the sunshine predominated. D. Butler, in his *John Wesley and George Whitefield in Scotland*, fairly summarizes the treatment which Wesley received.

He was everywhere received in Scotland with a dignity and a courtesy which were due to him as a Christian gentleman, scholar and teacher. He was received always with respect, and his reception speaks much for the civilization of the people as well as for their spiritual perception.[2]

With that, we may be sure John Wesley would have agreed.

Wesley's Irish congregations contained a large and often predominant Roman Catholic element. He must have been aware that, in including Ireland in his parish, he would have to face a new kind of opposition, but he regarded desperate opposition as a sign of desperate need, and accordingly went his way in good heart. In all, he made twenty-one visits to the Island, their combined durations being six years. There were a few terrible riots, as in Cork, but on the whole the opposition was far less both in strength and in malice than might have been expected. Curnock justly observes that 'if we except a few abnormal outbreaks, accounted for by special incitements, Wesley was almost as immune from persecution in Ireland as in Scotland'.[3]

[2] op. cit., p. 111.   [3] *Journal*, V.126.

For his Irish congregations, as a whole, he soon conceived a warm regard. Four days after his first arrival in the country (13th August 1747) he wrote to Ebenezer Blackwell:

For natural sweetness of temper, for courtesy and hospitality, I have never seen any people like the Irish. . . .

They receive the word of God with all gladness and readiness of mind. The danger is that it should not take deep root, that it should be as seed falling on stony ground.

During his third visit, in May 1749, there is evidence of his undiminished affection. 'What a nation is this!', he exclaims, 'every man, woman and child (except a few of the great vulgar) not only patiently but gladly "suffer the word of exhortation".' The following year found him in Ireland again, and his impressions are recorded in a letter to Ebenezer Blackwell:

I have had so hurrying a time for two or three months, as I scarce ever had before—such a mixture of storms and clear sunshine, of huge applause and huge opposition. Indeed, the Irish in general keep no bounds. I think there is not such another nation in Europe so
*impetuous in their love and in their hate.*⁴

The Papists, of course, organized opposition, but not to anything like the same extent as did some of the parish priests in England, and most of the *Journal* references to Roman Catholics are kindly (but not his references to Roman Catholicism as a system) and show Wesley's concern for them and their own desire to hear him. Frequently they defied the prohibitions of their priests, some of whom were occasionally present themselves. At Athlone (1st May 1748) he had an attentive congregation of Protestants and Roman Catholics and, being moved to speak particularly to the latter, was 'satisfied many of them were almost persuaded to give themselves up to the great Physician of souls'. A year later he had a similar audience in the same place, the 'poor Papists' being there 'maugre all the labour of their priests', so Wesley

called aloud, 'Ho, every one that thirsteth, come ye to the waters; and he that hath no money!'. Strange news to them! One of whom had declared frankly but a few days before, 'I would fain be with you, but I dare not; for now I have all my sins forgiven for four shillings a year; and this could not be in your church.'⁵

⁴ *Letters*, III.43.   ⁵ *Journal*, III.398.

So, great as were the barriers between him and the Papists, Wesley effected a more auspicious approach as time went on. The goodwill which he gained found unusual expression when he was in Aughrim (13th April 1773), for, as he made his way to preach in the market-place, he was greeted by a street full of people with a 'loud huzza'. There is a charming little picture of him at Portadown (10th April 1767), 'a place not troubled with any kind of religion', where

> I stood in the street and cried, 'Now God commandeth all men everywhere to repent'. The people gathered from all sides and, when I prayed, kneeled down upon the stones, rich and poor, all round me.

No account of Wesley's Irish congregations would be complete without reference to the Anglican clergy. His association with them was almost uniformly happy. From most he received a cordial welcome and they opened their churches and their homes to him. Surrounded as they were by a Roman Catholic population, they saw Wesley in a different light from that in which so many of the English clergy regarded him. He was a valued and timely ally, rather than an obnoxious interloper. They were frequently appreciative members of his congregations, and even sought his advice in spiritual affairs.

Of Wesley's Welsh congregations there is little that calls for special mention. Rarely did a year pass without a visit to the Principality and the *Journal* records forty-six in all. Wesley's activities were much hampered by his ignorance of the language, particularly in North Wales, where very little English was then spoken. In March 1748, the way to preaching seemed to open, and whilst waiting at Holyhead for weather that would allow of his crossing to Ireland, he addressed several congregations in the neighbourhood, seemingly with acceptance and success, encouraged thereto by a Mr Williams, who preached first in Welsh. Wesley records that many understood him and felt the power of God. At Llanfihangel the people were deeply moved. 'Oh, that we could declare to them, in their own tongue, the wonderful works of God!', he writes. On the Sunday of that visit, along with others, he worshipped in the morning at Llangefni church, but 'we understood little of what we heard'. Then he gives a loose rein to his feelings:

> Oh, what a heavy curse was the Confusion of Tongues! And how grievous are the effects of it! All the birds of the air, all the beasts of

the field, understand the language of their own species. Man only is a *barbarian* to man, unintelligible to his own brethren.

At Llanerchymedd (Anglesey. 1st April 1750) he was beset by 'the sons of Belial', and remarks:

I could just understand their oaths and curses, which were broad English and sounded on every side. The rest of their language was lost upon me, as mine was upon them.

Apparently these natives of Anglesey found English a more effective language for cursing and swearing, than Welsh.

The *Journal* records forty visits to South Wales, where there was little language difficulty and preaching was easy. At Margam (19th August 1746), for the benefit of those who did not understand English, 'one repeated to them in Welsh the substance of what I had said'; and near Bridgend (28th August 1771), seeing that his audience was largely Welsh, Wesley preached 'as deliberately as possible', and believed that therefore all could understand 'at least the substance of the discourse'.

As in Ireland, the Anglican clergy were mainly friendly, and many of their churches were opened to him. With the Welsh people in general he was on the happiest terms, and he refers to them in his *Journal* in such felicitous phrases as 'this loving, artless people'; 'a serious company of plain Welshmen'; 'a quiet, humane, courteous people'; 'a lovely congregation of plain, artless people'. After 'a great awakening', through Howell Harris, Wesley informed James Hutton, early in 1740, 'There is such a simplicity among the Welsh, who are waiting for salvation, as I have not found anywhere in England'.

PRISONERS

From Oxford days, Wesley paid special attention to prisoners. Hesitant at first, he and Charles consulted their father, and learned that he himself, when an Oxford undergraduate, had engaged in this type of ministry. So the Rector of Epworth encouraged them to proceed. 'Go on, in God's name, in the path to which your Saviour has directed you, and that track wherein your father has gone before you. . . . Walk as prudently as you can, though not fearfully, and my heart and prayers are with you.'[6]

Thereafter Wesley continued his prison ministry, which soon

---

[6] Tyerman, *Life of Samuel Wesley*, p. 407.

came to be recognized as specially characteristic of Methodist activities. It was not always an easy ministry to him. After preaching to prisoners in the Dublin Newgate (29th March 1748), he was 'afraid the Lord refuses His blessing to this place. Every time I have been here I have been as dead as a stone. A few more trials, and I have done with this house of woe.'

Soon after his return from Georgia Wesley preached in the prison at Oxford and ministered to a condemned malefactor. Such persons existed in the prisons in far greater numbers than they do today or ever will again. The penal code of the country shocks our moral sense. There were 160 offences for which a person might be condemned to death, such as picking a pocket for more than one shilling; stealing a horse or sheep; snaring a rabbit on a private estate. We must therefore beware of regarding all, or even the majority of these prisoners, as being sinners above all men and desperately wicked. No more terrible indictment of the criminal code is needed than a single entry in Charles Wesley's *Journal*: 'By half-hour past ten we came to Tyburn (viz., with condemned prisoners); waited till eleven; *then were brought the children appointed to die.*'[7]

Wesley made no outspoken criticism of the penal code. Whatever his private opinions may have been, he always maintained, as far as possible, an outward loyalty to the King's government. His more immediate concern was with the souls of these people and he availed himself of the opportunities which the law afforded of ministering to them. His compassionate attitude suggests a silent criticism of the system under which they suffered; again and again they are, to Wesley, 'the poor prisoners'. At Oxford, in October 1739, he noted how 'the poor prisoners . . . had none that now cared for their souls; none to instruct, advise, comfort and build them up in the knowledge and love of the Lord Jesus'.

But Wesley's ingrained respect for the King's Justice and the laws of the land did not prevent his criticism, when the occasion arose, of their administration. On 2nd January 1761, he wrote a letter to the *London Chronicle* which begins with a reference to the London Newgate.

Of all the seats of woe on this side hell, few, I suppose, exceed or even equal Newgate. If any region of horror could exceed it a few years ago, Newgate in Bristol did; so great was the filth, the stench, the misery and wickedness which shocked all who had a spark of humanity left.

[7] Charles Wesley's *Journal*, I.122.

He then goes on to express his gratified surprise at the changes which had taken place in Bristol and commends this example to keepers of prisons everywhere.

Wesley's prison congregations increased and he notes times of special power and blessing, as when (Bristol. 27th April 1739) 'all Newgate rang with the cries of those whom the word of God cut to the heart; two of whom were in a moment filled with joy, to the astonishment of those that beheld them'. In various parts of the country people came to look to him as, above all others, able and willing to speak to their condition. Thus, at Carrickfergus (25th July 1756):

The larger court-house being too small to contain the congregation, I the more readily complied with the desire of the prisoners to preach in the street, near the prison door.

At Bristol (21st September 1775):

At the earnest request of the prisoner, who was to die next day (and was very willing so to do, for, after deep agony of soul, he had found peace with God), I preached at Newgate to him and a crowded audience, many of whom felt that God was there.

At the Conference of 1778 official recognition was given to a ministry to prisoners, the question being asked:

Is it not advisable for us to visit all the gaols we can?

John Wesley clearly gives the answer:

By all means. There cannot be a greater charity.

Wesley was not always sanguine as to the results of his prison ministry. At Bristol (4th October 1781) he preached a kind of official sermon. 'I was importuned to preach the condemned sermon at Bristol. I did so, though with little hope of doing good, the criminals being entirely impenitent. Yet they were, for the present, melted into tears; and they were not out of God's reach.'

There is a harrowing and illuminating little word-picture under date 26th December 1784, when a more humane and merciful spirit was becoming manifest. It enables us to see John Wesley, in greater detail, facing these prison congregations, and to enter, more imaginatively, into his feelings.

I preached the condemned criminals' sermon in Newgate (London). Forty-seven were under sentence of death. While they were coming in there was something very awful in the clink of their chains. But no sound was heard, either from them or the crowded audience, after the text was named: 'There is joy in heaven over one sinner that repenteth, more than over ninety and nine just persons that need not repentance.' The power of the Lord was eminently present, and most of the prisoners were in tears. A few days after, twenty of them died at once, five of whom died in peace.

That Wesley could stand the emotional strain of such experiences is strong testimony to his health of body and of mind.

WORKHOUSES

Unfortunate persons were herded together in other places than the prisons. There were the poor-houses, as they were called, but there is little reference to Wesley's preaching there. He seems to have preferred to direct his energies to helping the poor and collecting for their needs, so as to keep them out of these places and restore them to a self-respecting position in society. He frequently preached at a poor-house in Bristol, on Saturdays, and notes, on 14th April 1739:

I preached at the poor-house; three or four hundred were within and more than twice that number without: to whom I explained those comfortable words, 'When they had nothing to pay he frankly forgave them both'.

It was probably one of his Methodists whom he was visiting in the same poor-house on 3rd April 1776, when he was

much moved to see such a company of poor, maimed, halt and blind, who seemed to have no one caring for their souls.

Therefore,

I appointed to be there the next day, and at two o'clock had all that could get out of bed, young and old, in the great hall. My heart was greatly enlarged toward them, and many blessed God for the consolation.

SOLDIERS

In the *Journal* there are many references to soldiers, for whom Wesley always entertained a warm regard. He met them constantly in his journeys and rejoiced to see them in his congregations, as at Canterbury (14th March 1757), where he 'preached in the evening with great enlargement of spirit, but with greater in the morning, being much refreshed at the sight of so large a number of soldiers'. Most of them, in those days, came from the lowest ranks of society: men almost wholly untouched by religion, generally because no man had cared for their souls or felt any responsibility for their moral and spiritual welfare; men drawn to the Army because they had failed in other directions, or desired a life of change and adventure in company with other dare-devil spirits, neither asking nor expecting much of life in the way of material success and rewards; inspired, probably, more by a spirit of loyalty to their friends than a fervent, disinterested patriotism. Wesley seems to have regarded them somewhat as Siegfried Sassoon:

> Soldiers are citizens of death's grey land,
>   Drawing no dividend from time's tomorrows.
> In the great hour of destiny they stand,
>   Each with his feuds and jealousies and sorrows;[8]

and he wanted to tell them of the Love of God, that brings men out of the land of darkness and the shadow of death. C. E. Vulliamy says that Wesley 'was nearly always popular with soldiers, who admired his pluck and his neat, manly bearing'.[9] That is true, but more remains to be said. Situated as they were, it is not surprising that Wesley found many of them susceptible to his appeals. He had a gospel which spoke to their inarticulate need and came to them as a revelation of a new order of existence, which God had made possible for them to share. Many of them joined his Societies and some, like John Haime and Sampson Staniforth, were received into the ranks of the first Methodist preachers.

In his earliest contacts with them, soldiers moved Wesley to compassion. In 1745 he wrote:

A soldier's religion is a by-word, even with those who have no religion at all. . . . Vice and profaneness in every shape reign among them without control; and the whole tenor of their behaviour speaks, 'Let us eat and drink, for tomorrow we die'.[10]

He was in Newcastle in October of the same year, after the defeat of the Government troops at Prestonpans, and when the whole town and neighbourhood were in the hands of the military

---

[8] 'Dreamers', *Collected Poems* (1947), p. 71.
[9] *John Wesley*, p. 191.   [10] *Works*, VIII.173.

authorities. What he then saw moved him to such horror and pity that he addressed a letter to the Mayor.

My soul has been pained day by day, even in walking the streets of Newcastle, at the senseless, shameless wickedness, the ignorant profaneness, of the poor men to whom our lives are entrusted. . . .

Is there no man that careth for these souls? Doubtless there are some who ought so to do. But many of these, if I am rightly informed, receive large pay and do just nothing.

I would to God it were in my power in any degree to supply their lack of service. I am ready to do what in me lies to call these poor sinners to repentance, once or twice a day (while I remain in these parts), at any hour or at any place. And I desire no pay at all for doing this, unless what my Lord shall give at His appearing.[11]

Wesley would have made a successful and beloved army chaplain, and we know how greatly such men were needed. He knew how difficult it was for men in the ranks to persevere in the Christian way of life, and how, having joined his Societies, they needed loving counsel and wise shepherding beyond the ordinary. As far as possible he gave these himself.

His chief difficulty and disappointment with soldiers seems to have been their stupidity. At Newcastle (31st October 1745) he found that, 'although none attempted to make the least disturbance from the beginning to the end', he 'could not reach their hearts. The words of a scholar (by which he probably meant correct English) did not affect them like those of a dragoon or a grenadier', whose language was proverbially lurid and pungent.

It was usual for Wesley to receive courteous treatment at the hands of officers, especially in Ireland, and he records the occasions with evident pleasure. Sometimes the Commanding Officer would parade his men to hear Wesley preach, and when trouble seemed to be brewing, soldiers frequently intervened to protect him and guarantee him a hearing and fair treatment, as at Malton (16th July 1766), where the people were inclined to be restless and inattentive, but 'a whole troop of Oxford Blues, who stood together and were deeply serious, kept them in awe; so they all behaved decently, and many of the soldiers were present again in the morning'. Sometimes they did even more than that, as at Fort Kinsale (25th August 1752), where, on a neighbouring hill, there was 'a large, deep hollow, capable of containing two or three thousand people', and Wesley says: 'On one side of this

[11] *Letters*, II.52.

the soldiers soon cut a place with their swords for me to stand, where I was screened both from the wind and sun, while the congregation sat on the grass before me.'

Wesley rejoiced most when, through his contacts with these men, they were converted, became Methodists and joined his Societies. As early as 1744 there were little groups of Methodists in the Army itself, meeting for spiritual fellowship and offering the blessings of the gospel to others. It was surely a Methodist whom Wesley met at Nenagh (12th May 1749), where he had no intention of preaching, 'but one of the dragoons quartered there would take no denial. So I ordered a chair to be carried out and went to the market-place. Presently such a congregation was gathered round me as I had not seen since I left Athlone. To these I spake, as I was able, the whole counsel of God.' When at Limerick, in June 1750, Wesley found in the Society about sixty soldiers of a Highland Regiment: 'men fit to appear before princes. Their zeal, "according to knowledge", has stirred up many; and they still speak for God and are not ashamed.'

THE COMMON PEOPLE

In Wesley's congregations there was one constant and never-failing element: *the Common People*, amongst whom he won his greatest triumphs; the 'poor', as they almost invariably were in those days: the folk who carried the heavier end of humanity's burden, oft-times with astonishing gaiety of heart. From early days these people roused his sympathy and to their service he deliberately dedicated his life. In various ways that do not concern us here, he served their interests and relieved their distresses, and their presence in his congregations gave him the deepest satisfaction. Here was material which offered good chance of success, and it was out of the Common People that Methodism took shape; and through them, by the grace of God, there came a measure of healing to an afflicted generation.

The Wesley Hymns are full of the poor and lowly, who are so often the needy and the sinful also. They are continually in mind in the great 'invitation' hymns.

> He hath opened a door,
> To the penitent poor,
> And rescued from sin,
> And admitted the harlots and publicans in.[12]

[12] *M.H.B.*, No. 262.

In a hymn wide in the scope of its sympathies, Charles Wesley rejoices that 'gospel salvation is preached to the poor',[18] and always the highest note of gladness is struck when 'the humble poor believe'.

There is a striking passage in the *Journal* (17th November 1759) in which Wesley discloses, in unusual circumstances and with transparent sincerity, the yearning of his heart over the poor and lowly.

I spent an hour agreeably and profitably with Lady Gertrude and Sir Charles Hotham. It is well a few of the rich and noble are called. Oh, that God would increase their number! But I should rejoice (were it the will of God) if it were done by the ministry of others. If I might choose, I should still (as I have done hitherto) preach the gospel to the poor.

One feels, in reading the *Journal*, how refreshing it was to John Wesley's tired body and spirit, to minister to a truly worshipping congregation of his Methodists. Here were no 'beasts of the people': no hooligans: no contemptuous, superior people: no coming and going: no jostling crowds, jeering, curious or indifferent. These beloved people ministered to him, and he could say, as at Rotherham (16th April 1766):

What a blessing it is to be with those who are alive to God!

M.H.B., No. 329.

CHAPTER VIII

MOBS AND HOOLIGANS

THE RULE OF the House of Hanover in the eighteenth century was not undisputed. Apart from the Stuart pretensions there were the unformulated pretensions of 'King Mob', to whom Horace Walpole refers as 'our supreme governors, the mob'.[1] Tobias Smollett knew them. His *Matthew Bramble* describes the mob as 'a monster I never could abide, either in its head, tail, midriff or members; I detest the whole of it as a mass of ignorance, presumption, malice and brutality',[2] and there is much justice in the indictment. Today we can hardly imagine how terrible were these expressions of popular and largely irrational feeling, inspiring widespread fear and disgust. The Wesleys were familiar with them, and not the anti-Methodist mobs alone. Charles Wesley, who was in London during the Gordon Riots, was profoundly moved by his experiences and his pity for the Roman Catholics, and his letters attest the ferocity of the rabble's onslaught.

John Wesley frequently refers to the mobs as 'the beasts of the people' or 'the sons of Belial', and some of his encounters with them he describes, in good scriptural language, as 'fighting with wild beasts at Ephesus'. He seems at times to have regarded the mob as something complete in itself and possessed by a satanic power, as when he writes (26th October 1740), 'the many-headed beast began to roar again'. Probably no man knew these eighteenth-century mobs, by first-hand experience, better than he, and the *Journal* has vivid descriptions of wild, tumultuous scenes, which became fewer and less murderous in their tendencies as time went by. They seem to have ceased, at any rate effectively, about the year 1766. Certain features recur. Wesley had at times to appeal to magistrates for the protection of the law, but not always with success. Sometimes the magistrates were themselves lawless. There were terrible scenes in Cornwall, where, on one occasion in 1745, two men rode into the midst of his congregation

[1] Letter to Sir Horace Mann, 7th September 1743.
[2] *Humphrey Clinker*, 23rd April.

and seized him, with the intention of pressing him into the King's service. Presently they discovered that Wesley knew more about the law in such matters than they had suspected and at once set him free. Numerous were the devices to silence him. Many mobs were organized by local 'gentry' and clergy, who circulated deliberately false statements about his preaching and his intentions, in order to spur the people on to outrage. At times, but rarely, Wesley suffered personal violence, being struck on the face and beaten to the ground. Cattle and other beasts were driven in among his hearers. Mobs burst into buildings where he was preaching, smashing windows and generally wrecking the place; even maltreating the people. Stones and dirt were common missiles. Church and hand-bells were rung; soldiers beat their drums; one mob, provided with horns by the local curate, blew them lustily. Clubs and sticks were used. On some occasions the public fire-engine was requisitioned and water pumped over the congregation. Wesley tells how, at North Tawton, in 1765, some would-be disturbers 'brought a huntsman with his hounds; but the dogs were wiser than the men, for they could not bring them to make any noise at all'.

John Wesley early discovered that command of the situation would probably pass into his own keeping if he could come face to face with the ringleader of the disturbance. 'It was', he says, 'my rule, confirmed by long experience, always to look a mob in the face.'[3] So, as T. B. Shepherd finely puts it, 'He walked out calmly to face mobs, rather like a French aristocrat during the Revolution.'[4] In St Ives he won a complete victory (18th September 1743) by actually laying hold of the leader, hauling him to the front and arguing with him. So the mobs did not, as a rule, have things all their own way. There was a typical instance in London (16th September 1740), when

Many more, who came in among us as lions, in a short space became as lambs; the tears trickling down their cheeks, who at first most loudly contradicted and blasphemed.

During the riots in Cornwall, in the summer of 1745, when Wesley preached at Tolcarn, it was personal contact and conversation that averted what threatened to be an ugly incident. It had been reported that 'a great company of tinners, made drunk on

[3] *Journal*, III.250.
[4] *Methodism and the Literature of the Eighteenth Century*, p. 253.

purpose, were coming to do terrible things', and the *Journal* entry runs:

Hearing the mob was rising again, I began preaching immediately. I had not spoken a quarter of an hour before they came in view. . . . As I stood on a high wall, and kept my eyes upon them, many were softened and grew calmer; which some of their champions observing, went round and suddenly pushed me down. I light upon my feet, without any hurt, and, finding myself close to the warmest of the horsemen, I took hold of his hand and held it fast while I expostulated the case. As for being convinced, he was quite above it: however, both he and his fellows grew much milder, and we parted very civilly.

Such a friendly, unsuspicious approach to a crowd often worked wonders, as at Galway (5th June 1765), where

the beasts of the people . . . roaring louder and louder, I walked through them without any hindrance or affront, and returned quietly to my lodgings. A large retinue attended me to the door, but it was only to gape and stare.

He preached at Lowestoft (11th October 1764) in the open-air, and tells us 'a wilder congregation I have not seen; but the bridle was in their teeth'. Thomas Tripp, a devoted Lowestoft Methodist, was present on that occasion, and his *Memoir* records that

his (Wesley's) sermon was with such power that it is not forgotten to the present day. It is highly probable that the presence of so venerable a person restrained the multitude; his flowing eloquence charmed their ears as well as affected their hearts; but with all his superior advantages he only just escaped being insulted, for the people were ready for mischief, but Divine providence over-ruled at that time.[5]

In spite of his penetrating voice and commanding personality Wesley did not always prevail against the mob and secure a hearing. Sometimes one has the impression that he did not try. Physically and mentally weary he must often have been, and it may be that there were times when he refused to cast his pearls before swine, or was mindful of the words of our Lord: 'As many as receive you not, when ye depart from that city, shake off the dust from your feet for a testimony against them.' At Newcastle (10th July 1743), after spending nearly an hour in singing and prayer and being unable to obtain a hearing, 'I thought it best

[5] *W.M.M.* (1811), p. 149.

to adjourn to our own house'. At Limerick (15th May 1785), the people were

> *Wild as the untaught Indian's brood.*
> They made such a wonderful noise that I judged it best to give them the ground, and retired to our own house.

If Wesley could forestall possible mob action he did so. At Pocklington (25th April 1752) he noticed the 'unusual bitterness' of persons in the street, and when a certain yard was proposed as a preaching-place he declined it, because 'it was plentifully furnished with stones; artillery ready at hand for the devil's drunken companions'.

In Ireland he from time to time faced opposition organized by Roman Catholics and their priests. There were some wild scenes in Cork (May 1750), and when, the next day, he reached Bandon, he learned that after his departure the mob of Cork had 'marched in grand procession and then burnt me in effigy near Daunt's Bridge'. Wesley probably appreciated the honour and enjoyed the humour of it.

Not only were there mobs, but hooligans: individuals who were out to gain popularity and a reputation for gallantry by publicly assailing Wesley and his companions and urging the not always obedient crowd to follow their examples. There was often a humorous side to their behaviour, as we have seen, and the comic element in the situation frequently worked to Wesley's advantage. Laughter induces tolerance, and a laughing crowd will not fling brickbats, though a jeering crowd may. At Athlone (14th July 1765), Wesley tells how

> A Popish miller ... got up to preach over against me; but some of his comrades throwing a little dirt in his face, he leaped down in haste to fight them. This bred a fray, in which he was so roughly handled that he was glad to get off with only a bloody nose.

At Bradford (Wilts. 19th October 1769), there was a person

> called a gentleman, who had filled his pockets with rotten eggs; but, a young man coming unawares, clapped his hands on each side and smashed them all at once. In an instant he was perfume all over; though it was not so sweet as balsam.

On some occasions Wesley's defenders emerged from the crowd itself. In July 1745, there were furious scenes in Falmouth, where the rabble roared out, 'Bring out the Canorum. Where is the

Canorum?';—'an unmeaning word', says Wesley, 'which the Cornish generally use instead of *Methodist*'. Wesley stepped bareheaded into their midst and asked permission to speak, which was at once granted. The leaders of the mob then became his protectors and swore that not a man should touch him. It is good to know that on that occasion a local clergyman and some of the gentry intervened on his behalf. At Reading (2 November 1747), a large company of bargemen attended the preaching, who, it was rumoured, had been hired to pull down the preaching-house, but

> in the conclusion of my sermon one of them, who used to be their captain, being the head taller than his fellows, rose up and, looking round the congregation, said, 'The gentleman says nothing but what is good: I say so; and there is not a man here who shall dare to say otherwise.'

Apparently no one did. Dictators were evidently not unknown in the days of John Wesley.

Sometimes the defence came from a quite unexpected quarter, as at Sunderland (11th July 1743), when Wesley was rescued from the mob by a burly, drunken fish-wife who challenged them not to touch her 'canny man'. At Hull (24th April 1752) it was a lady who afforded him protection of a different kind. He tells how

> many behaved as if possessed by Moloch. Clods and stones flew about on every side. . . . When I had finished my discourse, I went to take coach; but the coachman had driven clear away. . . . A gentlewoman invited my wife and me to come into her coach. She brought some inconveniencies on herself thereby, not only as there were nine of us in the coach, three on each side and three in the middle, but also as the mob closely attended us, throwing in at the windows (which we did not think it prudent to shut) whatever came next to hand. But a large gentlewoman who sat in my lap screened me, so that nothing came near me.

When he was at Passage, near Waterford (14th June 1769) Wesley preached to

> as dull a congregation as I have seen. They would have been rude enough, too, but that they stood in awe of Mr Freestone, who gave one and another, when they did not regard his signs, a stroke on the head with his stick. By this means the whole multitude was tolerably quiet, and many seemed much affected.

Wesley does not say whether this was by the stick or the preaching.

One gets the impression that many of these crowds were, in the first instance, much like children: trustful and pliable in the hands of those who first solicited their sympathies: easily persuaded and won over by persons not only of strong personality, but of superior social status, and, if won over for an evil purpose, rapidly passing from the guilelessness of children to the destructive madness of the wild beast. The crowd has then become a mob. Many of the crowds that became mobs around Wesley were deliberately marshalled by individuals who should have known better: by parsons, squires, magistrates and prominent persons. In a few cases their evil opinions of Wesley and his preaching may have been genuine, however mistaken, but their neglect to verify the accuracy of them was inexcusable. In other cases the instigators were moved by sheer, brutal malevolence; in others by love of a big row; in others by a desire for notoriety. Consciously or instinctively they were aware of their power to inflame the ignorant 'beasts of the people' and to collect a mob bent on obstruction and even destruction. This they did, in the main, by the dissemination of false ideas, engendering a common, unifying emotion of hatred and fear—that Wesley was a Jesuit; that he was an agent of the exiled house of Stuart, his mission being to foment rebellion against the reigning house; that he preached doctrines opposed to those of the Church of England and sought the overthrow of the Establishment; that, somehow, he was a threat to their liberties as British subjects, and as such he ought to be opposed by every patriotic individual and reduced to impotence and silence.

It was easy to inculcate such ideas into the minds of such people. Their conditions of life deprived them almost entirely of any power of private judgement. They were, for the most part, illiterate; life was hard and they were oppressed by dire poverty. They dwelt in stinking, ill-furnished hovels, where elementary decency and cleanliness were hardly possible. Cultural interests were almost non-existent. The gin shops knew them, but the churches scarcely at all, and few people had pity for them. Their amusements were such as appealed to and stimulated the brutal element in human nature and they found pleasure in sheer cruelty, which they regarded as 'sport'. The gulf between them and the 'upper classes' was, in almost every respect, immense, but these privileged persons did not hesitate to cross it when they needed the people on the other side to serve their evil purposes.

Bonamy Dobrée suggests that in some cases persons were roused to resentment by being told by Wesley that they were sinners; by interference with their cock-fighting, drinking and lusts; and by the discomfort experienced in a family when some of its members became Methodists.[6] It may well be that it was through the distorting medium of some such feelings that a few people looked at John Wesley, and hated him and his works in consequence. Some, as we have seen, were moved by a professed regard for Church or State. But the ordinary people who formed the crowds had little real or intelligent regard for either. Why should they? What had either done for them? Their devotion, on these occasions, to the Established Church, was due mainly to an inarticulate belief that it was a strong safeguard against a Roman Catholic domination which was then generally feared. As for the State, the conditions in which these people lived were its sufficient condemnation. Much was rotten in the State of Britain, but the fickle mob forgot many of its grievances when a pseudo-patriotism gave it an excuse for baiting the Methodist preachers. When the carefully instilled idea, that Wesley was a danger to the community, really possessed it, it became a raging, murderous rabble.

But amongst them were many who were moved by no such sentiments. They had no personal feeling against Wesley; they just loved a row. Here was a row, so they must be in it. It broke the monotony of life and provided a welcome variation of what they regarded as 'sport'; instead of cock-fighting, a personal encounter with another human being; and instead of bear-baiting, man-baiting. Sometimes they were reluctant to engage, lest they should fare badly in the contest or come up against the law, with serious consequences to themselves. Often they had to be plied with drink and given monetary and other encouragements to keep up their courage and determination, and, as they sobered, these stimuli had to be renewed. A mob was often a costly luxury for the man who employed it. Save for a few, these desperadoes do not appear to have been greatly moved by the pernicious ideas presented to them, but they provided a plausible excuse for wanton mischief and brutality. Perverted patriotism offered a convenient cudgel with which to exercise their sadistic instincts.

[6] *John Wesley*, pp. 105-6.

Gradually these attacks on Wesley and his preachers became less violent and frequent; less the collective upsurging of mob passions than the exhibitionist extravagancies of individuals. At Worcester (8th July 1777) he finds that 'even the beasts of the people are now tame, and open not their mouths against them' (viz. the Methodists). Barnsley was 'formerly famous for all manner of wickedness. They were then ready to tear any Methodist preacher in pieces'; but now (30th June 1786), 'not a dog wagged his tongue'.

On a broad survey it would seem that the mobs were a benefit, rather than a hindrance, to Wesley's ministry. A crowd attracts a crowd, especially if it is a riotous one. Many who came to curse remained to pray, and the day when they joined the mob became the birthday of their souls. News of these mobs and their atrocities spread through the land and became a magnificent advertisement for Wesley and his preachers. People came, out of sheer curiosity, to see and hear these men who had 'fought with beasts' at Walsall, Devizes, Cork and in Cornwall; and in this ordering of things, even the wrath of men was used to the glory and praise of God. Wesley discovered how true are the words of Ignatius: 'Christianity is a thing of might, whensoever it is hated by the world.'[7]

There are few aspects of the Methodist Revival which have so caught the popular imagination as the mobs and their violence, and there are echoes of those far-away encounters in some of the hymns that we still sing. We do not, today, sing such verses of Charles Wesley as,

> Slaughter and cruel threats they breathe,
> And endless battles wage,
> And gnash upon us with their teeth,
> And tear the ground with rage;[8]

but our hymnbook enables us, if we wish, to sing:

> Jesu's tremendous name
> Puts all our foes to flight;
> Jesus, the meek, the angry Lamb,
> A Lion is in fight.
>
> By all hell's host withstood,
> We all hell's host o'erthrow;
> And conquering them, through Jesu's blood,
> We still to conquer go;[9]

[7] *Epistle to the Romans*, Sec. 3.   [8] *P.W.*, IV.30.   [9] *M.H.B.*, No. 481.

and
>   Stand then against your foes,
>   In close and firm array;
>   Legions of wily fiends oppose
>   Throughout the evil day:
>   But meet the sons of night;
>   But mock their vain design,
>   Armed in the arms of heavenly light,
>   Of righteousness divine.[10]

Such verses are included in our hymnbook today because they describe the conflicts which are waged on spiritual battlefields, against spiritual hosts of wickedness, but their phraseology is born of those mundane battlefields where John Wesley and his preachers fought with beasts of eighteenth-century England.

Yet one thing remains to be said. As, in imagination, we see John Wesley facing those hostile crowds, we are impressed not only by his courage in the presence of physical danger, but by the courage with which he suppressed his own natural inclinations. When those raucous voices were bawling around him and even clamouring for his blood, and when those revolting faces, distorted by devilish malice, were thrust close to his and their foul breath assailed him, how often must his thoughts have turned, with something of a heartache, to joys and amenities of life that he had voluntarily surrendered; to his rooms in Lincoln College, haunt of ancient peace! to students with whom, even in that moment, he might have been reading his beloved Greek and Latin classics; to 'the High', and Christ Church and Magdalen Tower by the bridge; to those ancient college halls and libraries and chapels, with their

>   storied windows richly dight,
>   Casting a dim, religious light;[11]

to all that sculptured loveliness which is Oxford, and which had helped to fashion him into the Christian scholar and gentleman that he was; where he might have dwelt until his earthly course was run, listening to her 'whispering from her towers the last enchantment of the Middle Age'.[12]

Yes, Wesley made an immeasurable sacrifice when he became an itinerant preacher to illiterate mobs. He loved the cloistered life of Oxford, probably above any other kind of life on earth.

[10] *M.H.B.*, No. 484.   [11] Milton, *Il Penseroso*, l. 159.
[12] Matthew Arnold, *Essays in Criticism:* Preface to First Series.

But it was not to be. Nevertheless, *it might have been,* and then there would have been no mobs—*and no Methodism.* So, with a courage such as few have shown, John Wesley went out

> To meet the sons of night,
> To mock their vain design,[13]

and to 'keep right on to the end of the road' which he had chosen.

[13] *M.H.B.,* No. 484.

CHAPTER IX

JOHN WESLEY'S SUBJECTS

TOWARDS the end of his life John Wesley published eight volumes of sermons, some of which had appeared forty years earlier, whilst others had been printed from time to time in the *Arminian Magazine*. What is known as the First Series contains fifty-three discourses, forty-four of which are part of the doctrinal standards of Methodism. The Second Series is contained in the remaining four volumes, consisting of fifty-five discourses. After Wesley's death a Third Series was issued, containing eighteen sermons which had been printed in the *Magazine* but had not been revised by him. A Fourth Series consists of seven sermons which Wesley had published in separate form but never included in any collection. A Fifth and final Series presents eight discourses which were found in manuscript among his papers and which, apparently, he had never intended to publish.

We have assumed that what Wesley published he also preached; not necessarily in the same literary style, but proclaiming sum and substance in words which the common people could understand. It is not possible to conceive of any powers of oratory or intensity of zeal for the souls of men that could commend these sermons, as they stand, to the many people whose illiteracy was a disgrace to their age and country, and who probably formed the majority of Wesley's out-of-doors hearers.

As we read the Sermons and the many references in the *Journal* to Wesley's subjects and texts, we notice that they fall conveniently into three broad classes. In the first class are those that deal with what he rightly regarded as the fundamental doctrines of the Christian Faith; doctrines that can be brought to the pragmatic test of workability. They are based, first, upon Scripture, and are then, for the most part, verifiable in experience. Outstanding amongst them are those doctrines upon which Methodism has always laid special emphasis: what Wesley called 'our doctrines', although there is nothing about them that is peculiar to Methodism. It cannot be too strongly insisted that Methodism has no esoteric doctrines that distinguish it from every other Christian communion.

Its peculiar association with these doctrines lies solely in the recognition of their value and the emphasis in consequence placed upon them. They are entirely in accord with the teaching of the New Testament and the standards of the Church of England and the Protestant Churches generally. What Wesley did was to rescue them from neglect and partial oblivion and apply them to the desperate needs of his own day, with a success that was evidence of their virility. There can be no more deadly indictment of Wesley's clerical opposers than their own charge against him, that his doctrines were 'new'.

In brief, they are the doctrines of

1. Salvation by Faith, often described as Justification or the Forgiveness of Sins, involving Regeneration, or the New Birth.

2. Christian Assurance, or the Witness of the Spirit to the believer's acceptance into the Family of God, so that he is no longer a child of God by creation only, but also by Redemption: the Assurance that Charles Wesley expressed again and again in such lines as:

> My God, I am thine,
> What a comfort divine,
> What a blessing to know that my Jesus is mine!
> In the heavenly Lamb
> Thrice happy I am,
> And my heart it doth dance at the sound of His name;

and which was so great a comfort to old Samuel Wesley as he lay upon his death-bed—'The inward witness, son, the inward witness! That is the proof, the strongest proof, of Christianity.'[1]

3. Sanctification, which is that growth in grace which marks the life of the true Christian, culminating in what is variously styled 'Christian Perfection', 'Holiness', 'Perfect Love'. This use of the word 'perfect' led occasionally to misunderstandings which Wesley had to remove. He briefly defined the doctrine as 'the loving God with all our heart, mind, soul and strength. This implies that no wrong temper, none contrary to love, remains in the soul; and that all the thoughts, words and actions are governed by pure love.'[2] Wesley believed there could be no vital Christianity where this doctrine was neglected.

Within this first category of subjects fall the doctrines of Sin and Repentance. As Wesley toured the country and became

[1] Tyerman, *Life of Samuel Wesley*, p. 444.
[2] *Works*, XI.394. (*A Plain Account of Christian Perfection.*)

familiar with the barbaric character of masses of the people, he realized that nothing was possible towards their regeneration until they had a sense of sin and consequent need. The eyes of the spiritually blind had to be opened and the ears of the deaf unstopped, and this he attempted with the fervour of a prophet of old. In his *Earnest Appeal to Men of Reason and Religion* (1743), sections 65 and 66, Wesley gives a clear statement of how he preached to those who had delivered themselves into the bondage of sin. It is too long to be included here, and should be read at this point. It is not our intention to discuss these topics further, as they are fully dealt with in the many books that treat of the Methodist emphasis on Doctrine.

The second class of Subjects deals with those bearing upon speculative theology. In one form or another these doctrines are a part of the orthodox Christian Faith, their teaching being incorporated in the ancient creeds. They are based primarily upon Revelation, as given either explicitly or implicitly in the Scriptures, and can neither be derived from nor established by experience, though experience may strengthen their credibility. Prominent amongst them are the doctrines of the Holy Trinity; the Person and Work of Christ and the Nature of the Atonement; of His Second Advent and the Final Judgement; of Heaven and Hell.

On these subjects Wesley seems rarely to have preached specifically. For the most part he assumed the truth of these doctrines and their acceptance by his hearers in general. In addressing his mixed, open-air audiences, he had to convince men of sin and point them to the Saviour of the world, and in so doing to assume the truth of the Divinity of Christ and the efficacy of His atoning work; the certainty of final judgement; the reality of Heaven and Hell; and all this on the basis of Scripture revelation, which would not be questioned by a mixed crowd of his time, to anything like the extent to which it would be questioned by a similar crowd today. This he did, as a rule, without those niceties and discriminations in detail which mark the work of the professional theologian and apologist.

As Christian preaching is essentially 'preaching Christ', we pause here to inquire what John Wesley understood by this. There is a passage in his sermon on *The Law Established through Faith* that is so informative on this point as to warrant inclusion here.

It is our part to preach Christ by preaching all things whatsoever he hath revealed. We may indeed, without blame, and with a peculiar blessing from God, declare the love of our Lord Jesus Christ; we may speak, in a more especial manner, of 'the Lord our Righteousness'; we may expatiate upon the grace of God in Christ, 'reconciling the world unto himself'; we may, at proper opportunities, dwell upon his praise, as 'bearing the iniquities of us all, as wounded for our transgressions and bruised for our iniquities, that by his stripes we might be healed': . . . .

But still we should not preach Christ according to his word, if we were wholly to confine ourselves to this: we are not ourselves clear before God, unless we proclaim him in all his offices. To preach Christ, as a workman that needeth not to be ashamed, is to preach him, not only as our great High Priest, 'taken from among men, and ordained for men, in things pertaining to God'; as such 'reconciling us to God by his blood', and 'ever living to make intercession for us';— but likewise as the Prophet of the Lord, 'who of God is made unto us wisdom'; who, by his word and his Spirit, is with us always, 'guiding us into all truth';—yea, and as remaining a King for ever; as giving laws to all whom he has bought with his blood; as restoring those to the image of God, whom he had first re-instated in his favour; as reigning in all believing hearts until he has 'subdued all things to himself',—until he hath utterly cast out all sin, and brought in everlasting righteousness.[3]

The subjects of the third class are miscellaneous, dealing with matters of morals, expediency and general decency. Many of the people to whom the word of Wesley and his preachers had come with saving power, needed careful instruction in the art of Christian living. Some of them had existed on a plane of semi-barbarism and were ignorant of the elementary graces of life. These converts had, in the familiar phrase, 'accepted Christ'. What, now, were they to do with Him? Or, what were they willing for Him to do with them? To answer these questions they needed guidance. Faculties, hitherto dormant, had to be related to, directed by, that Christ to whom they had surrendered. At that point they turned to John Wesley and said: 'Tell us how to live; tell us what to do and we will do it.' Having rightly estimated their own need and incapacity, in turning to him they showed a wisdom of choice which was a testimony to their sincerity of heart.

It was no light task that Wesley accepted. Amongst the maxims

[3] *Works*, V.461.

of Epicurus which have come down to us is one on the art of living, which runs:

> It is not possible to live pleasantly (or, happily: ἡδέως) without living wisely (φρονίμως), nobly (καλῶς) and justly (δικαίως), nor to live wisely, nobly and justly, without living happily.[4]

It is this 'living happily' which every man is concerned to ensure, and Wesley and his converts no less than others. Epicurus has fairly stated the conditions. It remains to see how John Wesley put a Christian content into the three words, wisely, nobly, justly.

First, a word of warning! Wesley knew how necessary it is to insist that the Christian life does not wholly consist in the observance of rites and ceremonies, however helpful some of them may be. The prevalent idea, among those who thought about religion at all or made any profession of it, was quite otherwise, though few, in all probability, would have expressed themselves with such freedom and pungency of speech as a woman whom Wesley encountered at Newlyn, when he preached, on 11th September 1757, to

> a huge multitude, and one only seemed to be offended—a very *good sort of woman*, who took great pains to get away, crying aloud, 'Nay, if going to church and sacrament will not *put us to heaven*, I know not what will.'

We then notice that Wesley expounded the practical teaching of the *Sermon on the Mount* in thirteen published sermons, and these, in one form of words or another, he frequently preached. Those virtues and graces which our Lord pronounced to be 'blessed' to those who possessed them—meekness, mercy, purity and the like—are subjects too familiar to call for more than a passing reference. They are dispositions of the heart which lead to certain kinds of conduct, which we instinctively associate with Christianity. Richard Green says of these sermons that 'they are perhaps the most beautiful examples of ethical teaching Wesley ever penned, and the best reply to the charge that Methodism had no ethical message'.[5]

Beyond this sphere of essential Christian conduct and character, Wesley preached to them on some very practical matters, all embraced in that 'living wisely' of Epicurus. Most of these themes

---

[4] Diogenes Laertius, *The Sovran Maxims or Principal Doctrines of Epicurus* (Κύριαι Δόξαι), No. 5.
[5] *John Wesley: Evangelist*, p. 314.

would have evoked little, if any, response from a spiritually unawakened crowd and would almost certainly have invited derision from some. A man has to be released from the grip of old evil before he acquires the power and freedom to work all the works of the Christian life, or even to perform some of the actions which common prudence dictates. In a general kind of way, Wesley distinguished between preaching to believers and to unbelievers. This is apparent as early as 1745, when the question was asked in Conference: 'Do we preach as we did at first? Have we not changed our doctrines?' The answer runs:

At first we preached almost wholly to unbelievers. To those, therefore, we spake almost continually of remission of sins through the blood of Christ, and the nature of faith in His blood. And so we do still, among those who need to be taught the first elements of the Gospel of Christ. But those in whom the foundation is laid, we exhort to go on to perfection.

'Perfection' is a jewel with many facets, and these, as we shall see, Wesley presents in astonishing variety.

As we should expect, he preached to his Methodists about their *Health*, and insisted upon their care of it as a Christian duty. In his sermon on *Heaviness through Manifold Temptations*, amongst the causes of sorrow in Christian believers he instances 'all bodily disorders', particularly 'acute diseases and violent pains of every kind, whether affecting the whole body, or the smallest part of it'.

In close connection with Health, he repeatedly returned to the subject of *Sleep*, on which he could advise with undoubted authority. In his sermon on *Redeeming the Time*, he warns against the dangers of excess, and pleads for 'that measure of sleep every night which nature requires, and no more; that measure which is most conducive to the health and vigour both of the body and mind'. He describes how he himself ascertained the amount of sleep which he needed, telling how he 'waked every night about twelve or one and lay awake for some time'. This he attributed to 'lying longer in bed than nature required'. He therefore rose an hour earlier on successive mornings and found that by rising at four he secured a night of unbroken rest. He urged his Methodists, by the same experiment, to discover how much sleep they individually needed. His own general conclusion is that healthy men require a little above six and healthy women a little above seven hours. Wesley contends that excessive sleep hurts the health; induces flabbiness of flesh and tends to weaken the eye-sight. A graver objection is that it hurts the soul and is a sin against God, as being a waste of valuable time; it breeds sloth, and unfits us to 'endure hardships as good soldiers of Jesus Christ'. He then exhorts those who are a prey to over-indulgence to begin at once to break the habit: to seek the grace of God: to retire early: 'Keep your hour, notwithstanding the most pressing business. Lay all things by till the morning.' They must, in the same way, keep their hour of rising. 'Do not rise two mornings and lie in bed the third; but what you do once, do always.' Wesley then points out that early rising is not sufficient to make a man a Christian, but 'that single point, the not rising, may keep you a heathen, void of the whole Christian spirit'.

Having got his Methodists out of bed, Wesley proceeded to dress them. There are times when one receives the impression that he would have made a very effective sergeant-major. One published sermon is wholly devoted to the subject of *Dress*, the text being 1 Peter 3^{3-4}. Wesley cautions his people at the outset against *slovenliness*, which he hated. 'Slovenliness is no part of religion.' On 24th April 1769, he wrote to Richard Steel, one of his preachers in Ireland:

Whatever clothes you have, let them be whole; no rents, no tatters, no rags. These are a scandal to either man or woman, being another fruit of vile laziness. Mend your clothes, or I shall never expect you to mend your lives. Let none ever see a ragged Methodist.

In justice to the recipient, there is nothing to suggest that either he or his fellow-preachers had fallen below the standards of common decency, but, in Ireland, there was a danger of it.

Wesley contends that uniformity of Dress is not demanded of Christians. He allows, on Scriptural authority, the wearing of 'gold and costly apparel' on the part of those in certain official positions, but, on the same authority, forbids it to Christians in the middle and lower walks of life. Over-indulgence may impoverish the family and engender pride, vanity and the craving for admiration. It may also 'tend to create and inflame lust'. The more people spend in this way, the less they have for works of mercy and Christian charity. So intensely may a Christian come to cherish these things that 'the inward work of the Spirit' may stand still. At the close of the sermon a personal note steals in and he pleads with his people:

I conjure you all who have any regard for *me*, show me before I go hence that I have not laboured, even in this respect, in vain, for near half a century. Let me see, before I die, a Methodist congregation full as plain dressed as a Quaker congregation. Only be more consistent with yourselves. Let your dress be cheap as well as plain. . . . I pray, let there be no costly silks among you, how grave soever they may be. Let there be no Quaker-linen—proverbially so called, for their exquisite fineness; no Brussels lace, no elephantine hats or bonnets—those scandals of female modesty. Be all of a piece, dressed from head to foot as persons *professing godliness*, professing to do everything, small and great, with the single view of pleasing God.

These words will not meet with unqualified approval today, but there is a core of good sense in them, as in almost everything that Wesley wrote. As a musician transposes a simple tune from one key to another and the tune remains the same, so an intelligent reader of Wesley's writings will find that he can transpose them from the 'key' of the eighteenth century to that of the twentieth and their essential truth will still be there.

Interesting evidence of the importance which Wesley attached to the subject of *Dress* was forthcoming at the opening of the City Road Chapel, on Sunday, 1st November 1778, which was a long-anticipated and red-letter day in his life. From a contemporary newspaper cutting we learn that

the first quarter of an hour of his (Wesley's) sermon was addressed to his numerous female auditory on the absurdity of the enormous dressing of their heads; and his religious labours have so much converted the women who attended at that place of worship that widows, wives and young ladies appeared on Sunday without curls, without flying caps and without feathers; and our correspondent further says the female sex never made a more pleasing appearance.[6]

Wesley's advice on Dress appears less unreasonable after an examination of the fashion-plates of the period. He was certainly in advance of the general understanding of his age, in discerning a connection between clothing and health, for in the Preface to his *Primitive Physic* he informs his readers that 'the fewer clothes any one uses by day or night, the hardier he will be'. What Wesley preached he also practised, as appears in the following

[6] *Journal*, VI.216n.

description of his personal appearance, published soon after his death.

> In dress, he was a pattern of neatness and simplicity; a narrow plaited stock; a coat, with a small upright collar; no buckles at his knees; no silk or velvet in any part of his apparel; and a head as white as snow, gave an idea of something primitive and apostolical; while an air of neatness and cleanliness was diffused over his whole person.[7]

Wesley had now to see his Methodists properly *married*. Remembering his own unfortunate marriage as the outstanding calamity of his life, opinions will differ as to his fitness for advising on so grave an undertaking. Is the man whose marriage has been a failure better fitted than he who has been wholly fortunate? A case can be made out for either, and the former, especially when such a man as John Wesley, is worthy of careful attention. He knows, at least, what should be avoided, and that knowledge makes more clear what should be sought.

In his sermon on *A Single Eye*, Wesley refers to the marriage of young people from Methodist homes. Wealth or position alone must never be a prevailing consideration.

> How great is the darkness of that execrable wretch . . . who will sell his own child to the devil, who will barter her own eternal happiness for any quantity of gold or silver.
> Are any of you that are called Methodists thus merciful to your children? Seeking to *marry them well*? (as the cant phrase is): that is, to sell them to some purchaser that has much money, but little or no religion? . . . Are ye, too, regarding God less than Mammon? Are ye also without understanding? Have ye profited no more by all ye have heard? Dare *you* also sell your child to the devil? You undoubtedly do this (as far as in you lies) when you marry a son or a daughter to a child of the devil, though it be one that wallows in gold and silver.

In his sermon on *Family Religion* Wesley says much the same thing, but in milder terms, and becomes more emphatic again in the one on *Friendship with the World*.

> We should tremble at the very thought of entering into a marriage-covenant, the closest of all others, with any person who does not love or at least fear God. This is the most horrid folly, the most deplorable madness, that a child of God could possibly plunge into; as it implies every sort of connexion with the ungodly which a Christian is bound in conscience to avoid. No wonder, then, it is so flatly forbidden of

---

[7] J. Hampson, *Memoirs of John Wesley*, III.168.

God; that the prohibition is so absolute and peremptory: 'Be not unequally yoked with an unbeliever.' Nothing can be more express.

It was an age that needed both to hear and to heed such teaching. Marriage for money was a popular *motif* in many a stage play, as witness Goldsmith's Croaker, urging his son to marry Miss Richland, for her fortune 'must not go out of the family; one may find comfort in the money, whatever one does in the wife';[8] a sally which probably roused many an approving horse-laugh. Leonora's aunt, in Fielding's *Joseph Andrews*, crudely expressed a common view of marriage, without any trace of moral content, when she urged her niece to jilt one lover in favour of another who was more showy and apparently more wealthy, asserting:

I know the world very well. . . . I have lived longer in it than you; and I assure you there is not anything worth our regard besides money; nor did I ever know one person who married from other considerations, who did not afterwards heartily regret it. . . . Will any woman hesitate a moment whether she shall ride in a coach or walk on foot all the days of her life?[9]

Lord Chesterfield probably expressed the highest ethical conception of marriage generally held, when he counselled his godson:

There are but two objects in marriage, love or money. If you marry for love, you will certainly have some happy days, and probably many very uneasy ones; if for money, you will have no happy days and probably no uneasy ones; in this latter case let the woman at least be such a one that you can live decently and amicably with, otherwise it is a robbery; in either case, let her be of an unblemished and unsuspected character, and of a rank not indecently below your own.[10]

Here is worldly wisdom, with a slight infusion of kindly decency, but those deeper, sacred considerations and that religious approach for which Wesley contended, are absent. Against such a background he appears as a preacher with a potent message for his own time, in relation to prevalent social evil. Here was something which was cutting at the very roots of the nation's vigour and happiness. He denounced it in weighty terms and pleaded for the better way. We know that his Methodists, for the most part, took that way, to their increasing comfort and joy and to the steady building up and strengthening of Methodism itself, of whom his own brother Charles is a shining example.

[8] *The Good-Natured Man*, Act I. [9] op. cit., Book II, ch. iv.
[10] Letter to his Godson (Everyman Edn), p. 301.

Wesley preached to his people about their *Children* and how to *train* and *educate* them, and he vehemently insisted that his preachers should do the same, for upon success in this direction depended the very existence of Methodism in the future. At some of his advice on this subject we may smile today, and over some of it the modern psychologist will certainly grunt his disapproval, especially when he ponders over the Rules for Kingswood School. But there remains a good foundation of healthy teaching. Wesley is concerned that Education should be a real check upon such evil tendencies as become manifest in children, and he insists that 'the only end of education is to restore our rational nature to its proper state'. He had all the respect of the Greeks for reason and rationality, though not going so far as to believe that doing the right is the inevitable consequence of knowing what the right is. Children must be encouraged to treat others as they themselves would wish to be treated: 'to walk in love, as Christ also loved us and gave himself for us'; to mind that one point, 'God is love: and he that dwelleth in love, dwelleth in God and God in him'.[11] In Wesley's view, which he constantly declared, true education is inseparable from religion. We know today how right he was.

Of course Wesley preached on the *Use of Money*, and because he had seen so much of the blighting effects of riches on the finer qualities of the human spirit, he did so frequently and as forcefully as he could. Few people have had firmer right to give counsel to others about getting and spending and to caution them against miserliness than the man who explained to subscribers to his *Notes on the Old Testament* that he had not undertaken so laborious a work for love of gain.

> Does anyone who knows anything of *me* suppose that I would drudge thus for *money*? What is money to me? Dung and dross. I love it as I do the mire in the streets. But I find enough that want it; and among these I disperse it with both hands, being careful only to owe no man anything.[12]

It might be said of John Wesley, as of William Blake, that 'he feared nothing so much as being rich, lest he should lose his spiritual riches'.

---

[11] *Works*, VII.86 (The Education of Children).

[12] *Letters*, V.13–14. See also Sermon on *The More Excellent Way* (*Works*, VII.36). There Wesley tells of a young Oxford Methodist who, as his annual income rose from £30 to £120, continued to live on £28 *per annum* and gave away the remainder to the poor. We know that this young man was Wesley himself.

Wesley's teaching on the subject is summed up in his sermon on *The Danger of Riches*, with its impassioned appeal to Methodists: 'O, ye Methodists, hear the word of the Lord!' There are three famous divisions: (1) Gain all you can. (2) Save all you can. (3) Give all you can. The importance which Wesley attached to the subject was clearly shown when, in 1788, he re-published the four volumes of standard sermons and included this. It remains one of the official and accepted standards of Methodist teaching today, and should be consulted by the reader at this point. There are, of course, many references elsewhere, as in the sermon on *Spiritual Idolatry*, where he declares that the love of money for its own sake is 'the lowest, basest idolatry of which the human soul is capable'.

Wesley knew that the Methodist manner of life, with its regard for honourable dealing and the trust thereby inspired, must lead, in many cases, either to opulence or a comfortable economic position. There lay a subtle danger. In the *Arminian Magazine* for 1787 he surveyed the rise and development of Methodism and asked 'how the case stands with us at present'. His concern is almost wholly with Riches, on which he is very downright and explicit. The wide circulation of the *Magazine* assured Wesley of a large field of influence, and his people read and pondered warning and exhortation which need little change of phraseology to make them apposite for this and every generation.

I fear, wherever riches have increased, (exceeding few are the exceptions), the essence of religion, the mind that was in Christ, has decreased in the same proportion. . . . Religion must necessarily produce both industry and frugality; and these cannot but produce riches. But as riches increase, so will pride, anger and love of the world in all its branches.

How, then, is it possible that Methodism, that is, the religion of the heart, though it flourishes now as a green bay tree, should continue in this state? For the Methodists in every place grow diligent and frugal; consequently, they increase in goods. Hence they proportionately increase in pride, in anger, in the desire of the flesh, the desire of the eyes and the pride of life. So, although the form of religion remains, the spirit is swiftly vanishing away.

Is there no way to prevent this; this continual declension of pure religion? We ought not to forbid people to be diligent and frugal; we must exhort all Christians to gain all they can and to save all they can; that is, in effect, to grow rich. What way, then, (I ask again), can we take, that our money may not sink us to the nethermost hell? There is one way, and there is no other under heaven. If those who 'gain all they can', and 'save all they can', will likewise 'give all they can'; then, the more they gain, the more they will grow in grace and the more treasure they will lay up in heaven.

There must have been great searchings of heart in Wesley's congregations as he preached on this subject that touched many people so intimately, and his hearers would probe their consciences still further when they stood up to sing such verses as that which Charles Wesley wrote on 'the love of money is the root of all evil', and published in *Short Hymns on Select Passages of the Holy Scriptures*:

> Is that cursed root in me
>   From whence all evils grow?
> Thou the vile idolatry,
>   And Thou alone canst show:
> Searcher of the treacherous heart,
>   To me, O God, discover mine,
> Then the idolater convert,
>   And fill with love divine.[13]

Sometimes Wesley preached to his Methodists about the duty of *Making a Will*, if they had any earthly possessions to leave. He had been impressed by the evil that is often created and the passions that are aroused when a person dies intestate. He records the death of such a person, who had intended that his money should be put to good use after his decease, but, as he was stricken down unexpectedly, he 'left all his money to—be scrambled for'. A few weeks later he records (9th December 1779):

In speaking on those words, 'set thy house in order, for thou shalt die and not live', I took occasion to exhort all who had not done it already to settle their temporal affairs without delay. Let not any man who reads these words put off a day longer.

He preached from the same text seven years later, commenting:

It is a strange madness which still possesses many, that are in other respects men of understanding, who put this off from day to day, till death comes in an hour when they looked not for it.[14]

It is good to find John Wesley from time to time preaching the virtue of *Courtesy*. None could do so more congruously than this man, who, being assailed and maligned with the foulest invective,

[13] *P.W.*, XIII.103. [14] *Journal*, VII.231.

both in press and pulpit, never stooped below the level of a Christian scholar and gentleman in the trenchant replies that plain duty demanded of his unwilling spirit. 'How amiable is courtesy joined to sanctity!' he once wrote: 'why should they ever be divided?'[15] In his reply to the scurrilous attack upon him by Richard Hill, entitled *Farrago Double-Distilled*, he gives his traducer 'a few advices', including:

Be courteous. Show good manners, as well as good nature, to your opponent, of whatever kind. 'But he is so rude.' You need not be so too. If you regard not him, reverence yourself.[16]

In his sermon on *Pleasing All Men*, Wesley enjoins Courtesy towards all as a Christian virtue.

See that you are courteous towards all men. It matters not, in this respect, whether they are high or low, rich or poor, superior or inferior to you. No, not even whether good or bad, whether they fear God or not. Indeed, the *mode* of showing your courtesy may vary, as Christian prudence will direct; but the thing itself is due to all; the lowest and the worst have a claim to your courtesy. It may be either inward or outward; either a temper or a mode of behaviour; such a mode of behaviour as naturally springs from courtesy of heart.... This may subsist, even in a high degree, where there has been no advantage of education. I have seen as real courtesy in an Irish cabin, as could be found in St James's or the Louvre.

He then proceeds to link this with the Christian gospel.

What is the source of that desire to please, which we term courtesy? Let us look attentively into our heart, and we shall soon find an answer. The same Apostle that teaches us to *be courteous*, teaches us to *honour all men*. Join these together, and what will be the effect? A poor wretch cries to me for an alms; I look, and see him covered with dirt and rags. But through these I see one that has an immortal spirit, made to know and love and dwell with God to eternity. I honour him for his Creator's sake.... I love him for the sake of his Redeemer. The courtesy, therefore, which I feel and show toward him, is a mixture of the honour and love which I bear to the offspring of God; the purchase of his Son's blood, and the candidate for immortality. This courtesy let us feel and show toward all men; and we shall please all men to their edification.[17]

It was this doctrine that, as Methodists received it into their hearts and lived it out day by day, helped largely to create that

[15] Quoted in *Wesley Studies* (C. H. Kelly, 1903), p. 203.
[16] *Works*, X.445.   [17] ibid., VII.145.

atmosphere in the Societies which assured a welcome and a blessing to many lonely and unhappy souls, and which is characteristic of Methodism still. How heartily, in this matter of Christian Courtesy, would Wesley have agreed with William Combe!

> To every act it gives a grace;
> It adds a smile to every face;
> And Goodness' self we better see
> When dressed by gentle Courtesy.[18]

SMUGGLING

Then, as now, there were people who would have scorned to defraud their neighbour, but who would light-heartedly defraud the revenue if the opportunity offered. Wesley refused to discriminate between the two practices and regarded them as equally evil. He tells how, at St Ives (26th July 1753),

> I began examining the Society, but I was soon obliged to stop short. I found an accursed thing among them; wellnigh one and all bought and sold uncustomed goods. I therefore delayed speaking to any more till I had met them all together. This I did in the evening, and told them plain, either they must put this abomination away, or they would see my face no more.

The next day,

> they severally promised so to do. So I trust this plague is stayed.

In his sermon on *The Use of Money* Wesley urges:

> We may not engage or continue in any sinful trade; any that is contrary to the law of God or of our country. Such are all that necessarily imply our robbing or defrauding the King of his lawful customs. For it is, at least, as sinful to defraud the King of his right, as to rob our fellow-subjects; and the King has full as much right to his customs as we have to our houses and apparel.

Experience strengthened Wesley's conviction that smuggling is inimical to the spiritual life of man, especially as he saw a revival of that life in Societies that had once practised, but at length renounced it. He notes an example at Dover (3rd December 1765), where he found 'a little company more united together than they have been for many years. Whilst several of them continued to

---

[18] *Dr Syntax in Search of the Picturesque.* Canto xvii.

rob the King, we seemed to be ploughing upon the sand; but since they have cut off the right hand, the word of God sinks deep into their hearts.'

TEMPERANCE

Of course, Wesley preached what we today call 'temperance' sermons. The miseries wrought by intoxicants, especially by gin, were devastating among the poorer classes, but the full extent of the evil was not as widely recognized, even by Christian people, as one might expect. Cole and Postgate, in *The Common People*, quote Henry Fielding, writing in 1751: 'Gin is the principal sustenance of more than a hundred thousand people in this Metropolis.' They then go on to say:

Dram drinking had probably a good deal of the responsibility for making London so turbulent a place, and the re-action from it was largely the making of the Methodist movement.[19]

Intemperance and drunkenness were, of course, condemned in those circles where there was sincere religion, but there was not that insistence on total abstinence which developed later. Even on the part of men and women of eminence, it was not regarded as particularly shameful to appear drunk in public. Alexander Pope once received an invitation to a social gathering from a Duchess, probably the Duchess of Kingston. It was written by her secretary, and began:

Sir,—My lady Duchess being drunk at this moment, so as not able to write herself, has commanded me to acquaint you, Etc.[20]

Apparently the lady's drunken condition was regarded in much the same way as a temporary indisposition, like headache, is regarded today. So profoundly was John Wesley moved by the horrors and miseries caused by strong drink, which glared at him everywhere as he moved about the country, that he let himself go on the subject in words of more than usual vehemence. In his sermon on *The Use of Money* he introduces the topic thus:

Neither may we gain by hurting our neighbour *in his body*. Therefore we may not sell anything which tends to impair health. Such is, eminently, all that liquid fire, commonly called drams or spirituous liquors. . . . All who sell them in the common way, to any that will buy, are poisoners general. They murder His Majesty's subjects

[19] op. cit. (1938 edn), p. 56.
[20] Quoted by Edith Sitwell, *Alexander Pope*, Ch. xi.

wholesale, neither does their eye pity or spare. They drive them to hell like sheep. And what is their gain? Is it not the blood of these men? Who then would envy their large estates and sumptuous palaces? A curse is in the midst of them: the curse of God cleaves to the stones, the timber, the furniture of them. The curse of God is in their gardens, their walks, their groves; a fire that burns to the nethermost hell.

Wesley did not hesitate to use the strongest language of denunciation for an evil whose curse lay so heavily upon the land, and he urged his Methodists to be specially compassionate towards its victims.

I beseech you, brethren, by the mercies of God, despise not poor drunkards. Have compassion on them. Be instant with them in season and out of season. Let not shame, or fear of men, prevent your pulling these brands out of the burning. Many of them are self-condemned: they despair; they have no hope of escaping . . . and they sink still deeper, because none else has any hope for them.

But there is a word of God for these people, which Wesley himself has effectively delivered. He declares that he has known hundreds to whom this word has come with saving power.

Cast not away thy hope. I (the Lord) have not forgotten thee. He that tells thee there is no hope is a liar from the beginning. Look up. Behold the Lamb of God, who taketh away the sin of the world. This day is salvation come to thy soul: only see that thou despise not him that speaketh. Just now he saith unto thee, 'Son, be of good cheer. Thy sins are forgiven thee.'[21]

In passing reference or in more detailed treatment Wesley dealt with almost every disposition of the heart and mind of man and every human action, in their relation to religion. In his sermon on *National Sins and Miseries*, preached in St Matthew's Church, Bethnal Green, on Sunday, 12th November 1775, he touched on a variety of pertinent topics. *Deceit* and *Lying* are strongly condemned. One common form that they take is *Flattery*. It is significant that there is no accusation which a man more strongly resents than of being a *Liar*. Wesley thinks it possible that an *Epicure* is an even more detestable character. The main study of many is 'to enlarge the pleasure of tasting'. He declares that *Luxury* in *Food*, *Dress*, *Furniture* and *Equipage* has never been so great in Britain as at that time. *Luxury* leads to *Sloth*. 'Every

[21] *Works*, VI.302–3.

Glutton will in due time be a *Drone*.' He then attacks the prevailing *Profaneness*, declaring that 'not one nation under the canopy of heaven can vie with the English' in this respect. Let each one ask, 'Lord, is it I?'

A different order of topics is touched upon in such a sermon as that on *The More Excellent Way*. *Private Prayer* should not be confined to set forms. *Business* should be conducted 'in the spirit of Christ', putting the will of God before one's personal will. The Christian should be *temperate* in his *eating* and take his *food* with a thankful heart. He should study his *Conversation*, so that it may be good and on good subjects and so to the edification of those taking part. Wesley then dwells on the *Use of Leisure*, giving an outline of the diversions in which men foolishly or wisely engaged. Cock-fighting and bull-baiting he condemns as 'foul remains of Gothic barbarity', and he looks askance at fox hunting and hare coursing. In such amusements as plays, balls, masquerades and cards, he himself could not conscientiously engage, but 'I am not obliged to pass any sentence on those that are otherwise minded. I leave them to their own Master: to Him let them stand or fall.'

The *Reading* of 'plays, novels, newspapers and the like' are 'quite innocent diversions', but there are more excellent occupations. Wesley recommends gardening, the reading of History, Poetry and Natural Philosophy (viz. Science) and conducting scientific experiments. To these he adds Music and urges that all our employments be 'interfused' with Prayer.

The whole passage should be read, as illustrating Wesley's charitable attitude towards those whose opinions were contrary to his own, and also as descriptive of amusements current at the time. Let us remember that he is referring to these diversions as they were practised (e.g. the Stage) in the eighteenth and not the twentieth century.

CONTROVERSIAL PREACHING

Although Wesley intensely disliked controversy, given the pressing occasion he took up the challenge, not only in the press and by private correspondence, but, if the issue appeared to warrant it, in the pulpit also. This was notably so in the case of *Calvinism* in its crudest form, for which one illustration may suffice, as the subject is not a 'living' one today. He tells how, at Norwich (13th November 1776):

finding many of our friends had been shaken by the assertors of the Horrible Decree, I employed the three following mornings in sifting the question to the bottom. Many were confirmed thereby, and, I trust, will not again be removed from the genuine gospel.

He preached against *Baptismal Regeneration*, as at Islington (14th December 1739), when he 'stood in the garden and showed them how vainly they trusted in Baptism for salvation, unless they were holy of heart.' The doctrine of *Stillness*, promulgated by some of the Moravians, could not pass unchallenged, so Wesley preached, in a controversial spirit, on the necessity for and efficacy of the ordinary means of grace, that is, the Reading of Scripture, Prayer and the Sacrament of the Lord's Supper. At York (3rd July 1776) he

preached . . . on the fashionable religion, vulgarly called morality (viz. the current so-called *Deism*); and showed at large, from the accounts given of it by its ablest patrons, that it is neither better nor worse than Atheism.

Wesley was keenly alive not only to the overt sins which men committed, but to those specious doctrines, inimical to the purity of the Christian life, which masqueraded in the guise of religion and had such a suggestion of New Testament teaching as to make them alluring and dangerous to those who were disposed toward the Christian way of life, but who were strangers to clear thinking. Wesley thought for them, preached his thoughts to them, aided them to think for themselves, and so helped to 'guide their feet into the way of peace'.

POLITICAL SERMONS

It is difficult to imagine Wesley preaching what we describe today as 'a political sermon'; that is, advocating from the pulpit the claims of a particular political party against all others. By *Politics* he usually meant any kind of criticism of the King and his Ministers. He was always peculiarly sensitive to the various New Testament injunctions to 'honour the King' and those in authority under him, and stressed such loyalty and reverence as an important duty of a Christian. He records how (3rd February 1777),

hearing there was some disturbance at Bristol, occasioned by men whose tongues were set on fire against the Government, I went down (from London) in the diligence, and on Tuesday (the following day) evening strongly enforced those solemn words, 'Put them in mind to be subject to principalities and powers, to speak evil of no man.' I believe God applied His word and convinced many that they had been out of their way.

In his tract on *Preaching and Politics* Wesley reveals to what extent he 'preached politics' in the usual sense of that word, and recommended it to others.

It is always difficult and frequently impossible for private men to judge of the measures taken by men in public offices. We do not see many of the grounds which determine them to act in this or the contrary manner. Generally, therefore, it behoves us to be silent, as we may suppose they know their own business best; but when they are censured without any colour of reason, and when an odium is cast on the King by that means, we ought to preach politics in this sense also; we ought publicly to confute those unjust censures: only remembering still, that this is rarely to be done, and only when fit occasion offers; it being our main business to preach 'repentance towards God and faith in our Lord Jesus Christ'.[22]

Wesley disclaimed being himself a party politician and decided that 'no politics shall have a place in the *Arminian Magazine*'.[23] In 1768, the year of the John Wilkes riots, when our relations with America and France were very strained and 'Junius' was attacking the Government, Wesley was invited to give his opinion on the general situation, and wrote in response a long and revealing letter. At the outset he pleads:

I am no politician; politics lies quite out of my province. Neither have I any acquaintance, at least no intimacy, with any that bear that character. And it is no easy matter to form any judgement concerning things of so complicated a nature. It is the more difficult because, in order to form our judgement, such a multitude of facts should be known, few of which can be known with tolerable exactness by any but those who are eye-witnesses of them.

He then proceeds in humorously scornful vein:

perhaps you will say, 'Nay, every Englishman is a politician; we suck in politics with our mother's milk. It is as natural for us to talk politics as to breathe: we can instruct both the King and his Council. We can in a trice reform the State, point out every blunder of this or that Minister, and tell every step they ought to take to be arbiters of all Europe.'

I grant every cobbler, tinker, porter and hackney-coachman can do

[22] *Works*, XI.155.   [23] *Letters*, VI.283.

this. But I am not so deep learned: while they are sure of everything, I am in a manner sure of nothing, except of that very little which I can see with my own eyes or hear with my own ears. However, since you desire me to tell you what I think, I will do it with all openness. Only please to remember I do not take upon me to dictate either to you or to anyone. I only use the privilege of an Englishman to speak my naked thoughts, setting down just what appears to me to be the truth, till I have discovered better information.[24]

Wesley did not, however, recommend precisely the same aloofness from politics on the part of his Methodists that he prescribed for himself. Probably the greatest factor that kept him out of the political arena was the lack of necessary time. The supreme work of his life demanded every moment that he could give to it, and active participation in politics he had to leave to others. But at least he could tell them how and in what spirit to proceed, and this he did. Amongst the Methodists were freeholders, people who had votes and recorded them by a show of hands. These men were solicited to sell their votes, and it was customary for the candidate who made the highest offer to receive the suffrage. Wesley saw this, rightly, as an abomination not to be tolerated among Christian people. It was bribery, corruption and the breaking of a solemn vow which every freeholder had ordinarily to re-affirm every seven years. The subject was so important that Wesley issued a four-page sermon-pamphlet entitled *A Word to a Freeholder*. He begins with a reminder of the oath. There must be no perjury; no receiving of any 'gift or reward, directly or indirectly, nor any promise of any, on account of your vote'. To exercise a vote is a highly solemn, even sacred duty; therefore 'act as if the whole election depended on your single vote, and as if the whole Parliament depended (and therein the whole nation) on that single person whom you now choose to be a member of it'.

For whom shall the vote be cast? Wesley's answer is simple and contains no trace of party feeling. 'For the man that loves God.' He may be known by his fruits. If there is no such candidate, 'vote for him that loves the King'. Wesley contends that love of King and love of country are inseparable. 'The welfare of one is the welfare of the other.' So we return to that loyalty to Throne and Constitution which was central in all Wesley's political thinking and teaching.[25]

[24] *Letters*, V.370.   [25] *Works*, XI.196.

So extended was the span of Wesley's life that before the end he found himself 'voyaging through strange seas of thought'. New ideas were abroad of kingship, of government and of the rights and responsibilities of men. It seemed to him that, exploited by cunning agitators, men were clamouring for a liberty they already possessed, both civil and religious. He was appalled by the sight of the hideous passions engendered by party strife. In his sermon on *National Sins and Miseries* (1775) he told his congregation:

If you saw, as I have seen, in every county, city, town, men who were once of a calm, mild, friendly temper, mad with party-zeal, ready to tear out one another's throats and to plunge their swords into each other's bowels; if you had heard men, who once feared God and honoured the King, now breathing out the bitterest invectives against him, and just ripe, should any occasion offer, for treason and rebellion; you would not then judge this to be a little evil, a matter of small moment, but one of the heaviest judgments which God can permit to fall upon a guilty land.[26]

Right at the end the French Revolution came crashing into his world, but too late for him to appreciate its significance. He remained true to his central political idea: the Crown as the divinely appointed Head and Symbol of the State. His Methodists must strengthen the things that remain, that are ready to perish.

We look back at John Wesley today across intervening fields of human activity and development, many of which would have astonished him; fields in which men have been and are no longer hampered by those forms of monarchical and aristocratical government which Tom Paine saw as 'the base remains of two ancient tyrannies';[27] across many a blood-soaked battlefield and the body of many a young Lycidas,' dead 'ere his prime'; across exploded theories for human betterment, which failed either because of the falsity at the heart of them or the falsity in the hearts of those whom they were designed to succour and to bless. So regarding him and pondering his words and his ways, we see how wise he was: how great a humanitarian, and how sound the core of his judgement; how, through purity of political thought and action he saw one means to national well-being, knowing and declaring that the only road to the ideal human society lies through Christian loyalties: through those individual lives that have become new creations in Christ Jesus. Such lives were his

[26] *Works*, VII.403.   [27] *Common Sense* (1776).

legacy to that New World, from whose threshold he passed through death triumphant home.

ADDENDUM

'THE TERRORS OF THE LORD'

There is one subject on which Wesley preached to which passing reference must be made, not so much because of its intrinsic importance, but rather because to ignore it would expose the writer to a charge of *suppressio veri*. We know from references in the *Journal* and from several of the published sermons, in particular No. lxxii, *Of Hell*, that Wesley preached occasionally on what he called *The Terrors of the Lord*. Let us admit that he expressed views about Hell and Future Punishment which are very rarely met with today. They were based upon a very literal interpretation of certain passages of Scripture, a method which has been considerably modified since his day. It should be borne in mind that these views were in accord with the intellectual climate of contemporary Christian orthodoxy and were by no means peculiar to John Wesley. They were, in fact, a part of the Christian tradition going back to very early times.

One feels that Wesley was not at his best nor wholly happy in expounding them, and only did so when there seemed to be no other line of approach to the unawakened consciences of his hearers. He much preferred to preach on *The Love of God*, which was, indeed, the prevailing theme of his sermons. Like an ellipse by its two foci, Wesley's mental life was constrained by two centres of authority: 1. The 'plain' meaning of Scripture; 2. Reason. When these were in agreement—and such agreement he continually sought—his mind was at rest; when they were not, there was tension in his inner life. That was so in respect of this type of preaching. One feels that there was much against which both his Reason and his Emotions revolted, but, on the other hand, there was, what seemed to him and to many others, the 'plain' teaching of Scripture, and in such a conflict the authority of Scripture took precedence of all else.

Much more might be written on this subject, for it opens up the whole question of Wesley's ideas of Inspiration and Revelation, but for our present purpose it is sufficient to bear these simple but important considerations in mind.

CHAPTER X

A CLOUD OF WITNESSES

WHEN WE consider the vast number of people who, at one time or another, heard John Wesley preach—perhaps a majority of the people in England—it is surprising that so few accounts of his preaching have come down to us; and many of these are references, rather than accounts. Hundreds of descriptive letters must have been written by persons who came under the spell of his preaching and who wished to acquaint their friends of the fact, as a piece of exciting news; and there must have been scores of diary entries and private memoranda, all of which would have been invaluable, had they survived to our own day. One of the earliest accounts refers to 24th August 1744, when Wesley preached in St Mary's Church, Oxford: a duty which fell to his lot, as Fellow of a College, about every third year. There are the two references in the *Journals* of John and Charles Wesley, and an exceedingly full description of the whole service by Dr Kennicott, then about 24 years of age and an undergraduate of Wadham College. He tells how, on that Friday morning, Wesley

came to St Mary's at ten o'clock. There were present the vice-chancellor, the proctors, most of the heads of houses, a vast number of gownsmen and a multitude of private people, with many of Wesley's own people, both brethren and sisters. He is neither tall nor fat; for the latter would ill become a Methodist. His black hair, quite smooth, and parted very exactly, added to a peculiar composure in his countenance, showed him to be an uncommon man. His prayer was soft, short, and conformable to the rules of the university. His text was Acts 4^{31}. He spoke it very slowly, and with an agreeable emphasis.

After a description of the sermon the account continues:

When he came to what he called his plain, practical conclusion, he fired his address with so much zeal and unbounded satire as quite spoiled what otherwise might have been turned to great advantage; for, as I liked some, so I disliked other parts of his discourse extremely. I liked some of his freedom, such as calling the generality of young gownsmen 'a generation of triflers', and many other just invectives. But, considering how many shining lights are here, that are the glory of the Christian cause, his sacred censure was much too flaming and strong, and his charity much too weak in not making large allowances. But, so far from allowances, he concluded, with a lifted up eye, in this most solemn form, 'It is time for Thee, Lord, to lay to Thine hand'; words full of such presumption and seeming imprecation, that they gave an universal shock. This, and the assertion that Oxford was not a Christian city, and this country not a Christian nation, were the most offensive parts of the sermon, except when he accused the whole body (and confessed himself to be one of the number) of the sin of perjury; and for this reason, because, upon becoming members of a college, every person takes an oath to observe the statutes of the university, and no one observes them in all things. Had these things been omitted, and his censures moderated, I think his discourse, as to style and delivery, would have been uncommonly pleasing to others as well as to myself. He is allowed to be a man of great parts, and that by the excellent Dean of Christ Church (Dr Conybeare); for the day he preached, the Dean generously said of him, 'John Wesley will always be thought a man of sound sense, though an enthusiast.' However, the vice-chancellor sent for the sermon, and I hear the heads of colleges intend to show their resentment.[1]

Another independent reference to this service has also survived, in a letter written by William Blackstone, the famous lawyer, who, like John Wesley himself, was an alumnus of Charterhouse School.

We were last Friday entertained at St Mary's by a curious sermon by Wesley the Methodist. Among other equally modest particulars he informed us; first, that there was not one Christian among all the Heads of Houses; secondly, that pride, gluttony, avarice, luxury, sensuality and drunkenness were the characteristics of all Fellows of Colleges, who were useless to a proverbial uselessness. Lastly, that the younger part of the University were a generation of triflers, all of them perjured, and not one of them of any religion at all. His notes were demanded by the Vice-Chancellor, but on mature deliberation it has been thought proper to punish him by a mortifying neglect.[2]

The sermon should be read carefully at this point by all who wish to understand and appreciate Wesley as a preacher. Its title is *Scriptural Christianity*, and soon after its delivery Wesley published it as a pamphlet, with the explanation:

[1] Tyerman, *Life of John Wesley*, I.448.
[2] Quoted by J. Lawson, *Notes on Wesley's Forty-four Sermons*, pp. 25, 35.

It was not my design, when I wrote, ever to print the latter part of the following sermon; but the false and scurrilous accounts of it which have been published almost in every corner of the nation, constrain me to publish the whole, just as it was preached, that men of reason may judge for themselves.

Having read it, we can understand the consternation and hostility that were aroused in the academic and clerical world of Oxford, and we realize, at the same time, how malicious was Blackstone's report.

In several respects this sermon is unique in Wesley's long ministry. It is not wholly beyond criticism. There are those who consider, with some plausibility, that the interests of Christianity and of Methodism in Oxford would have been better served by a less severe message and a more pleading tone; and that in his attack on 'perjury' his judgement was somewhat at fault. These matters do not, however, primarily concern us. It is Wesley the *Preacher* whom we must keep before us, and rarely did he act with purer intention and with finer courage than on this outstanding occasion in this outstanding place.

Wesley's first open-air sermon, on 2nd April 1739, marked the beginning of a new life for at least one of his hearers, who left a brief record of the event. This was William Webb, of Bristol, who was then about thirty years of age. Fifty years later he told how

I went to the place appointed, out of curiosity, and heard that great and good man; but with much uneasiness all the time, not knowing what was the matter with me; nor could I relate any part of the sermon, being much confused in my mind and filled with astonishment at the minister. For I had never seen such proceedings before, it being quite a new thing to preach in the open air and not in a church or chapel. This was the first sermon Mr Wesley preached in Bristol. When it was ended I was induced to follow him, but, at the same time, knew not why I did so, being shut up in ignorance and gross darkness, through the multitude of my sins and the hardness of my heart. . . . But O!, how great was the goodness of God to me, who drew my heart with love to follow that dear minister of Jesus Christ, whose name I revere and esteem![3]

The writer goes on to tell how ultimately he entered into 'the peace and joy of Faith'. He is an early example of the power of Wesley's preaching to create in others a strong attachment to himself. One has only to browse through the *Methodist Magazines*

[3] *W.M.M.* (1807), p. 416.

for fifty and even sixty years after Wesley's death to find how common this was. Under conviction of sin and in great spiritual distress, it seemed to such people that little remained in their world on which they could rely, save this man, who must surely have power with God on their behalf. There was, for example, George Walker of Chester, who wrote in the trustees's minute book an account of the beginnings of Methodism in that city and included this loving and reverential reference to Wesley.

In June 1752, that bright luminary of the Christian World, Mr Wesley, paid his first ministerial visit to the Chester Society. Here he was hailed as an Angel of God, respected as the servant of the Most High. From this period his visits ... became a regular part of his engagements, and it may be said, on the part of his adherents, they sincerely loved him and ever held his approach among them as a high, a festival and a Jubilee day.[4]

In order to attend his ministry there were people who would surmount difficulties and endure hardships. Having heard him once, they would go to great lengths to hear him again. Such was Dame Summerhill, of Bristol, who, at the age of 104, met Adam Clarke and told him of her first meeting with Wesley, fifty years before, and how powerful was his attraction.

When he (Wesley) first came to Bristol I went to hear him preach; and, having heard him, I said, 'This is the truth.' I inquired of those around, who and what he was. I was told that he was a man who went about everywhere preaching the Gospel. I further inquired, 'Is he to preach here again?' The reply was, 'Not at present.' 'Where is he going to next?', I asked. 'To Plymouth', was the answer. 'And will he preach there?' 'Yes.' 'Then I will go and hear him. What is the distance?' 'One hundred and twenty-five miles.' I went, walked it, heard him and walked back again.[5]

When Wesley preached at Rode Hall, near Congleton, Thomas Buckley, who lived at Astbury, more than five miles away, determined to hear him. He left on record how

when night came, six or seven of us went. My wife carried a child which was eight months old in her apron. When we arrived, there was Mr Wesley and three more preachers. Mr Wesley preached from Romans 3^{23}: *For all have sinned and come short of the glory of God.* He gave notice for preaching at five o'clock on the following morning. We got

---

[4] F. F. Bretherton, *Early Methodism in and around Chester*, p. 30.
[5] J. W. Etheridge, *Life of Adam Clarke*, pp. 120–1.

leave of Roger Moss to sit by the fire all night. We brought some little books to read. When preaching was over we returned well pleased with our journey. Mr Wesley gave notice for preaching at the end of the month. We all resolved to go, which we did.[6]

Wesley was cheered by many fresh and frank confessions like that of Sarah Clay, a Londoner, who wrote to him:

In the year 1739 I went one Sunday morning to Islington Church. There was a great stir among the people. I was very inquisitive to know the cause and gave great attention. At last I heard them say, 'One of the Wesleys is to preach.' When you went up into the pulpit I fixt my eyes on you and thought you were more than man. Your text I have forgot; but you spoke so plain to the rich and great that it delighted me. I went home and told my mother, I had heard a man in Islington Church that I would go ten miles to hear again. I felt myself strangely drawn after something, but I could not tell what. The next Sunday I went again. Now I had nothing to do with others; for, as Nathan said to David, *Thou art the man*. I found my soul greatly alarmed, so that I never omitted going to the Church till they turned you out. After I had lost you for some time, I grew very careless and indifferent again.

Later, on Kennington Common, she heard him give out the hymn:

> Angel of God, whate'er betide,
> Thy summons I obey;
> I ever take thee for my guide,
> And walk in Thee my way,

and 'found such a warmth come into my soul, that I thought I could have gone all over the world to hear you. I went home very much affected and my soul was drawn out after the Lord'. Presently thereafter she entered into the Peace of God.[7]

To the end, Wesley's personal attractiveness remained and, indeed, seems to have increased as he became more venerable in appearance. Many a time it predisposed people to hear him, as in the case of James Mort, who had become careless and had 'shaken off his early good impressions'. In June 1788, Wesley preached in the church of John Hampson, in Sunderland, and we learn that when James Mort

---

[6] Dyson, *History of Methodism in the Congleton Circuit*. Quoted *Journal*, III.175.
[7] *W.M.M.* (1783), p. 529.

saw the venerable man moving down the aisle with tremulous step, leaning on the arm of Mr Hampson . . . his heart melted, and in order to conceal his tears he sat down and covered his face.[8]

Charles Wood was born at Banwell in 1757, and when he was about sixteen years of age,

> the fame of Mr Wesley brought him to South Brent to hear the Word of God; but, his mind having been much prejudiced against the Methodists, he resolved to be on his guard, lest, to use his own words, he 'should be taken in'. But how happily was he disappointed! He beheld, with unexpected reverence and delight, an aged minister of Jesus Christ, whose very appearance, still fresh in the memory of thousands, commanded the highest esteem and respect.[9]

Of a different order was the attraction experienced by George Osborn of Rochester.

He had heard much of Wesley, had read his writings and had an ardent desire to see him. About the year 1784 Mr Wesley made a visit to Rochester. . . . Mr Osborn was captivated with the Founder of Methodism, and said the first impression made upon his mind by what he saw and heard from Mr Wesley was 'This man is a scholar'. Others had represented Wesley to him in a different light, as fanatical and ignorant. Mr Wesley's frequent references to recent publications, his natural and unostentatious manner of quoting the original Scriptures, his whole bearing and demeanour, even to the manner of his handling the pulpit books, were all noticed as bearing on this point, and Mr Osborn concluded that, so far as these indications might be relied on, there was no more fanaticism in the Founder of Methodism than in any of the more dignified and wealthy clergymen he had been accustomed to hear at the Cathedral.[10]

Mr Osborn was twenty years old at this time, and he at once joined the Methodist Society. He has a special interest for students of Methodist history, in that he was the father of Dr George Osborn, who figured so prominently in Wesleyan Methodism during the middle period of the following century; who was the Tutor in Theology in Richmond College from 1868 to 1884 and was twice elected to the Chair of the Conference.

A specially interesting testimony, as coming from a distinguished foreigner, is that of Professor J. H. Liden, of Upsala, who

---

[8] *W.H.S.*, XIV.76.

[9] *W.M.M.* (1809), p. 402.

[10] Wakeley, *Anecdotes of the Wesleys*, p. 261. See also J. G. Stevenson, *Methodist Worthies*, I.360, and *W.M.M.* (1839), p. 785.

visited England in 1769 and met both John and Charles Wesley. Under date Sunday, 15th October of that year, he wrote in his *Journal*:

Today I learned for the first time to know Mr John Wesley, so well known here in England, and called the spiritual Father of the so called Methodists. . . . He preached today at the forenoon service in the Methodist Chapel in Spitalfield for an audience of more than 4,000 people. His text was Luc. i.68. The sermon was short but eminently evangelical. He has not great oratorical gifts, no outward appearance, but he speaks clear and pleasant. . . . He is a small, thin old man, with his own long and strait hair, and looks as the worst country curate in Sweden, but has learning as a Bishop and zeal for the glory of God which is quite extraordinary. His talk is very agreeable, and his mild face and pious manner secure him the love of all rightminded men. He is the personification of piety, and he seems to me as a living representative of the loving Apostle John.[11]

That, given a fair field and no favour, Wesley, by personality and preaching combined, could go a long way towards winning his hearers, is frequently exemplified. There is the amusing story of how he came to preach on Sunday, 20th July 1766, in the church of St Saviour-gate, York, whose rector, the Rev. Mr Cordeux, had warned his congregation against hearing 'that vagabond Wesley'. In Tyerman's words:

Wesley, after preaching in his own chapel at Peasholm Green, went in his canonicals to Mr Cordeux's church. Mr Cordeux saw that he was a clergyman, and, without knowing who he was, offered him his pulpit. After service he asked his clerk if he knew who the stranger was. The clerk replied, 'Sir, he is the vagabond Wesley, against whom you warned us.' 'Aye, indeed!' said the astonished rector, 'we are trapped; but never mind, we have had a good sermon.'[12]

The general impression was, indeed, so good, that when Wesley next visited York the rector renewed his offer of his pulpit and Wesley preached on the Beatitudes.

Robert Moss, of Gainsborough, heard Wesley in the years 1779 and 1780. He considered himself too young at that time to become a member of Society, but he left on record, after the second occasion, how

here I solemnly covenanted, in the presence of God, angels, the Rev. John Wesley and the church there assembled, that I would be

[11] *W.H.S.*, XVII.2–3.   [12] Tyerman, *Life of Wesley*, II.571.

a Methodist as soon as I was old enough. . . . But, O, what a privilege I have ever felt it to have received my first principal impressions under the ministry of the Founder of Methodism![13]

Methodists have on many occasions been charged with 'worshipping' John Wesley; with giving him a place of honour in their Communion comparable to that of the Virgin Mary among Roman Catholics. Those who know both Methodism and Roman Catholicism smile at the accusation, knowing how easy it is for the uninitiated to misread their devotion. They have even been accused by the ultra-foolish of worshipping him as *God*. For example, we read how, in April 1790, at Bradshaw, near Halifax,

A considerable group of persons was assembled near the chapel, anxiously waiting Mr Wesley's arrival, but a considerable time having elapsed without any sign of his approach, a woman in the crowd, of the name of Wilson, mocked the patience of the expectant multitude by shouting—'they are looking for their God, but he does not come!'

We are further informed that thereupon she fell speechless to the ground and died the following day.[14]

Wesley is no *divus* in the Church of his creation, nor ever has been, but it is easy to understand how such a belief could be entertained by illiterate people when his followers wrote of him in such ecstatic and heart-warming terms as Robert Moss. He invokes four witnesses to his vow: God, the Church Triumphant, or the angelic hierarchy, the Church Militant, and—John Wesley!! And he puts Wesley between angels and men. Was this by design? If so, one feels that Robert Moss had strong and sufficient reason. John Wesley was for him, as for many another, the link between the Church on earth and the Church in Heaven: between the seen and the unseen: between himself and others like him, and the Lord who had redeemed them. Under God they owed everything to him. There was probably no one in this country at that time, who, with greater justice and in a more ingenuous sense, could have claimed to be a 'mediating priest' than John Wesley, but his ambitions were far indeed from being of that particular order.

Wesley's preaching was by no means uniform in its effects upon his hearers, which, human nature being so diverse, is what we should expect. Amongst the most sincere and enthusiastic accounts

---

[13] *W.H.S.*, XX.71.   [14] J. U. Walker, *Methodism in Halifax*, p. 181.

are those given by men who in time became his travelling preachers, and especially by those who owed their conversion directly to him. One of the most distinguished of these men was John Nelson, a Yorkshireman, who, when nearly thirty-two years of age and working in London at his trade as a stonemason, heard John Wesley preach in Upper Moorfields on 17th June 1739. He describes his recent unhappiness and search for spiritual enlightenment and guidance and continues:

I was like a wandering bird, cast out of the nest, till Mr John Wesley came to preach his first sermon in Moorfields. Oh, that was a blessed morning to my soul! As soon as he got upon the stand he stroked back his hair and turned his face towards where I stood, and I thought fixed his eyes upon me. His countenance struck such an awful dread upon me, before I heard him speak, that it made my heart beat like the pendulum of a clock; and, when he did speak, I thought his whole discourse was aimed at me. When he had done, I said, 'This man can tell the secrets of my heart: he hath not left me there; for he hath showed the remedy, even the blood of Jesus.' Then was my soul filled with consolation, through hope that God for Christ's sake would save me.

A few weeks later Nelson found 'the true peace of God'.

About this time Nelson overheard a soldier in Westminster talking to fellow-soldiers and some Welsh women, and was so impressed by his story that he recorded it in his own *Diary*. Both James H. Rigg and W. H. Fitchett appear to have read the *Diary* rather carelessly at this point, for they confuse the two men and take the soldier's story to be a continuation of Nelson's own. Unfortunately, this involves ascribing to Nelson excesses of evil from which he would have shrunk in horror and to which he was a complete stranger. After confessing to almost every imaginable wickedness except murder, the soldier continues:

I was desperate in wickedness and did not put a restraint on any lust or appetite; till one day, as I was coming out of the country by Kennington Common, Mr John Wesley was going to preach and I thought I would hear what he had to say; for I had heard many learned and wise men say he was beside himself. But when he began to speak, his words made me tremble. I thought he spoke to no one but me, and I durst not look up; for I imagined all the people were looking at me. I was ashamed to show my face, expecting God would make me a public example, either by letting the earth open and swallow me up, or by striking me dead. But before Mr Wesley concluded his sermon he cried out, 'Let the wicked forsake his way, and the unrighteous man his thoughts; and let him return unto the Lord, and he will have mercy upon him; and to our God, for he will abundantly pardon.' I said, 'If that be true, I will turn to God today.' I immediately went home and began to read and pray, keeping out of bad company for about a fortnight, and hearing Mr Wesley as often as I could.

He then tells how he slipped back into the old ways for a very short time, but after hearing Charles Wesley preach and partaking of the Lord's Supper in Whitehall Chapel, he

found power to believe that Jesus Christ had shed his blood for me, and that God, for his sake, had forgiven my offences. Then was my heart filled with love to God and man; and since then sin hath not had dominion over me.[15]

There is such broad similarity in the testimonies of William Webb, John Nelson, the unknown soldier and others, that they must be generally descriptive of the experiences of thousands of people who passed away and left no personal record of these transcendent matters. We note the consciousness of sin. This may or may not have been very strong before they heard John Wesley, but the stronger it was, the more arresting his preaching proved to be, and the more eagerly they listened. Often these people were prejudiced against him by evil report, but in most cases this was speedily overcome. There is also the strong impression, that we have previously noted, that Wesley was to them, for the time being almost *in loco Dei*. They wanted to hear him again and again. He was their fountain of hope and rock of refuge in a perplexing and changing personal world. Frequently it seemed that his words were directed purposely to them. Usually a bond was forged between him and them on that first day that time strengthened, and they had few happier or prouder boasts than that of calling him Friend.

For the spiritual edification and encouragement of his readers, Wesley regularly printed in his *Magazine* letters from correspondents about personal conversions and experiences during life and at the time of death. In all fairness, we must make allowance for some of the expressions used. They may sound strange and crude, even repulsive in some cases to modern ears, but, in the language of the time, and in figures of speech only now current in a few obscure circles, they express that great change which the Spirit

[15] *Veterans*, III.10ff.

of God works in the human heart, when he 'raises men from the death of sin to the life of righteousness'. It would be the very folly of criticism to allow this terminology to obscure, and the critic himself to contemn, the profound and basic fact of a new spiritual creation.

The testimonies of some of his Preachers, now published under the title of *Wesley's Veterans*, are of peculiar value and reference has already been made to that of John Nelson. There was Alexander Mather, one of the earliest of the band, who became, in 1792, the second President after Wesley's death. In a letter to Wesley, written about the year 1780, he says:

> You (Wesley) preached at West Street, April 14 (1754): it was the first time I ever saw or heard you. Under that sermon God set my heart at liberty, removing my sins from me as far as the east is from the west—which the very change of my countenance testified before my tongue could utter it. I had no great transport of joy; but my load was gone, and I could praise God from the ground of my heart, all my sorrow and fear and anguish of spirit being changed into a solid peace.[16]

William Hunter, who began to 'travel' in 1767, wrote warmly to Wesley confessing his indebtedness to his preaching.

> It pleased God to bring me to hear you at Newcastle. You preached, I well remember, from the First Epistle of John, i.9: 'If we confess our sins, God is faithful and just to forgive us our sins, and to cleanse us from all unrighteousness.' This was a precious time to me. While you were preaching, a divine light shone in upon my heart with the word, and I was clearly convinced of the doctrine of sanctification and the attainableness of it. I came home with full purpose of heart not to rest till I was made a living witness of it. I had now a clear view of the holiness of God . . . and of the purity and perfection of His law . . . and I felt my great unlikeness to both.[17]

Thomas Rutherford, who travelled as a Preacher from 1772 to 1806, testifies to the charm of Wesley's personal appearance and the power of his preaching.

> In the month of May (1770), I, for the first time, saw and heard that extraordinary man, the Rev. Mr John Wesley, at Morpeth. He was in the pulpit when I went into the chapel. His apostolic and angelic appearance struck me exceedingly. He appeared like one come down from heaven to teach men the way thither. His text was

[16] *Veterans*, II.88–9.   [17] ibid., IV.177.

Heb. viii.10–12. . . . He opened the words in a concise and easy manner, and spoke from them with such perspicuity and simplicity, and, at the same time, with such wisdom and authority, as I never heard before. To me he seemed like one of the apostles going about, confirming the churches. . . . I and the friends who accompanied me returned highly satisfied, and thankful to the Lord, who had given us to see and hear such a venerable and eminent minister of Christ.[18]

The account which another early Methodist Preacher, Thomas Rankin, gives of his first meeting with John Wesley, is of special interest.

In the beginning of June (1761), being informed that Mr Wesley was to preach at Morpeth at one o'clock, we (Rankin and five or six friends) set forward (from Sunderland); but when we came to Morpeth we found he had preached at twelve. . . . We were not too late, however, for the divine blessing. As soon as I came near to hear the words of the (last) hymn, I was so struck with the presence of God that, if I had not leaned on a friend's arm, I should have fallen to the ground. . . . As I had read all Mr Wesley's *Works*, and in particular his *Journals*, I had formed a very high opinion of him; and the moment I distinctly saw him and heard his voice, such a crowd of ideas rushed upon my mind, as words cannot express. The union of soul I then felt with him is indescribable.

I had long considered Mr John Wesley as the Father of the Methodists, under God. . . . I could not help saying in my mind, 'And is this the man who has braved the winter storm and summer's sun, and run to and fro throughout Great Britain and Ireland, and has crossed the Atlantic Ocean to bring poor, wretched sinners to the knowledge of the Lord Jesus Christ? I looked at him with a degree of astonishment, and from my very soul could bless God that He had so highly favoured me as to let me see this eminent servant of the King of Kings and Lord of Lords. . . . I have a thousand times over blessed the God of heaven that ever I saw his face or heard his voice.[19]

Rankin spent five years of his ministry in America, and there are many references to him in Wesley's *Journal*.

Thomas Tennant was one of the less prominent of the early Preachers: a quiet man, who, for twenty-two years, wrought an effective ministry. In a letter, written in 1779, he gives a short account of how John Wesley's preaching affected him.

Frequently, when I have heard you preach, I thought you appeared as with a sword in your hand, with which you cleft me asunder. At such times the word was indeed quick and powerful, piercing and

[18] *W.M.M.* (1808), p. 437.   [19] *Veterans*, VI.148–54.

wounding my inmost soul; it was indeed a discoverer of the thoughts and intents of my heart.[20]

Richard Moss, who became one of Wesley's Preachers and later went as an Anglican missionary to the West Indies, describes his strangely vicious youth and tells how, about Easter, 1740, a friend

called and said, 'There is one come to town whom you never heard preach: Mr John Wesley; you will like him.' We came, a little before the service began, and sat down in the foremost seat of the lower gallery, fronting the pulpit. When Mr Wesley came . . . I rose up to look at him. I felt something I had never felt before. I thought, 'I have read or heard of saints: surely this is one.' He went up into the pulpit, but I could not keep my eyes off him. He prayed, and I thought, 'Well, this is such a prayer as I never heard in my life.' Then he gave out a verse of a hymn. Immediately I felt much love in my heart, and such joy, that I could not refrain from tears. I was ashamed anyone should see this, and leaned my face against the boards. But then I wanted to see him: so I could not help looking up again. Now I was happy: now I was in heaven: the hymn, the singing, all was heavenly around me. And I knew that till this hour I had never known what happiness meant.

I listened to the sermon and I knew it was all right. I found all my prejudice vanish away and I had such a love, both to the preachers and to all the people, as I cannot express.[21]

There followed a period of doubt and unsettlement, till

on Sunday, Feb. 5 (1744), I communicated at the chapel in the morning and in the afternoon went to the Foundery. Mr John Wesley was preaching. In the middle of the sermon I found myself overshadowed by a divine power. I was lost in God. I knew the Father, as well as the Son and Holy Spirit. The whole Godhead was revealed. I supposed that I was saved from all sin. I was more in heaven than on earth. I felt nothing of the body. I saw nothing but heaven and God. When I came to myself, toward the latter end of the sermon, I was upon my knees. I was filled with the divine fulness. My soul and body were a habitation of God through the Spirit.[22]

This language, so reminiscent of St Paul, is remarkable and cannot be lightly dismissed. It was to this man's desperate need that Wesley appealed, and out of its depths his soul went forth in hopefulness and gratitude to meet the preacher and accept his message. He was typical of many. One feels that these short,

[20] *Veterans*, VI.238.   [21] *W.M.M.* (1798), p. 7.   [22] ibid., p. 56.

staccato sentences were a sincere attempt to express the inexpressible tumult within, and the sense of forgiveness and divine favour that had come to him.

From a brief account of Robert Winter, of the Minories, London, who was born in 1704, we learn that

> when Mr Wesley came to preach in Moorfields, one of his (R. Winter's) neighbours saying to him, 'There is a clergyman come to preach in Moorfields: I think you would like him, if you would go and hear him', he did not care to displease his friend, but thought, 'Neither you nor the clergyman can tell me more of religion than I know already.' However, to oblige his neighbour he went to the Foundery, which was then but a desolate place. He thought, if the preacher was like the place, he should admire neither; however, he stayed to hear Mr Wesley; and God worked upon him in so powerful and effectual a manner, as he had never felt before. When they came out his neighbour said, 'Well, sir, what do you think of this preacher?' 'Think of him!', said he, 'I never heard such a preacher before. He is more fit to stand before kings and teach them, than to stand before and teach these old women.' His neighbour had no need to invite him to go afterwards; he ran at every opportunity for above forty years.[23]

We may be sure that Wesley would have preferred the old women to the kings.

A testimony, deeply interesting and probably unique, was given by David Jeffries of Cambridge and Blewbury, near Salisbury, who appears to have been a Tertiary of the Order of St Francis. It occurs in a published letter of twelve pages (1743) by 'A late Roman Catholic (viz. Jeffries) to a former confessor, concerning his leaving the Romish Profession'. The whole letter should be read, of which the following extract is germane to our purpose.

> As soon as I providentially heard the Rev. Mr John Wesley preach free, universal salvation by faith in Jesus Christ alone, it pleased the Lord mercifully to open my eyes, to shake my carnal security and show me the weakness of the doctrine of that pretended infallible church I had so long profest myself a member of.
>
> Amaz'd to find I had hitherto known nothing of Christianity, till it pleased the guide of good men and angels to bring me within the sound of this godly man's voice, I could not help saying with joy: *This is the Lord's doing, and it is marvellous in our eyes.*
>
> Finding, after strictly searching the oracles of God to see if things were really so, that what this zealous champion for the Lord of Hosts

[23] *W.M.M.* (1791), p. 74.

taught from the pulpit, and what he had written in his sermon on Salvation by Faith... and in his discourse on the Doctrine of Salvation, Faith and Good Works, was exactly consonant to the dictates of the Holy Ghost; yet contrary to the dogmatical faith of the great Council of Trent, the very Bulwark and Standard of the Church of Rome; I was struck with admiration and thoroughly convinced that unless I believed and felt what he, or rather God through him, laid down for true Christianity, I should be damned in spight [sic] of all my good works, confessions, indulgencies, holy peregrinations and absolutions.[24]

There is something peculiarly pleasing and gracious about the testimony of Howell Harris, the Welsh evangelist, separated as he was from John Wesley on the issue of Calvinism. He had previously expressed 'some prejudice against him, because he did not hold the Perseverance of the Saints and the doctrine of Election', but four years later (12th May 1743) he wrote to George Whitefield:

Last Sunday I heard Bro. John Wesley preach upon the seventh of the Romans. He was very sweet and loving, and seemed to have his heart honestly bent on drawing the poor souls to Christ.[25]

The young and thoughtless also came under the spell of Wesley's preaching and personality, and life for many of them took on a new and joyous meaning. There was, for example, Rebecca Mason, of Shadwell, who, in 1739, when only sixteen years of age,

was invited by a friend to hear the Rev. Mr Wesley at the Old Foundery. They waited some time at the door, in the midst of a great crowd, before Mr Wesley arrived. The delay led her to think of the parable of the ten virgins, and was the occasion of exciting a serious desire that she at last might be found ready to enter into the Marriage-Supper of the Lord. The approach of the minister was announced by 'Here he comes!' As soon as they entered and the congregation was settled, (for seats they had none), Mr Wesley gave out the following hymn:

> Behold the Saviour of mankind,
> Nailed to the shameful tree.

These words were accompanied with a divine influence and fixed her attention to that man of God, whom, from that time, she never ceased highly to esteem. When she returned home, being asked by her mother how she liked the preacher, she replied, 'I never saw such a people; I will go again.'[26]

[24] *W.H.S.*, V.193-4.
[25] A. H. Williams, *Welsh Wesleyan Methodism*, p. 24; also *Journal*, III.77n.
[26] *W.M.M.* (1804), p. 126.

She lived to be eighty, and these words were written nearly thirteen years after Wesley had passed away.

One of the most adventurous romances of the days of Wesley is the life story of Silas Told. This was written by himself and vouched for by John Wesley, who published it in serial form in his *Magazine*. In 1790 it was issued in one volume.

The author's early life at sea has almost all the elements of a first-class schoolboy 'thriller'. When his seafaring days were over Told heard Wesley preach and his conversion followed. For a time he was a master in Wesley's school at the Foundery. He will be ever remembered for his amazing and sacrificial devotion to the spiritual welfare of the inmates of prisons and workhouses in and around London. Many of the prisoners he accompanied to the scaffold and was at times mistaken by the crowd for one of the condemned malefactors themselves. He has left a long and illuminating account of his first encounter with John Wesley. He tells how he became friendly with a young bricklayer named Charles Greaves, in July 1740. When Greaves asked him to go to hear Wesley, Told 'begged him, for God's sake, never to ask him so any more'. Ultimately the two men went to the Foundery together at four o'clock one morning, and the story proceeds:

When we entered the place . . . I was tempted to gaze about me; and finding it a ruinous place, I began to think it answered the report given of it. Greaves stood close behind me to prevent my going out, to which I was strongly tempted; and had it not been for the multitude of people and the profound seriousness which evidently appeared in the countenance of almost every person, I should have given way to the temptation. Exactly at five a whisper was conveyed through the congregation, 'Here he comes! Here he comes!' I was filled with curiosity to see his person, which, when I beheld, I much despised. The enemy of souls suggested that he was some farmer's son, who, not able to support himself, was making a penny in this manner. He passed through the congregation into the pulpit, and, having his robes on, I expected he would have begun with the Church service; but, to my astonishment, he began with singing a hymn, with which I was almost enraptured; but his extemporary prayer was quite unpleasant, as I thought it savoured too much of the Dissenter. His text was, *I write unto you, little children, because your sins are forgiven you.* The enemy now suggested that he was a Papist, as he dwelt so much on forgiveness of sins. Although I had read this Scripture many times before, yet I never understood that we were to know our sins forgiven on earth; supposing that it referred only to those to whom the Apostle was then writing; especially as I had never heard this doctrine preached in the Church. However, my prejudices quickly abated, and I plainly saw I could never be saved without knowing my sins forgiven. At the close of which, however strange it may appear, a small, still voice entered my heart with these words, 'This is the truth!', and instantly I felt it in my soul. My friend, observing my attention, asked me how I liked Mr Wesley. I replied, 'As long as I live, I will never part from him.'

Under this sermon my soul was filled with a hatred for sin and also with zeal for the truth. Accordingly, I broke off at a stroke all my old acquaintance in iniquity.[27]

There is one testimony to Wesley's preaching which may well be unique, in the true sense of that much misused word; that of Miss E.R., who tells how she dreamt that she heard him preach 'a sweet sermon' from 'O that I had the wings of a dove! Then would I fly away and be at rest.' 'It was food to my soul', she remarks, and the good lady actually goes on to give an outline of the 'dream sermon' under two heads.[28] It may, of course, have been a dream repetition of an actual experience, when the sleeper drew upon what was stored below the level of conscious memory. However the psychologist may attempt to account for such a dream, it suggests a rarely recognized sphere of religious influence. Hundreds of people must have had dreams in which Wesley figured and even preached, though few, if any, in which his sermon was delivered and remembered in such minute detail. There may be a ministry of dreams, as the Bible writers recognized, whether or not we agree with their theory of it. A dream, in the language of philosophy, is a 'fact'; it has 'reality', though on a different plane from the facts of our waking life in the objective world, and as such it may exercise an influence for good or for ill. These 'facts' of the dream world may be complementary to those of the waking world, as was the case with Miss E.R. As John Wesley was aware of her experience, he is certain to have regarded it as divine in origin. In his sermon on *Human Life as a Dream*, he dwells on the mysterious nature of dreams in general and how none can tell their essence, but continues:

From the divine treasury of knowledge (Scripture) we learn that, on some extraordinary occasions, the great Father of spirits has manifested

[27] *W.M.M.* (1787), p. 627. *The Life of Mr Silas Told* has been re-published by The Epworth Press (1954).
[28] ibid. (1790), p. 51.

himself to human spirits, 'in dreams and visions of the night'. But which of all these arise from natural, which from supernatural influence, we are many times unable to determine.[29]

In the main this view would commend itself to the devout and intelligent people of the time. We note that Wesley's presence, his sermon and the comfort he gave, were all *true facts* in the experience of the dreamer. He exercised a *ministry of dreams*, unconsciously, as others have done, whose extent and fruitfulness cannot be determined. But such a ministry was only possible because John Wesley was, in his active life, a faithful ambassador of Jesus Christ.

There is ample evidence of the prejudices of people against Wesley being overcome when they heard him preach. A notable example is John Newton, in his early life serving on a vessel engaged in the slave trade, but later a convert to the Christian Faith, incumbent of Olney and friend of William Cowper. Nelson entertained Calvinistic views and did not wholly approve of Wesley's presentation of the Gospel. Some of these early prejudices were removed when, at last, he heard Wesley preach and he very humbly expressed contrition for his former uncharitable attitude.

The remaining power of bigotry in me has received a blow which (I would hope) will keep me low hereafter. I would hope that, since the Lord has taken so gracious and favourable a way to correct my ignorance and presumption, I shall no more venture to censure and judge without hearing, or dare confine the Spirit of the Lord to those only who tally in all things with my sentiments.[30]

The following testimony is not only valuable as evidence of the power of Wesley's preaching, but it deserves to be rescued from oblivion as a contemporary reply to the malicious detractors of the early Methodists. Under the initials M.F.S., a correspondent wrote to John Wesley on 21st February 1783. The writer was, without doubt, Miss Mary Freeman Shepherd, the lady who is regarded as partly responsible for the secession of Samuel, Charles Wesley's younger son, to the Church of Rome about the year 1784. He was never a convinced Romanist, and his always shaky and critical allegiance at length faded out entirely. James T. Lightwood, Samuel's biographer, says of Miss Shepherd that she

[29] *Works*, VII.319.   [30] Josiah Bull, *Life of John Newton*, p. 93.

A CLOUD OF WITNESSES 125

occupies a high rank amongst the literary gossips of her day. She was an Englishwoman by birth, though descended on the maternal side from the ancient and noble house of the Falletti, of Piedmont. She was educated at a convent in Rome, and brought up a strict Roman Catholic. She possessed a strong mind, and had well-defined opinions, which she expressed on every possible occasion. Her knowledge of languages, classic and modern, was extensive, and she greatly appreciated their beauties. She had a wide acquaintance with the best literature, and was as fond of imparting knowledge as of acquiring it.

She was born in 1730, and the years from 1759 to the end of her long life she spent

in writing very lengthy letters to different people on various subjects, literary and theological. Although a devotee of the Catholic (Roman) faith, she had a broad outlook on religious questions generally. She held John Wesley in great esteem, and Adam Clarke's biographer went so far as to assert that 'she would willingly have merged her name in his'.[31]

The testimony of such an accomplished lady is of special value and interest. This is what she wrote to John Wesley.

The Methodists! I sing their praises every day. Perhaps there is not a body of people where there is so little *vulgarity* among those of the lower classes of life: so much good sense, and so much good manners. Do not think I despise the Methodists. I honour them exceedingly; and it is one of my motives for honouring you, that you have been such an instrument in the hand of God for restoring, with religion, her separable attendants, clear heads, sound judgements, good hearts, breathing forth in word and deed, love, good will, and civility between man and man.

One can readily understand the pleasure this letter would give to John Wesley, who knew how refining is the power of true heart religion upon even the crudest natures.

Most of the personal testimonies that have come down to us are by people to whom John Wesley came as a messenger of God, and who blessed the day and manner of his appearing; but there were exceptions. On Sunday, 5th October 1766, he preached in Lady Huntingdon's Chapel in Bath. Among the aristocracy there assembled was Horace Walpole, then aged 49, the bleakness of whose spiritual world chills one to the bone. On 10th October he wrote to John Chute:

[31] *Samuel Wesley: Musician*, p. 63; see also *Letters*, VII.230, and Etheridge, *Life of the Rev. Adam Clarke*, pp. 371 ff.

I have been at one opera, Mr Wesley's. They have boys and girls with charming voices, that sing hymns, in parts, to Scotch ballad tunes; but indeed so long, that one would think they were already in eternity, and knew how much time they had before them.... Wesley is a lean, elderly man, fresh-coloured, his hair smoothly combed, but with a *soupçon* of curl at the ends. Wondrous clean, but as evidently an actor as Garrick. He spoke his sermon, but so fast and with so little accent, that I am sure he has often uttered it, for it was like a lesson. There were parts and eloquence in it; but towards the end he exalted his voice and acted very ugly enthusiasm; decried learning and told stories, like Latimer, of the fool of his college, who said, 'I *thanks* God for everything.' Except a few from curiosity, and *some honourable women*, the congregation was very mean.

To suggest that John Wesley ever decried learning in itself is ludicrous, but this effusion will not disturb those who know their Horace Walpole. Without disparagement of his ability and good qualities, be it said that he was something of a snob, whose estimates of people needed to be revised by persons of sound and unprejudiced judgement. One of his biographers, Stephen Gwynne, says that one of the affectations which never left him was 'a sort of contempt for the serious affairs of life. Indeed, he was never seriously concerned for anything except when his affections were engaged'. The same writer continues: 'The truth may as well be spoken at once: Horace Walpole was a bad critic, and the worst kind of bad critic; one who tends to magnify himself by being supercilious.'[32] Those who, having read Walpole's references to John Wesley, feel the need of a strong sedative for their ruffled spirits, should turn to Lord Macaulay's pages, there to read, for example, that

The conformation of his (H. Walpole's) mind was such that whatever was little seemed to him great, and whatever was great seemed to him little. Serious business was a trifle to him, and trifles were his serious business.

Those who hesitate to accept the unqualified and sententious pronouncements of the Victorian sage may note, for their comfort, the words of Stephen Gwynne, on the last page of his book:

His friends who knew him best—we have it on his own word—always laughed at him a little;

and having re-read the objectionable letter, we conclude that it is best for us to laugh with them and leave it there.

[32] op. cit., pp. 54–5.

With few exceptions, contemporary references to Wesley's preaching are by men and women who never moved in the *beau monde* of the age, but who found, as they listened to him, what Horace Walpole and those like him missed, and all life was for them miraculously and superbly different thereafter. As we read their personal testimonies, in a kind of continuation of the *Acts of the Apostles*, and discover the manner of men they once were and ultimately became, we inevitably recall the words of St Paul:

For we beheld your calling, brethren, how that not many wise after the flesh, not many mighty, not many noble (εὐγενεῖς, nobly-born: blue-blooded) have part therein; but God chose the foolish things of the world, that he might put to shame them that are wise; and God chose the weak things of the world, that he might put to shame the things that are strong; and the base things, (τὰ ἀγενῆ, the things, or people, of no family: plebeian), and the things that are despised, did God choose; the things that are not, that he might bring to nought the things that are (τὰ μὴ ὄντα, ἵνα τὰ ὄντα καταργήσῃ): that no flesh should glory before God.[33]

Few who heard John Wesley had the power of literary expression, and for every such one there must have been hundreds who could only lisp their praises with a stammering tongue, and whose eloquence was confined to those quiet places of the human spirit where speech is lost in unutterable love and gratitude. But Charles Wesley helped them to break their silence and liberate their emotion in words which they could and did make their own. The finest testimonies to Wesley's preaching are in those hymns which his people sang, because his preaching, by the grace of God, had made their singing possible.

> For Jesus, my Lord, is now my defence;
> I trust in His word, none plucks me from thence;
> Since I have found favour, He all things will do;
> My King and my Saviour shall make me anew.[34]

[33] 1 Cor. 1$^{26-9}$.   [34] *M.H.B.* No. 420.

CHAPTER XI

SOME EFFECTS OF WESLEY'S PREACHING

(a) NEWNESS OF LIFE

WE HAVE NOTED the redeeming effects of Wesley's preaching upon individual men and women to whom the word came with convincing power. In the course of time a new kind of entry appears in the *Journal*, with increasing frequency. As Wesley passed from place to place he recalled former visits: his harsh receptions, the mobs, the widespread wickedness: and he notes the change which has taken place. There have been conversions, and scores of people have become Christians and Methodists, but that is not the full measure of the results of his preaching and of the daily witness of his own followers. He discovers in the place a new temper; a respect toward himself and a willingness to hear his message; an extensive reversion from vicious habits, which is a sign of the leaven of righteousness at work among the people. Though not all have entered into the peace and joy of a living faith in Jesus Christ, there is a marked improvement in their morals; ugly vices, where they still exist, have become shamefaced and sequestered, and life in general has become more serious and decent. John Wesley's heart must have swelled in gratitude to Almighty God as he penned such entries as this:

Arbroath. (5. May 1772). In this town there is a change indeed! It was wicked to a proverb; remarkable for Sabbath-breaking, cursing, swearing, drunkenness and a general contempt of religion. But it is not so now. Open wickedness disappears; no oaths are heard, no drunkenness seen in the streets. And many have not only ceased from evil and learned to do well, but are witnesses of the inward kingdom of God, 'righteousness, peace and joy in the Holy Ghost.'

Even in 1745 Wesley could present his 'living witnesses' to confront and confound the doubts, malice and opposition of his enemies; individuals who could testify clearly that 'whereas I was blind, now I see'. This he did in a long and important letter to the Rev. Thomas Church, Vicar of Battersea and Prebendary of St Paul's Cathedral, whom Wesley describes as 'a gentleman, a scholar and a Christian'. Wesley was seeking to justify his evangelism and the doctrines he preached, to a critic whom he respected.

By the fruits shall we know those of whom I speak; even the cloud of witnesses, who at this hour experience the gospel I preach to be the power of God unto salvation. The habitual drunkard that was is now temperate in all things. The whoremonger now flees fornication. He that stole, steals no more, but works with his hands. He that cursed or swore, perhaps at every sentence, has now learned to serve the Lord with fear and rejoice unto Him with reverence. Those formerly enslaved to various habits of sin are now brought to uniform habits of holiness. These are demonstrable facts. I can name the men, with their several places of abode. One of them was an avowed Atheist for many years, some were Jews, a considerable number Papists, the greater part of them as much strangers to the form as to the power of godliness.[1]

One of these 'living witnesses', after hearing Wesley preach at Kingswood, expressed the gladness of his heart at what he saw, in the unusual form of verse. He is simply described as 'a poor man', and was probably a collier. He hails John Wesley as a modern 'Druid' and a 'bard' of glad tidings. Kingswood is in his mind, and the unhappy, ignorant condition of the miners.

> Those dark, benighted slaves, alas! we find,
> Were to their dearest interests wholly blind.
> How gross their ignorance! Their hearts how dark!
> No ray of light was there,—no heavenly spark.
> But when a modern Druid did enquire,
> How sad their fate: he strung his tuneful lyre;
> Around his sounding lyre the miners throng,
> Charmed with his voice, they blest him as he sang.

There follows a description of the Advent of our Lord, and the preaching of John Wesley, and the verses continue:

> O happy day! O most stupendous Birth!
> In heaven was gladness, and good-will on earth.
> The attentive wood was ravished as he sung,
> While truths divine flowed sweetly from his tongue.
> Victorious heavenly love, it all o'ercame,
> Colliers looked mild and savages grew tame.
> Renewed by grace, enlightened by the Word,
> They now became true followers of the Lord.
> They worshipped God, and lived in love and peace,
> And daily found their happiness increase.[2]

[1] *Letters*, II.201.   [2] *W.M.M.* (1803), p. 48.

It is a tribute couched in rare form, by one who knew whereof he wrote, and, coming from such a quarter, there is something moving in its sincerity, and in the evident desire of the writer to honour John Wesley in rhyme and rhythm. One feels the aptness of a remark by William Wakinshaw:

It was said of Napoleon that he could stamp soldiers out of mud. By his preaching, Wesley surpassed this miracle. He fashioned saints out of slime.[3]

When he was seventy-five, Wesley wrote to Elizabeth Ritchie on the permanence of his work. (12th February 1779.)

The present revival of religion in England has already continued fifty years. And, blessed be God, it is at least as likely to continue as it was twenty or thirty years ago. Indeed, it is far more likely; as it not only spreads wider, but sinks deeper than ever, more and more persons being able to testify that the blood of Christ cleanses from all sin. We have therefore reason to hope that this revival of religion will continue, and continually increase, till the time when all Israel shall be saved and the fullness of the Gentiles shall come.

From the standpoint of that year, 1779, we see how, in a great act of faith and hope, Wesley had claimed these kingdoms of the human spirit for Jesus Christ, when the forces opposing him appeared irresistible. We read of a Roman citizen whose faith in the might of Rome was so unshakable that, when Hannibal was besieging the city, he paid a high price for a piece of land beyond the walls, on which the enemy was even then encamped. Such was Wesley's faith. At great personal cost, by the consecration of his whole life, he had purchased the spiritual freeholds of many lives, where was encamped and entrenched the Enemy of Souls. By the power of the preached word he had sought to enter into possession of his purchase, and where he was successful men and women were redeemed and there was a new creation in Christ Jesus. In all his preaching he had been sustained by hope, assured that 'by this anchor a Christian is kept steady in the midst of the waves of this troublesome world, and preserved from striking upon either of those fatal rocks—presumption or despair. . . . He neither apprehends the difficulties of the race set before him to be greater than he has strength to conquer, nor expects them to be so little as to yield in the conquest, till he has put forth all his strength.'[4] These were Wesley's own words when he

[3] William Wakinshaw, *John Wesley*, p. 80.
[4] *Works*, V.206 (*The Circumcision of the Heart*).

preached before the University of Oxford as early as New Year's Day, 1733. Such was the Hope that strengthened his life's purpose and saved him alike from presumption and despair. With its strong ally, Faith, it anticipated triumphs of grace that were yet to be, fruits of his preaching hidden in the heart of future years, but present in his imagination. 'Look', said John of Gaunt to Henry Bolingbroke,

> Look, what thy soul holds dear, imagine it
> To lie the way thou goest.[5]

That is what John Wesley did, and the great days came when the Enemy of Souls vacated his usurped possessions before the entry of the Prince of Peace, and then the heart of a dauntless Christian preacher rejoiced with exceeding great joy.

(b) SOULS IN TORMENT

There are certain effects of John Wesley's preaching which call for notice, as existing in a class apart. These are the states of hysteria and convulsion into which some of his hearers were thrown, particularly during his earlier ministry. One example must suffice.

12 June 1742. (At Epworth) While I was speaking several dropped down as dead, and among the rest such a cry was heard of sinners groaning for the righteousness of faith as almost drowned my voice. But many of these soon lift up their hearts with joy, and broke out into thanksgiving, being assured they now had the desire of their soul—the forgiveness of their sins.

S. G. Dimond gives a useful summary of these occurrences, as they are related in the *Journal*.

In some instances the whole congregation is described as breaking forth into tears or cries or groaning, but, apart from these general statements, I have examined two hundred and thirty-four individual cases enumerated and reported on during the years 1739–1743. Out of eighty-five cases of persons who 'dropped as dead', fifty-six occurred in Bristol, nineteen in London, seven in Newcastle and three in Cornwall. Two cases of persons struck blind (psychogenic blindness) are reported from Newcastle. Convulsive tearings, violent trembling, groaning, strong cries and tears, and other physical effects, are frequently recorded throughout the second and third volumes of the *Journal*. There are fourteen cases of madness and restoration, and

---
[5] Shakespeare, *Richard II*, I.iii.286–7.

nine cases of incurable insanity. From the distribution of these peculiar phenomena it is apparent that they occurred largely among the more primitive and less civilized types, in the neighbourhood of Bristol and Kingswood, and at Gateshead Fell and Chowden, which Wesley characterizes as 'the very Kingswood of the North'.[6]

Whilst there is nothing fresh to be said about these happenings, there are certain points which we should note.

1. It was by no means under the preaching of John Wesley alone that they occurred. They have been features of many 'religious revivals', both Christian and non-Christian, and some of Wesley's contemporaries had experience of them. Amongst these were his brother Charles; George Whitefield; John Berridge, Vicar of Everton and William Grimshaw, Rector of Haworth, the last-named of whom tells how, in 1742,

> my church began to be crowded, insomuch that many were obliged to stand out of doors. Here, as in other places, it was amazing to see what weeping, roaring and agonies my people were seized with at their apprehension of the sinful state and the wrath of God.[7]

2. Wesley himself was much perplexed at these scenes. It was natural to associate them with the New Testament stories of demon possession, but he did not like them. Were these distortions of body and mind of God or of the devil? It seemed to Wesley they might be of either, and it was therefore wise to observe them closely and judge each case separately. He is chary of venturing any statement that looks like an 'explanation'. He cites an extreme case of a young woman in Kingswood and comments: 'The fact I nakedly relate, and leave every man to his own judgement of it.'[8]

3. These phenomena were eagerly seized upon by the antagonists of John Wesley and Methodism. They were regarded askance by captious people and also by some of the better educated, who were otherwise inclined to look sympathetically upon his work as a whole. His enemies exploited these sneers and suspicions, in order to discredit Wesley and his works in the eyes of the people at large. Again and again, being challenged, he had to express an opinion about them.

On Sunday, 25th November 1759, he preached at Everton for John Berridge, and noted in his *Journal*:

[6] *The Psychology of Methodism*, p. 81.
[7] G. G. Cragg, *Grimshaw of Haworth*, p. 22.
[8] *Journal*, II.298.

SOME EFFECTS OF WESLEY'S PREACHING 133

a remarkable difference since I was here before, as to the manner of the work. None were now in trances, none cried out, none fell down or were convulsed; only some trembled exceedingly, a low murmur was heard, and many were refreshed with the multitude of peace.

The danger *was* to regard extraordinary circumstances too much, such as outcries, convulsions, visions, trances; as if these were essential to the inward work, so that it could not go on without them. Perhaps the danger *is* to regard them too little, to condemn them altogether; to imagine that they had nothing of God in them and were a hindrance to His work. Whereas the truth is: God suddenly and strongly convinced many that they were lost sinners, the natural consequence whereof were sudden outcries and strong bodily convulsions.

Wesley then expresses his belief, which would not appear strange as it does today, that 'Satan . . . mimicked this work of God, in order to discredit the whole work;' but 'He (God) will enable us to discern how far, in every case, the work is pure, and where it mixes or degenerates.' He continues:

Let us even suppose that, in some few cases, there was a mixture of dissimulation—that persons pretended to see or feel what they did not, and imitated the cries or convulsive motions of those who were really overpowered by the Spirit of God; yet even this should not make us either deny or undervalue the real work of the Spirit. The shadow is no disparagement of the substance, nor the counterfeit of the real diamond.

On 28th March 1768, Wesley wrote to Dr Thomas Rutherford, Regius Professor of Divinity at Cambridge, who had passed certain strictures upon 'bodily emotions of various kinds'. After replying to him in detail, Wesley, who was weary of the subject, thus concludes:

Upon the whole, I declare once for all (and I hope to be troubled no more upon the subject) I look upon some of those bodily symptoms to have been preternatural or diabolical, and others to have been effects which in some circumstances naturally followed from strong and sudden emotions of mind. These emotions of mind, whether of fear, sorrow or joy, I believe were supernatural, springing from the gracious influences of the Spirit of God which accompanied His word.[9]

These occurrences appear mysterious and irrational to us today, largely because we cannot wholly transport ourselves, in imagination, into the mental climate of the uncultured masses of the eighteenth century. The phenomena followed the impact of

[9] *Letters*, V.367-8.

Wesley's message upon a certain type of mind and a suddenly awakened conscience. Whilst we may justifiably claim the preaching as their immediate cause, we cannot claim them as a necessary and invariable effect. Neither did Wesley. In large crowds they were confined to a comparative handful of people or even to a single individual. Must we assume these people to have been the sole representatives of their particular mental type, present on the occasion? That is extremely unlikely. Further, the phenomena became less and less frequent and finally ceased. Does that mean that this type became practically extinct? Again, it is more than unlikely, though the type certainly becomes rarer as educational, physical and social conditions improve, and in an ideal society, such as that suggested by 'the Kingdom of God', would become non-existent and finally almost unimaginable. We therefore conclude that, whilst Wesley's preaching was their immediate cause, it was not their sole or more remote cause. There were subjective factors, physical, mental, and social, which, together with the preached word, helped very greatly to determine what the reaction of any particular individual would be.

On this subject Charles Wesley has a timely word for us. In the order of those who do not suffer fools gladly, he certainly held a more exalted position than his brother John, and he had a more discerning eye for imposture. He was early convinced that, for the most part, these were cases of what is called today 'exhibitionism', and the results of his methods of dealing with them tend to confirm that view. For example, he notes in his *Journal* (5th August 1740):

> I talked sharply to Jenny Dechamps, a girl of twelve years old; who now confessed that her fits and cryings out (above thirty of them) were all feigned, that Mr Wesley might take notice of her.

His entry for 4th June 1743, is both instructive and amusing.

> I went on at five expounding the *Acts*. Some stumbling blocks, with the help of God, I have removed, particularly the fits. Many, no doubt, were, at our first preaching, struck down, both soul and body, into the depth of distress. Their *outward affections* were easy to be imitated. Many counterfeits I have already detected. Today, one who came from the ale-house, drunk, was pleased to fall into a fit for my entertainment, and beat himself heartily. I thought it a pity to hinder him; so, instead of singing over him, as had been often done, we left him to recover at his leisure. Another, a girl, as she began her cry, I

ordered to be carried out. Her convulsion was so violent as to take away the use of her limbs, till they laid and left her without the door. Then immediately she found her legs and walked off. Some very unstill sisters, who always took care to stand near me, and tried which should cry loudest, since I had them removed out of my sight, have been as quiet as lambs. The first night I preached here half my words were lost through their outcries. Last night, before I began, I gave public notice that whosoever cried out so as to drown my voice, should, without any man's hurting or judging them, be gently carried to the farthest corner of the room. But my porters had no employment the whole night; yet the Lord was with us, mightily, convincing of sin and of righteousness.

Thomas Butts was a devoted Methodist, clear-sighted, rational and a trusted friend of John Wesley. In 1743 he wrote a pamphlet in which he touched upon these strange scenes, that were then arousing much controversy.

As to persons crying out or being in fits, I shall not pretend to account exactly for that, but only make this observation: it is well known that most of them who have been so exercised were before persons of no religion at all, but they have since received a sense of pardon, have peace and joy in believing, and are now more holy and happy than ever they were before. And if this be so, no matter what remarks are made on their fits.[10]

We may, with contented minds, leave the last word with wise Thomas Butts.

[10] Quoted by T. E. Brigden in *A New History of Methodism*, I.216. For *Thomas Butts* see, *inter alia*, Leslie F. Church: *More about the Early Methodist People*, p. 61.

CHAPTER XII

SERVICE: SERMON: STYLE

(*a*) In the nature of the case John Wesley could not confine the conduct of his services to one particular form, even if he had so desired. The form was determined by the occasion: whether he was conducting a normal service in a church of the Establishment, or preaching before the University of Oxford, or at the Bedford Assizes, or to prisoners in gaol, or to open-air crowds in some industrial or rural centre, or to his own people in one of their preaching-houses.

His personal preference was to preach in a church and use *The Book of Common Prayer*. It held a warm place in his heart and he had a reverence for its authority as being 'only less than that of the oracles of God'.[1] When he adapted it for use among Methodists, first in America (1784) and then in this country (1788), he declared, in his *Preface*:

I BELIEVE there is no LITURGY in the World, either in ancient or modern language, which breathes more of a solid, scriptural, rational Piety, than the COMMON PRAYER of the CHURCH of ENGLAND. And though the main of it was compiled considerably more than two hundred years ago, yet is the language of it, not only pure, but strong and elegant in the highest degree.

At the same time, he did not regard the Liturgy as being beyond criticism. Having read a book in which objections were taken to certain parts of it, he remarks that about one in ten of them appear to have weight and about one in five, plausibility. 'But', he says, 'who will supply a better?'[2]

In a letter to the Rev. Samuel Walker, of Truro, one of the evangelical clergymen of the time (20th November 1755), Wesley refers to the ejection of 1662. The Act of Uniformity, in accordance with which the ejectment took place, had demanded that every minister in a benefice should make a public declaration in these words:

I do here declare my unfeigned assent and consent to all and everything contained and prescribed in and by the book entitled 'The

[1] *Works*, VIII.101–2.   [2] *Journal*, III.491.

Book of Common Prayer and Administration of the Sacraments, and other rites and ceremonies of the Church, according to the use of the Church of England, etc.'

Wesley comments:

I should not dare to declare my assent and consent to that book in the terms prescribed. Indeed, they are so strong that I think they cannot safely be used with regard to any book but the Bible. Neither dare I confine myself wholly to forms of prayer, not even in the church. I use, indeed, all the forms; but I frequently add extemporary prayer either before or after sermon.

In a letter to the same correspondent (24th September 1755), Wesley states the position of his Methodists, which was clearly his own.

With regard to the Liturgy itself: though they allow it is in general one of the most excellent human compositions that ever was, yet they think it is both absurd and sinful to declare such an assent and consent as is required, to any merely human composition. Again: though they do not object to the use of forms, yet they dare not confine themselves to them. And in this form (the Book of Common Prayer) there are several things which they apprehend to be contrary to Scripture.

So Wesley asserted, both for himself and for his people, entire freedom from any tyranny of forms and ceremonies. 'God is a spirit, and they that worship Him must worship Him in spirit and in truth.' He had seen all too frequently how the spirit dies and truth becomes obscured when men are slavishly tied down to forms of worship, with no power spontaneously to express the emotions of any particular moment or occasion. The Liturgy belonged as much to the Methodists as to anyone else, but they used it wisely; it remained, and still remains, one of the varied forms which their corporate worship might take. At all costs, sincerity and reality must be preserved, for Wesley knew that without these all worship becomes vain repetition. Let rigidity and formalism once be established in her worship, and Methodism would cease to be an instrument in the hand of God for spreading scriptural holiness throughout the land.

Writing to a friend (20th September 1757), when Methodist preaching-houses were being erected all over the country, Wesley describes the usual method of conducting worship therein, which we may safely presume to be generally descriptive of his own.

The person who reads prayers, though not always the same, yet is always one who may be supposed to speak from his heart, one whose life is no reproach to his profession, and one who performs that solemn part of divine service, not in a careless, slovenly manner, but seriously and slowly, as becomes him who is transacting so high an affair between God and man.

Nor is it a little advantage, as to the next part of the service, to hear a preacher whom you know to live as he speaks, speaking the genuine gospel of present salvation through faith, wrought in the heart by the Holy Ghost, declaring present, free, full justification and enforcing every branch of inward and outward holiness. And this you hear done in the most clear, plain, simple, unaffected language, yet with an earnestness becoming the importance of the subject and with the demonstration of the Spirit. . . .

Add to this that the whole service is performed in a decent and solemn manner, is enlivened by hymns suitable to the occasion and concluded with prayer that comes not out of feigned lips.

(*b*) How did Wesley construct his sermons? Did he work by some principle that we can recognize? In respect of his preached sermons, only a tentative and inferential reply is possible. On Thursday, 28th April 1774, he opened 'the new house at Wakefield', and his sermon was taken down in shorthand and published as a pamphlet. There is nothing particularly revealing about it. Curnock remarks: 'It does not help us to account for the preacher's popularity.'[3] So we are driven back upon the published sermons and are at once faced with the tedious question of the relation between them and the spoken word.

During the Middle Ages sermons in this country were generally preached in the common tongue, and, if later committed to writing, were often transposed into Latin. There is a possible analogy here with John Wesley's practice. Not that he transposed into Latin, though he was as well able to do that as any man in the land, but into that terse, vigorous, clear English that makes all that he wrote such excellent reading. Probably, however, he worked in the reverse order: first the written sermon and then the preached one.

A slight examination of his sermons reveals their careful planning. Many of them are set out under three clear headings, with numerous subdivisions, and all so logically interrelated that it is easy to grasp the general outline. They are models of precise, definite, theological and ethical statement, their framework

[3] *Journal*, VI.17 and 248.

obviously designed by a man who knew exactly what he wished his framework to contain.

The chief sermons are on those subjects which helped to bring the Methodist Societies into existence and on which we know Wesley continually preached. There appears to have been no reason why he should not have used the general frameworks, which can hardly be improved upon. The same frame and the same subject may serve both a Raphael and a Picasso, but how different will be the treatment in each case! It is what is put into the frame that chiefly matters; that is, the subject, specifically treated in order to accommodate it to the intelligence and capacity of that section of the public whose sympathies it is designed to enlist. There is abundant evidence that the precise phraseology, the technical terms and the recondite quotations and allusions of the printed sermons gave way, in preaching, to a more colloquial style; to a phraseology, an exposition and illustrations that the ordinary man of the time could more readily understand. Perhaps the most we can say about the *construction* of John Wesley's preached sermons is that there is no reason why, in this respect, they should have differed greatly from the printed ones. The simplicity of his method would certainly enable the average hearer long to remember the outline of the discourse.

(*c*) From the time when Plato wrote the *Phaedrus* and the Third Book of the *Republic*, and possibly even before then, men have discussed the questions, '*What is Style?*' and '*What are the essentials of a good Style?*' The *Concise Oxford Dictionary* defines Style as

> the manner of writing, speaking or doing, especially as opposed to the *matter* to be expressed or the thing done; collective characteristics of the writing or diction or artistic expression or way of presenting things or decorative methods proper to a person or school or period or subject; manner exhibiting those characteristics.

Literary Style is our concern; in the case of preached sermons, diction: wording and phrasing.

If Walter Pater is right—and he is an excellent authority—that 'the chief stimulus of good style is to possess a full, rich, complex matter to grapple with',[4] then assuredly a good style was initially possible to Wesley, since the whole field of New Testament Christianity was his chosen subject. Matthew Arnold

---

[4] *Appreciations*, Ch. I, On Style.

advised, 'Have something to say, and say it as clearly as you can. This is the only secret of style.'[5] Wesley's published sermons pass such a test triumphantly, and, keen logician and practised debater that he was, it is hardly conceivable that he should have wholly forsaken such a style in preaching, however he may have modified his vocabulary and idiom in the interests of his audience of the moment.

We must not overlook the *personal* quality in style: what Georges de Buffon, Wesley's distinguished contemporary, meant when he said, *'le style est l'homme même'*; what Goethe had in mind when he told Eckermann that 'if any would write in a noble style, let him first possess a noble soul'; and what Sir Walter Raleigh meant when he wrote: 'All style is gesture, the gesture of the mind and of the soul.'[6] 'Style is like the colouring of a painter, a quality of the writer's vision, the rendering and revelation of the world of his unique perception.'[7] Wesley's style has this personal quality. It is, to his subject-matter, what light is to a painting; the glamorous light of a Vermeer: the centralized, compelling light of a Rembrandt. It illuminates his subject; does not confuse the understanding with shadows, half-lights, irrelevancies. Every word does its duty, nor does it encroach upon its neighbour's territory, but observes an etiquette *inter verba*. Moreover, Wesley so impressed his preachers with the importance of such a style that many of them acquired it by practice. In time it became one of the recognized characteristics of Methodist preaching, and led Dr Johnson to remark, on one occasion, that the success of Methodists

is owing to their expressing themselves in a plain and familiar manner, which is the only way to do good to the common people, and which clergymen of genius and learning ought to do from a principle of duty, when it is suited to their congregations; a practice for which they will be praised by men of sense.[8]

In his Preface to the second series of published sermons, dated 1st January 1788, Wesley refers to his own plainness of style in these words:

I dare no more write in a *fine style* than wear a fine coat. But were it otherwise, had I time to spare, I should still write just as I do. I should

---

[5] *Letters of Matthew Arnold to Arthur Hugh Clough* (Oxford), p. 65.
[6] Eckermann, *Conversations with Goethe* (14th April 1824). Sir Walter Raleigh, *Style*, p. 127.
[7] Quoted by L. Pearsall Smith in *Selected Passages from Jeremy Taylor*, p. lxii.
[8] Boswell's *Johnson* (Saturday 30th July 1763).

purposely decline, what many admire, a highly ornamental style. . . .

Only let his (the preacher's) language be plain, proper and clear, and it is enough. God himself has told us how to speak, both as to the matter and the manner: 'If any man speak', in the name of God, 'let him speak as the oracles of God'; and if he would imitate any part of these above the rest, let it be the First Epistle of St John. This is the style, the most excellent style, for every gospel preacher. And let him aim at no more ornament, than he finds in that sentence, which is the sum of the whole gospel, 'We love Him, because He first loved us.'

This admiration for St John's style lasted to the end of his life.

An obscure style annoyed him. He felt no obligation to complete his reading of a work badly written, unless the excellence of its matter helped to compensate for the uncouthness of its diction. We sense the vigorous reaction of the trained, concise mind, in such a Journal entry as that of 27th January 1759.

I began reading, with huge expectation, a tract written by a son-in-law of the great Bengelius, Mr Oetinger, *De Sensu Communi et Ratione*. But how was I disappointed! So obscure a writer I scarce ever saw before. . . . When I had with huge labour read fifty or sixty pages, finding the sense did by no means make amends for the time and pains bestowed in searching it out, I took my leave of him for ever.

In three letters, written in 1764 to his young clerical friend, Samuel Furly, Wesley is very explicit on this subject. 'A clergyman', he insists, 'should talk with the vulgar'; that is the ordinary, common, homely folk. With them he should use the vernacular. However costly in rhetoric and fine speech, Wesley calls for that utter clarity of expression which the urgency of the gospel message demands.

Write, imitating the language of the *common people* throughout, so far as consorts with purity and propriety of speech. *Easiness* . . . is the first, second and third point; and *stiffness*, *apparent* exactness, artificialness of style the main defect to be avoided, next to solecism and impropriety.[9]

In a letter to Samuel four months later, the subject recurs.

What is it that constitutes *a good style*? Perspicuity and purity, propriety, strength and easiness, joined together. Where any of them is wanting, it is not a good style. . . .

As for me, I never think of my style at all; but just set down the words that come first. Only when I transcribe anything for the press,

[9] *Letters*, IV.232.

then I think it my duty to see every phrase be clear, pure and proper. Conciseness (which is now, as it were, natural to me) brings *quantum sufficit* of strength. If, after all, I observe any stiff expression, I throw it out, neck and shoulders. . . .

Clearness in particular is necessary for you and me, because we are to instruct people of the lowest understanding. Therefore we, above all, if we think with the wise, yet must speak with the vulgar. We should constantly use the most common, little, easy words (so they are pure and proper) which our language affords. When I had been a member of the University about ten years, I wrote and talked much as you do now. But when I talked to plain people in the Castle or the town, I observed they gaped or stared. This quickly obliged me to alter my style and adopt the language of those I spoke to. And yet there is a dignity in this simplicity, which is not disagreeable to those of the highest rank. . . .

You are a Christian minister, speaking and writing to save souls. Have this end always in your eye, and you will never designedly use a hard word. Use all the sense, learning and fire you have; forgetting yourself, and remembering only these are the souls for whom Christ died.[10]

Here are interesting personal revelations. Telford tells us how, as a young man, Wesley once preached 'a highly finished sermon to a country congregation. The people listened with open mouths. He saw at once that they did not understand what he said. He struck out some of the expressions and tried again. Their mouths were now only half open. Wesley, however, was resolved to carry them entirely with him. He read the sermon to an intelligent servant, and got her to tell him whenever she did not understand. Betty's "Stop, sir", came so often that he grew impatient. But he persevered, wrote a plain word over every hard one, and had his reward in seeing that his congregation now clearly understood every word.'[11]

Returning to the subject, in October of the same year, Wesley writes to Furly:

Long sentences utterly confound their intellects; they know not where they are. If you would be understood by them, you should seldom use a word of many syllables or a sentence of many words. Short sentences are likewise infinitely best for the careless and indolent. They strike them through and through. I have seen instances of it a hundred times. Neither are the dull and stupid enlightened nor the careless

---

[10] *Letters*, IV.256–8.
[11] *John Wesley*, p. 315. See also Wesley's *Notes on the Old Testament*, Introduction, p.v.

affected by long and laboured periods half so much as by such short ones as these: 'The work is great. The day is short and long is the night wherein no man can work.' . . . But the main thing is, let us be all alive to God.[12]

We may therefore be sure that Wesley employed simple, common words, in short, sharp, stabbing sentences, and found that people listened, understood and responded.

Commenting on our Lord's *Sermon on the Mount*, Wesley writes:

Through this whole discourse, we cannot but observe the most exact method which can possibly be conceived. Every paragraph, every sentence, is closely connected both with that which precedes and that which follows it. And is not this the pattern for every Christian preacher? If any then are able to follow it without any premeditation, well; if not, let them not dare to preach without it. No rhapsody, no incoherency, whether the things spoken be true or false, comes of the Spirit of Christ.[13]

No account of Wesley's preaching would be adequate, which omitted reference to his Preface to the Sermons published in 1746. There he tells us:

The following sermons contain the substance of what I have been preaching for between eight and nine years last past. . . . Nothing here appears in an elaborate, elegant or oratorical dress. . . . I now write, as I generally speak, *ad populum*—to the bulk of mankind, to those who neither relish nor understand the art of speaking; but who, notwithstanding, are competent judges of those truths which are necessary to present and future happiness. I mention this, that curious readers may spare themselves the labour of seeking for what they will not find.

I design plain truth for plain people: therefore, of set purpose, I abstain from all nice and philosophical speculations; from all perplexed and intricate reasonings; and, as far as possible, from even the show of learning, unless in sometimes citing the original Scripture. I labour to avoid all words which are not easy to be understood, all which are not used in common life; and, in particular, those kinds of technical terms that so frequently occur in Bodies of Divinity; those modes of speaking which men of reading are intimately acquainted with, but which to common people are an unknown tongue. Yet I am not assured that I do not sometimes slide into them unawares: it is so extremely natural to imagine that a word which is familiar to ourselves is so to all the world. . . .

[12] *Letters*, IV.267–8.   [13] *Notes on the New Testament* (Mt. 5⁹).

I have set down in the following sermons what I find in the Bible concerning the way to heaven; with a view to distinguish this way of God from all those which are the inventions of men.

Here, in a phrase, is the reason *why* Wesley composed his sermons: that he might show people 'the way to heaven'; a simple yet comprehensive expression, which has fallen upon evil times, but at which only supercilious ignorance will smile.

But Wesley also tells us, in the same Preface, much about *how* he composed these sermons. Declaring himself to be, in respect of the Bible, *homo unius libri*—a man of one Book—he goes on to picture himself meditating the composition of a sermon.

Here, then, I am, far from the busy ways of men. I sit down alone: only God is here. In his presence I open, I read his book. . . . Is there a doubt concerning the meaning of what I read? Does anything appear dark or intricate? I lift up my heart to the Father of Lights— 'Lord, is it not thy word, "If any man lack wisdom, let him ask of God"? Thou "givest liberally and upbraidest not". Thou hast said, "If any be willing to do thy will, he shall know". I am willing to do, let me know, thy will.' I then search after and consider parallel passages of Scripture, 'comparing spiritual things with spiritual'. I meditate thereon with all the attention and earnestness of which my mind is capable. If any doubt still remains, I consult those who are experienced in the things of God; and then the writings whereby, being dead, they yet speak. And what I thus learn, that I teach.

Wesley did not regard his style as entirely independent of the grace of God; to some extent it was a divine gift, and in times of unusual urgency he traced the hand of God in his ability to meet the situation and to fit both speech and style to the occasion. Thus, he wrote on 31st May 1771:

Observing many fashionable people in the court-house at Castlebar, I spoke with such closeness and pungency as I cannot do but at some peculiar season. It is indeed the gift of God, and cannot be attained by all the efforts of nature and art united.

We know that there were cultured and discerning people who listened to John Wesley and found his style appealing and satisfying. His early biographers reproduce a character-sketch of him, written soon after his death by an anonymous person, who says:

His elocution was ready and clear, graceful and easy, accurate and unaffected. As a writer, his style, though unstudied and flowing with natural ease, yet for accuracy and perspicuity was such as may vie with the best writers in the English language.[14]

We have also the description given by John Hampson, Wesley's earliest biographer and, at one time, one of his preachers, who later became an Anglican clergyman.

> In point of style, his most distinguishing character is conciseness. He abhorred circumlocution, and constantly endeavoured to say everything in the fewest words. Hence he was sometimes abrupt; and the sententious turn of his expressions gave now and then a sort of bluntness to his writings. His conciseness, however, did not prevent his perspicuity. He knew how to separate ideas apparently similar; and his long habit of considering every subject in its most simple and direct view was the true reason that he rarely fell into obscurity.[15]

We have not, in all the foregoing, maintained any sharp distinction between style in writing and style in speaking or preaching. This is largely because, in the case of John Wesley, we are almost entirely restricted to working back from the former, which we know well, to the latter, which we only know specifically from few and rather scanty reports. It is more than improbable that a man with Wesley's lucid, direct literary style, could ever be wordy or ambiguous in his speech. Had he been an artist, we may be sure he would not have been of the Impressionist School; his 'art' was too decisive and peremptory. We may well say of him what Thomas Fuller said of a certain Archbishop of Spalato, that 'he had a controversial head, with a strong and clear style; nor doth a hair hang at the nib of his pen to blur his writings with obscurity; but, first understanding himself, he could make others understand him'.[16]

It was not a delayed or conditioned response that Wesley sought from his hearers: that of men going away to think over what the message they had just heard might or might not mean, and returning in due course with a carefully guarded answer. Life moved too swiftly with Wesley to allow for that and his message was too urgent. He sought a prompt response, and to that end stated the Gospel message in terms that the ordinary man could understand without question and which called for an immediate, unequivocal *Yes* or *No*.

[14] e.g., Richard Watson (Edn 1831), p. 351.
[15] Hampson, *Memoirs of John Wesley*, III.158.
[16] *Church History of Britain*, Bk. X.vi.1.

CHAPTER XIII

VOICE AND GESTURE

IN THE beginning of his ministry John Wesley recognized that, so far as preaching is concerned, all piety and all erudition, all purity and clarity of speech, all homiletic artistry and all evangelistic zeal, are of little account if the people in the congregation fail to hear or have difficulty in hearing the preacher. In his *Address to the Clergy* (1756) he asks: 'In our public ministrations, would not one wish for a strong, clear, musical voice and a good delivery, both with regard to pronunciation and action? I name those here, because they are far more acquirable than has been commonly imagined.'[1]

In 1749 Wesley published a penny tract entitled *Directions concerning Pronunciation and Gesture*, to which he refers as *Rules for Action and Utterance*.[2] The pamphlet may still be read with great profit. The first section is on *How we may Speak so as to be heard without Difficulty and with Pleasure*. Wesley urges an early start in the study of elocution, before bad habits have been formed. A speaker's first business is to make himself 'heard and understood with ease', for which a clear, strong voice is a great asset. He warns against speaking too loud and too low, or in a 'thick, cluttering manner', and points out the importance of good articulation, the clear pronouncing of every word. Speakers should guard against a too rapid and a too slow delivery, and especially against 'speaking with a *tone*', such as 'womanish', 'squeaking', 'singing', 'canting', 'swelling', 'theatrical', 'awful', 'whining', 'solemn', 'odd', 'whimsical'; all these should be avoided. Monotony is a great fault and he lays down the general rule, 'endeavour to speak in public just as you do in common conversation', with 'a natural, easy and graceful variation of the voice, suitable to the nature and importance of the sentiments we deliver'. The voice should be as soft as possible. He warns against straining it and drawling; the speech ought 'to flow like a gliding stream, not as a rapid torrent'.

Finally, Wesley gives some particular directions as to the

[1] *Works*, X.485.   [2] ibid., XIII.518-27.

management of the voice, appropriate to the emotional quality of the subject being dealt with, but this should operate naturally for the speaker who has mastered the general rules.

Whatever, then, is positively recommended, we may regard as characteristic of Wesley himself, and of this we have ample corroboration. His voice was clear and penetrating and could usually be heard above the raging of a mob. He contended valiantly with all opposing noises and, as a rule, emerged victoriously. He tells how, at St Ives (13th September 1760), he was 'afraid . . . that the roaring of the sea, raised by the north wind, would have prevented their hearing. But God gave me so strong and clear a voice that I believe scarce one word was lost.' When near Chapel-en-le-Frith (28th June 1745), 'the poor miller near whose pond we stood, endeavoured to drown my voice by letting out the water, which fell with a great noise. But it was labour lost; for my strength was so increased that I was heard to the very skirts of the congregation.' At Freshford, near Frome (25th September 1767), a table had been set near the churchyard to serve as a pulpit, and Wesley tells how

I had no sooner begun to speak than the bells began to ring, by procurement of a neighbouring gentleman. However, it was labour lost; for my voice prevailed and the people heard me distinctly: nay, a person extremely deaf, who had not been able to hear a sermon for several years, told his neighbours, with great joy, that he had heard and understood all, from the beginning to the end.

In order to ensure being heard, Wesley sometimes took special precautions. He preached in the Temple Church (6th October 1782) and wrote:

I now found how to speak here so as to be heard by everyone: direct your voice to the middle of the pillar fronting the pulpit.

On one occasion he caused the ground to be measured and found that he could be heard distinctly at a distance of 140 yards. When he preached in John Hampson's church in South Shields (1st June 1788),

it was doubted whether all could hear (he was then 85). In order to try, Joseph Bradford (one of his preachers) stood in the farthest corner, and he could hear every word.

After preaching to a large congregation in Manchester, on Easter Sunday morning, 1784, he comments: 'I have found no congregation which my voice could not command.' But there were exceptions, so rare, that Wesley evidently forgot them when writing the foregoing words, for he records how, at Leeds (26th April 1747) he addressed

an unwieldy multitude, several hundreds of whom soon went away, it being impossible for them to hear.

The clarity and carrying power of Wesley's voice contributed immensely to his success, and without it there would have been little success to record. Men had to *hear* before anything could happen to them; before ever their hearts and consciences could be reached and all the glorious possibilities of the Christian Life described to and realized by them. Homer tells us how

> All men's souls were startled when they heard
> The brazen war-cry of Aeacides.[3]

Wesley's 'war-cry' was that of a soldier of Jesus Christ. As such it had to be heard, and then it 'startled' the souls of men. A 'war-cry' that is unheard is as effective as the bleating of a sheep on a distant mountain side.

His preachers profited by his instructions, but some of them, in their anxiety to be heard, fell into the vice of shouting, which Wesley ruthlessly condemned as 'screaming'. His references to it are sometimes sorrowful, but more frequently sarcastic. He was quite convinced that it could be a contributory cause of premature death and regarded the practice as self-murder. He wrote to John King, one of his preachers (28th July 1775):

Scream no more, at the peril of your soul. God now warns you by me, whom He has set over you. Speak as earnestly as you can, but do not scream. Speak with all your heart, but with a moderate voice. It was said of our Lord, 'He shall not cry'. The word properly means, 'He shall not scream' ($\kappa\rho\alpha\upsilon\gamma\acute{\alpha}\xi\epsilon\iota\upsilon$). Herein be a follower of me, as I am of Christ. I often speak loud, often vehemently; but I never scream, I never strain myself. I dare not: I know it would be a sin against God and my own soul.

To Sarah Mallet, a lady whom he permitted to preach in the Societies, Wesley wrote a letter of advice (15th December 1789) including:

Never scream. Never speak above the natural pitch of your voice; it is disgustful to the hearers. It gives them pain, not pleasure, and it is destroying yourself. It is offering God murder for sacrifice.

[3] Homer, *Iliad*, Bk. XVIII (Trans. by Sir Wm. Morris, Oxford).

Wesley, then, was no 'ranter', and such a suggestion would have been highly abhorrent and offensive to him. It is clear also that he guarded against mannerisms and eccentric expressions and discountenanced them in others. He wrote, in his direct fashion to Thomas Wride, a 'difficult' brother (5th May 1790):

I hope you have *now* got quit of your queer, arch expressions in preaching, and that you speak as plain and dull as one of us.

By 'arch' Wesley would mean 'facetious, flippant', and by 'dull', 'without rhetorical flourish and ornamentation'.

The last section of his tract on Elocution, already referred to, deals with *Gesture*, which Wesley calls 'the silent language of face and hands'. To be effective, gesture

must be well adjusted to the subject, as well as to the passion which you desire either to express or excite. It must likewise be free from all affectation, and such as appears to be the mere, natural result, both of the things you speak and of the affection that moves you to speak them. And the whole is so to be managed, that there may be nothing in all the dispositions and motions of your body to offend the eyes of the spectators.

Wesley then proceeds to give minutely detailed advice. The movement of the body should not be incessant, but natural and graceful according to circumstance. The head should be kept 'modestly and decently upright', and its movement should be in harmony with that of the body. Most important of all is the face, 'which gives the greatest sense of life to action'. There should be nothing disagreeable in it and it should mirror the various emotions. The eyes should meet directly all the listeners in turn, 'with an air of affection and regard; looking them decently in the face, one after another, as we do in familiar conversation'. He warns against setting the mouth awry: biting or licking the lips: shrugging the shoulders and leaning on the elbow. Hands and arms claim great attention. There should be no clapping of the hands and no thumping of the pulpit. The right hand should be used more than the left. Hands and eyes should always act in concert. 'Seldom stretch out your arms sideways more than half a foot from the trunk of your body.' He counsels observation of other speakers and the practice of these rules in private until they become habitual.

So detailed are these instructions that we feel, were a speaker to memorize them for pulpit exercise, he would be so intent upon their performance that whatever he might be saying would be largely mechanical. The division of attention between matter and manner would be so distracting that both would suffer. It seems clear that what Wesley was advising was just those gestures and actions which came naturally and fittingly to himself, a man of taste and education. But that which was so natural to him, and whose performance in no way detracted from his mind's intentness upon his sermon, could only be acquired with difficulty by those preachers whose upbringing had been so widely different from his own, apart from any instinctive genius that some of them might possess. In writing his tract Wesley must not only have recalled what he had noticed in listening to acceptable and convincing preachers and speakers, but must also have been an imaginary spectator of himself. The tract is a bit of self-portraiture, and it enables us, in clearer detail than any other writing we possess, to hear Wesley preaching and see his instinctive gestures. He never included these rules in the *Large Minutes*, where, in respect of these matters, he simply directs:

> Let your whole deportment before the congregation be serious, weighty and solemn.
> Take care of anything awkward or affected, either in your gesture, phrase or pronunciation.
> Beware of clownishness, either in speech or dress.[4]

We gather, then, that Wesley laid himself out, first of all, to capture the interest of his hearers. Not until that had been achieved could he obtain the consent of their minds to the preached word, and, beyond that, the consent of their wills, issuing in complete surrender to the claims of Jesus Christ and the glad, new life that follows. To that end he employed every means in his power, not being content with the message itself, but with its delivery also. A man who relies solely upon the verbal message today might just as well stay at home and supply a gramophone record for the pulpit. Wesley's message was alive and arresting because Wesley himself was alive. 'This one thing I do', and he did it with body, mind and spirit. George Herbert might have been writing of John Wesley, when, over seventy years before the great evangelist was born, he wrote:

> When he preacheth, he procures attention by all possible art, both by earnestness of speech, it being natural to men to think that where

[4] *Mins.*, pp. 527, 529.

there is much earnestness there is something worth hearing; and by a diligent and busy cast of his eye on his auditors, with letting them know who marks, and who not, and with particularizing his speech, now to the younger sort, then to the older: now to the poor and now to the rich.[5]

As we have noticed, Wesley preached for *decision*, for only so could his dreams come true. He refused to believe that inexorable fate may supervene upon man's spiritual indecision and render impossible the day of his salvation. But there is danger in delay. Indecision can be tyrannical over the human spirit. So he insisted, with the zeal of an Old Testament prophet, 'Seek ye the Lord, while he may be found; call ye upon him while he is near', and he could say with Moses, 'I call heaven and earth to witness against you this day, that I have set before thee life and death, the blessing and the curse; therefore choose life, that thou mayest live'.

Wesley coveted these men and women, their decision for *life* having been made, as allies in the great crusade against evil to which he had dedicated his own life. Hence this matter of arresting speech was of supreme importance. We are told that when men heard Cicero they would frequently remark, 'What a fine orator!'; but when they listened to Demosthenes they said, 'Arise, let us go and fight Philip.' Wesley's 'oratory', if of him that word is permissible, was of the order of Demosthenes, and, hearing him, there arose those valiant Methodist preachers and people, who went out to fight the forces of the Prince of Darkness and to shake the gates of Hell.

Provided always that men did not 'scream', Wesley regarded preaching as conducive to physical health and longevity. On his eighty-fifth birthday, he gave, as one reason for his long life and general good health, his 'constant preaching at five in the morning for above fifty years'. The following year (8th October 1789) he wrote regretfully, 'My strength is much lessened, so that I cannot preach above twice a day', and four months later he told a correspondent (13th February 1790), 'It does me no harm, but rather good, to preach once or twice a day.' So Wesley had proved for himself the health-giving virtue of preaching, especially in the early morning, and it is not surprising that he should recommend it to others for that reason, as to his brother Charles: 'Preach as much as you can and no more than you can.'[6]

[5] Quoted by A. L. Rouse, *The English Spirit*, p. 151.   [6] *Letters*, VI.152.

To his assistant, Thomas Taylor, he wrote (30th October 1775), after giving him sundry advice on his health, 'then you will find preaching, especially in the morning, one of the noblest medicines in the world'. Perhaps his valiant comrade-in-arms, William Grimshaw of Haworth, was one of Wesley's converts to this view of preaching, for he once wrote to Thomas Lee, a Methodist preacher,

I hope your love abides in full strength, and that you can preach twenty times a week. If you can preach oftener, do. Preaching is health, food and physic to me, and why not to thee, my brother?.[7]

[7] G. G. Cragg, *Grimshaw of Haworth*, p. 79.

CHAPTER XIV

ILLUSTRATIONS AND QUOTATIONS

(a) ILLUSTRATIONS

IT IS impossible to say to what extent John Wesley used illustrations in his preaching. There is almost nothing to enlighten us in the accounts of those who heard him preach. Apparently they were more concerned to report their own emotional reactions than to give a succinct account of the sermon that produced them. John Hampson is one of the very few exceptions. He tells us that many have remarked that when Wesley

fell into anecdote and story-telling, which was not seldom, his discourses were little to the purpose. . . . We have scarcely ever heard from him a tolerable sermon in which a story was introduced.[1]

But we need to be cautious in reading Hampson.

Though we have decided that, with a few exceptions, the sermons published cannot be transcripts of those preached, we naturally turn to the latter for preliminary information on this subject. What we find is meagre in the extreme. There are, of course, metaphor and simile, devices common to all speakers and writers, and occasionally Wesley draws an analogy between things spiritual and things material, as in his treatment of *The New Birth*. He also illustrates by simply citing examples, either incidents or personal characteristics, of the subject he is expounding, but these are not impressive to the modern mind. Sometimes these examples are *ideal* or *imaginary*, being detailed descriptions of certain types of persons, as when he dwells at large upon the individual who has only 'a form of godliness', and gives an elaborate account of his characteristics, both positive and negative. So he builds up a kind of lay figure, draping it in the particular virtues or vices with which at that moment he is concerned. In this way he describes the *Almost Christian*, *The Natural Man*, *The Enthusiast*, *The Man of Catholic Spirit*, *The Bigot*, and others meet us in the series of sermons on the Beatitudes.

[1] J. Hampson, *Memoirs of John Wesley*, III.170

At times he made use of *History*, usually in a general kind of way, either to commend or to condemn past events in the light of his subject. Thus, in his sermon on *The Mystery of Iniquity*, he describes the declension of Faith and Morals which befell the Church after the era of primitive Christianity: the evil consequences of the patronage of Constantine the Great and the imperfect results of the Reformation, continuing to his own day. In preaching on *Eternity*, he names some of the most ancient of existing things, such achievements of skilful human craftsmanship as the Pyramids, and declares how infinitely Eternity transcends them all in duration.

Contemporary Persons and *Current Events* and *Conditions* also furnished Wesley with matter for illustration. In dealing with *Mercy* as one of the graces of the Christian character, he deplores the widespread lack of it amongst the professedly Christian nations of his time, referring to wars, parties, factions and 'these Christian cities where deceit and fraud, oppression and wrong, yea, robbery and murder, go not out of their streets!'

Wesley also made use of the *Scientific Knowledge* of the day, in which few laymen were better versed. He dwells upon the Wisdom of God, as manifested in the phenomena of the heavens and the earth. Much of his sermon on *The Imperfection of Human Knowledge* is an account of what was then known of the wonders of Nature, which should lead to a deeper knowledge of God; but there comes a point beyond which human curiosity and probing cannot pass. From the consciousness of this ignorance we should learn lessons of Humility, of Confidence in God and of Resignation. In the sermon on *What is Man?*, he enlarges upon the awe-inspiring vastness of the astronomical universe and then goes on to declare the peculiar love of God for Man: this 'speck of creation', this 'poor little creature of a day', for whom 'He hath given His Son, His only Son, both to live and to die'. In *The Great Assize* he refers to possible ways in which the world may come to an end: by the impact of a comet: by lightning, earthquake, or fire.

Illustrations drawn from Wesley's *Personal Experiences* are fairly numerous. They occur mainly in the later discourses and are far from striking. Occasionally he makes use of *Anecdotes*, other than incidents in his own life, as when he uses a story told by Herodotus of King Psammitichus of Egypt.

Few of the illustrations in the published sermons are of real distinction. As we have noticed, some of them are merely apposite

ILLUSTRATIONS AND QUOTATIONS

allusions to the subject matter; others are references to individuals or incidents, exemplifying certain actions or qualities, and selected from the fields of History, Biography or Experience. Such are not the most arresting kind of illustration. An example is a hard fact, and, having once been cited, there is little more to be said about it. There is no feeling of a tantalizing, evasive 'something' at the heart of it, that awaits and invites discovery. On the other hand, a telling illustration lays hold of the imagination and suggests or unfolds a deeper meaning in the speaker's words; it lingers in the memory and keeps fresh and enduring the message that has been proclaimed.

On the whole, then, we conclude that, many and varied as were John Wesley's gifts, that of sermon illustration was not conspicuous amongst them. He left untouched the field of Mythology, so fruitful for those in search of apposite illustration for religious or moral themes. This is the more surprising as, being an accomplished classical scholar, he would be familiar with the fables of Greece and Rome. It is quite likely that he was too fastidious to introduce into a Christian discourse stories which were the product of pagan imagination. Also, that he declined the use of any illustration that was unrelated to actuality, or, at least, to possibility, and a glance at the kind he did use seems to confirm this. They all, so to speak, have their feet upon the solid ground and are untouched by fancy or pure imagination. No statue, wrought by some devout Pygmalion, quivers into rosy life at his earnest prayer; no Argonauts sail the wine-dark sea, seeking some mystic Golden Fleece.

Most surprising of all is how little influenced by our Lord's method of teaching by parables Wesley seems to have been: that is, so far as we can judge by the published sermons. So diligent a student of the New Testament must have been impressed repeatedly by their significance and the frequent and effective use which Jesus made of them. Did Wesley, in connexion with his own preaching, ever ponder St Mark's words: *Without a parable spake he not unto them*? His comment on this passage in his *Notes on the New Testament* is: 'that is, not at that time; at other times he did'. Can we be sure of that? It is too bold an assumption to make, and one with no warrant in the gospel records. It is obvious that we have there a far from complete account of what Jesus said during the years of his ministry, and it may well be that there is no complete record of what he said on any particular occasion. Is it not better to take the words of St Mark as a plain statement of fact—χωρὶς δὲ παραβολῆς οὐκ ἐλάλει αὐτοῖς? How definite it is! Just such a forthright statement as Wesley himself might have made! One wonders if, in his comment, Wesley was sub-consciously seeking to justify his own neglect of this method of preaching.

But we have been considering only the published sermons. Did he fail, in his public ministry, to profit by the examples presented to him in the New Testament? He might, with advantage, have pondered upon John Bunyan's *Apology* for writing *The Pilgrim's Progress* in the form of an allegory:

> I find that Holy Writ, in many places,
> Hath semblance with this method, where the cases
> Do call for one thing, to set forth another;
> Use it I may then, and yet nothing smother
> Truth's Golden Beams: Nay, by this method may
> Make it cast forth its Rays as light as day.

Did he ever consider the popularity of Bunyan's book and the probable cause thereof? He must have connected our Lord's use of parable, or allegory, with the fact that the common people heard him gladly. Knowing the same class of people of his own day as intimately as he did, Wesley must have realized the value of such a method of approach to them, and we are driven to the conclusion that what he so largely failed to do in his published sermons, he did more liberally in those which he preached. But the evidence for this is not factual. The most that we can say is that it is highly probable. We remind ourselves that he was prepared to accept and incorporate in his schemes and methods almost anything that would enable him more effectively to achieve his purpose: to win the souls of men for God. To that end he broke with convention when he saw it to be an obstacle to progress. He accepted lay preachers and field-preaching and such innovations as made for the strengthening of an expanding Methodism, because he saw their inestimable worth. The type of preaching prevalent in his day was ineffective for evangelism, and in any case Wesley scorned it. And here, straight from the pages of the New Testament, was the supreme example of the unconventional, effective preaching of Jesus; these illustrations, or parables, so often drawn from incidents which had come under his own notice: the lost piece of silver, the treasure hidden in a field, the prodigal son, the good Samaritan. Probably there was no man in England at that time whose life was so rich in incident, in personal contacts and in material for effective illustration of a similar kind, as that of John Wesley. It is incredible that he should be wholly unaware of this, or fail entirely to draw upon these resources for some parable charged with a more profound meaning than the superficial one, in the manner of our Lord. Jesus did not, for example, tell the quite commonplace story of a woman seeking a lost coin, as an example of right regard for money, or wise economy or care of small things, but as illustrating the solicitude of God for any solitary soul that is astray from the Kingdom of Heaven; nor even then has the story yielded up the whole of its secret. In writing his published sermons, particularly the Standard ones, Wesley sought to expound certain very important Christian Doctrines for the reader who is prepared to study serious themes in a serious way. But when preaching to a crowd of eighteenth-century semi-barbarians something very different was demanded. There was an unchanging basic message to be delivered—sin, repentance and the offer of God's forgiving and redeeming grace in Christ Jesus. But surely not in the language of the schools! How magnificently these human contacts of his would serve him here! Surely, also, he must have discovered the power of some appropriate story, even some allegory, to arrest attention and make more attractive and comprehensible the Word of Life, as he must have illuminated that Word by describing some of the wonders of grace which he himself had seen, of souls new-born into the Life of God.

> What we have felt and seen,
> With confidence we tell.

Of this we may be sure: that whatever illustrations Wesley used as he preached to mixed crowds, they would always be consistent with human experience. If he ever drew upon his imagination, it would be in strict accord with the *dictum* of John Macmurray: 'Imagination always transcends fact, but it is only rational when it is also immanent in fact.'[2] In the eighteenth century there was no more convinced 'rationalist', in the true sense of that tortured word, than John Wesley.

[2] *The Structure of Religious Experience*, p. 64.

(b) QUOTATIONS

With the exception of those from Scripture and the Wesley Hymns, quotations in the sermons are surprisingly few. Wesley knew Edward Young's comment on their use, for he includes the satire in which it occurs in his *Collection of Moral and Sacred Poems*.

> Some for *Renown* on Scraps of Learning doat, [*sic*]
> And think they grow immortal as they *quote*.
> To Patch-work learn'd Quotations are ally'd:
> Both strive to make our *Poverty* our *Pride*.[3]

This may have been Wesley's way of regarding their use, which 'our great poet',[4] as he calls Young, would help to confirm. Be that as it may, for a man so deeply and widely read as John Wesley, the number of quotations which he makes throughout 141 sermons is small indeed. In the earlier and more important ones they rarely occur, but gradually increase as discourse follows discourse.

Wesley uses them in the ordinary way: chiefly to emphasize some teaching or to express his thoughts in the striking words of another person. They are frequently inaccurate, which is not surprising when we consider how much of his writing Wesley did on his journeys, having only his memory upon which to rely; but he always gives the sense of the passage, nor ever, in respect of poetry, lays violent hands upon the metre.

The number of writers from whom he quotes is smaller still, and he does not always give their names. Among prose writers we notice Baxter, Addison and William Law, with a few who are less known. English poets include Donne, Cowley, Herbert, Farnell, Pope, Young, Milton, Sir John Davies and Matthew Prior. The two last-named he held in particularly high esteem.

Latin authors quoted include Horace, Ovid, Juvenal, Velleius Paterculus, Virgil and Terence, for whose plays he had entertained a warm admiration from his youth up. Tertullian and Cyprian are used, and also Epiphanius and Macarius. He quotes Hesiod, in English, and frequently gives the Greek of New Testament passages. The Latin quotations are sometimes given without a following translation. This is usually so in regard to Virgil. Did Wesley assume an English rendering of his verse to be unnecessary? If so, he was surely paying too great a compliment to a large number of his readers.

[3] op. cit., II.44.   [4] *Works*, VII.64.

If further evidence were required that the preached sermons were not absolutely identical with the printed ones, it lies ready to hand in the untranslated passages from Latin writers, running even to eight lines. Had John Wesley been a member of either House of Parliament, he could have indulged his taste in this direction quite freely, knowing that it would provoke no surprised comment and that he would be generally understood. *Sed . . . fugit inreparabile tempus!!*[5] But only a fatuous humorist could suggest that Wesley quoted Horace or Virgil, in preaching to the common people who gathered about him, either to curse or to bless.

[5] Virgil, *Georgics*, III.284. 'But time flies beyond recall', or 'Those days can never return'. (Seemingly!)

CHAPTER XV

THE PUBLISHED SERMONS

THE PUBLISHED sermons are the surest guide that we possess to the subjects of Wesley's preaching, whether he was addressing a crowd of spiritually unawakened people: or backsliders: or a company of more or less professing Christians: or his Methodists, either in their regular worship or in the intimacy of a Society Meeting. To the mixed multitude he preached the substance of his sermons on Sin, Repentance, Faith, Forgiveness, and Regeneration, in words suited to the level of their intelligence. It is likely that as he preached to those who had emerged from spiritual darkness, and were becoming increasingly intelligent in consequence, his words would approximate more and more closely to those of the printed text.

We have noted elsewhere the general scope of these discourses, but more remains to be said. When, in the early years of his evangelical ministry, his doctrines were assailed and derided by ignorant and malicious people, including both parish clergymen and dignitaries of the Anglican Church, he deemed it expedient to publish a number of sermons, showing to the world what these doctrines were; that they were, in fact, exactly those which every Anglican clergyman professed to believe and was pledged to teach. In his Preface to the first volume (1746), Wesley declares that:

the following sermons contain the substance of what I have been preaching for between eight and nine years last past. During that time I have frequently spoken in public on every subject in the ensuing collection; and I am not conscious that there is any point of doctrine on which I am accustomed to speak in public which is not here, incidentally, if not professedly, laid before every Christian reader. Every serious man who peruses these will therefore see, in the clearest manner, what these doctrines are which I embrace and teach as the essentials of true religion.

These include the great discourses on Salvation by Faith, The Almost Christian, Scriptural Christianity, Justification by Faith, the Spirit of Bondage and Adoption, The Witness of the Spirit, etc. Wesley continues:

> I am thoroughly sensible these are not proposed in such a manner as some may expect. Nothing here appears in an elegant or oratorical dress. . . . I now write, as I generally speak, *ad populum*,—to the bulk of mankind, to those who neither relish nor understand the art of speaking; but who, notwithstanding, are competent judges of those truths which are necessary to present and future happiness.

It does not follow from this statement that Wesley's written word was identical with his spoken word. To *write ad populum* is not necessarily the same as to *speak ad populum*. Most people would find it easier to understand Wesley's sermons by reading them, than by hearing them read. He explains:

> I design plain truth for plain people. . . . My design is, in some sense, to forget all that ever I have read in my life. I mean to speak, in the general, as if I had never read one author, ancient or modern (always excepting the inspired). I am persuaded that, on the one hand, this may be a means of enabling me more clearly to express the sentiments of my heart, while I simply follow the chain of my own thoughts, without entangling myself with those of other men; and that, on the other, I shall come with fewer weights upon my mind, with less of prejudice and prepossession, either to search for myself, or to deliver to others, the naked truths of the gospel. . . .
>
> I have accordingly set down in the following sermons what I find in the Bible concerning the way to heaven; with a view to distinguish this way of God from all those which are the inventions of men. I have endeavoured to describe the true, the scriptural, experimental religion, so as to omit nothing which is a real part thereof, and to add nothing thereto which is not.

These are words of complete honesty of purpose. Candour and integrity can do no more. Wesley told Henry Moore that when he retired to Lewisham to write the first volume, he took with him 'only the Holy Scriptures in the original tongues'.[1] Ultimately the Sermons extended to eight volumes.

Their popularity, particularly of the First Series (Vols. i–iv.), is evidenced by the many editions through which they passed, and which still continue to be issued. They were widely read in Wesley's day, both by people within and without the Methodist Societies. Even before 1742, the year in which Fielding's *Joseph Andrews* was published, there was a good sale for such of the

---

[1] Henry Moore, *Life of Wesley*, II.403.

sermons as had appeared in pamphlet form, for the bookseller in that work declined to publish the sermons of Parson Adams because 'sermons are mere drugs. The trade is so vastly stocked with them that really, unless they come out with the name of Whitefield or Wesley, or some other such great man, as a bishop, or those sort of people, I don't care to touch.'[2] Throughout most of the nineteenth century the Conference regarded tract distribution as a valuable means of Christian propaganda, and during the year 1840 it issued seventy-seven, of which thirty-two were 'Mr Wesley's Sermons'. Many of the early Methodists recommended the sermons to their friends and there are various testimonies to blessings received, even spiritual conversion, either through reading them or hearing them read.

Of special interest is the following extract from a letter written to the Wesleyan Methodist Missionary Society by the Rev. Robert Carver, dated *Madras, 12th January, 1836*.

Mr Wesley's Sermons are making such progress that they are delivered and read in many congregations where we could never come. A great change in one military man took place, and he immediately wanted sermons to read to the people under his charge; he obtained Mr Wesley's from me, and values them above gold; and great has been the benefit that he has received and done by them. He is still going forward in the new state of happiness into which the truth has led him.

These sermons are demanded at stations some hundreds of miles from us, where no Chaplain or Missionary resides. Into Tamul we have rendered one on *Salvation by Faith*; and, as time permits, it is my intention to do what I can towards putting these truths before the natives.[3]

Nor was Tamul the only foreign tongue into which Wesley's Sermons have been translated. Two Protestant ministers of Prussia visited the London Conference of 1816, whose members decided that

two sets of the Works of Mr Wesley and of Mr Fletcher, with Copies of our Large Hymn Book, and of Mr Benson's *Apology for the Methodists*, shall be presented . . . to the Rev. Messrs Sac, of Berlin; in token of our Christian affection for them, and as a memorial of the high gratification which the Conference derived from their friendly visit and interesting communications, in its sitting of Tuesday, August 6.[4]

[2] op. cit., Bk. II, ch. 17. For sermons published by Wesley up to 1742, see R. Green's *Bibliography*, Nos. 5, 8, 11, 28, 29.
[3] *W.M.M.* (1836), p. 711.
[4] *Minutes of Conference* (1816).

To this there was a pleasing sequel. In May 1825, just prior to his second Presidency, Joseph Entwisle met Dr Tholuck, Professor of Theology in the University of Berlin, and recorded in his *Diary*:

> Dr Tholuck appears to be a holy man; his heart is given to God. He gave us an account of a great work of God in Berlin, Pomerania and Weimar, which originated in the reading of Mr Wesley's Sermons, copies of which were presented to two Prussian clergymen at our Conference in London, in 1816. These sermons have been read with avidity, and many have been brought to God in consequence. . . . The Professor has a commission to procure all our standard works.[5]

Reference to these religious movements on the continent of Europe is made in the Address of the Conference of 1825 to the Methodist Societies.

> It is a pleasing testimony to the excellence and influence of the writings of Mr Wesley, that the recent translation of parts of them into two of the languages of the continent of Europe has been eminently useful to several influential persons, who are taking an active part in that very promising revival of religion which has occurred in France and in Prussia.

In the *Magazine* for 1836 there is a highly appreciatory review of a French translation of selected sermons, made by T. Marzials, Pasteur de l'Eglise Protestante à Lille, where the writer states:

> Mr Wesley's Sermons are too well known and too much esteemed in the Methodist Connexion, to need any recommendation on our part. For purity of doctrine, clearness of style and strength of argument, we think they are superior to all other sermons in the English language. It has always appeared to us alike creditable to the piety and good taste of the body at large, that these sermons should continue to find an extensive and still extending sale in all parts of the world where Methodism is known and the English language understood; and we do not hesitate to express our belief that the time will come when they will be read in all the languages of the world.
>
> We have now the high satisfaction of seeing a neat volume, containing twenty-nine sermons on the most important subjects of experimental and practical Christianity, rendered into French by a master of that language. M. Marzials is evidently well qualified for his work, as he has, in addition to his critical knowledge of the two languages, a minute acquaintance with Wesleyan theology. It is no mean praise to say the translator of Wesley has transfused the spirit of Wesley into his native tongue.

[5] *Memoir of Joseph Entwisle*, by his Son, p. 329.

The reviewer gives several selected passages, from which one extract will suffice to show how lucid and faithful is the translation and how closely it keeps to the style of Wesley. It is the well-known passage from the sermon on *The New Birth*, II.5.

Il paraît clairement de cela, quelle est la nature de la nouvelle naissance: c'est ce grand changement que Dieu opère dans une âme, quand il l'appèle à la vie, et qu'il l'a ressuscité de la mort du péché à la vie de la justice;—c'est ce changement produit dans toute l'âme par le puissant Esprit de Dieu, quand elle est créée de nouveau en Christ, quand elle est renouvellée à l'image de Dieu, en justice et en vraie sainteté.[6]

In the report of the Wesleyan Methodist Missionary Society for 1861 reference is made to various Christian agencies in Italy, 'among which the translation of certain of Mr Wesley's Sermons deserves to be mentioned here. Twelve of these admirable discourses have been translated by a converted Italian resident in London, and will be printed in Italy, with a view to a more ready and extensive circulation than they would otherwise obtain.'[7] In the *Magazine* for 1859 there is a notice that 'twenty select Sermons of Mr Wesley, translated into the vernacular of the Friendly Islands (Tonga), and edited by the Rev. Thomas West, possess far more than literary interest. The version is said (by competent judges) to follow closely the style and force of the original.'[8] The first translation into Welsh was of one sermon, in 1797.

Nor were the people of Spanish-speaking and Roman Catholic countries forgotten as time went on, for in the *Proceedings of the Wesley Historical Society* for December 1924 (Vol. xiv.), we read that:

an edition of five hundred copies of a Spanish translation of the first volume of Wesley's *Sermons*, mainly for use in Protestant Missions in Mexico, the Argentine Republic and other Spanish-speaking American countries was published a few years ago. A copy was sent to the Wesleyan Mission House in London, as likely to be of use in connection with our Spanish work.

For the most part Wesley's published sermons have evoked high praise from readers competent to judge. We have noted how, in writing them, he discarded all aids except the Bible in its

---

[6] *W.M.M.* (1836), p. 47.   [7] ibid. (1861), p. 559.   [8] ibid. (1859), p. 95.

original tongues. A little consideration might have suggested that to us. Extensive as was his knowledge of the sub-apostolic writings and subsequent outstanding works on Divinity, there is almost no echo of earlier dissertations. He seems to have approached his task *de novo*, like a pioneer in an undiscovered country, knowing nothing, assuming nothing, except that this Bible contains a revelation from God to men, of such spiritual truths as mankind needs to know. What is that Revelation? How, from all the diffuse and intricate matter of the Scriptures, can the essential truths of Christianity be extracted and set forth in clear and unambiguous terms? In seeking an answer to these questions Wesley relied only upon the enlightening Spirit of God, operating through his own trained intelligence. It was not an easy task, and it was rendered more difficult by his refusal to take counsel with those who had gone the like way before him. Apparent contradictions had to be reconciled, such as those associated with Arminianism as against Calvinism, and the relation between Faith and Works. We know what his chief method was; in his own words it was 'comparing Scripture with Scripture', and for that exacting task he was eminently fitted, having been trained to it in his father's parsonage from early youth onward.

There was something else which aided him. From his own religious experience he knew the truth and power of the fundamental, transforming doctrines of the Christian Faith. He had proved them for himself and had observed their revolutionary effects in the lives of others. That experimental knowledge must have been a valuable guide to the meaning of many Scripture passages and have helped to suggest the form of words into which their teaching was ultimately cast.

One feels, too, that in composing the sermons, especially those on the great doctrines, Wesley was clarifying his own mind and crystallizing his ideas. This procedure is specially valuable in the sphere of religion, where, perhaps more than elsewhere, there is a tendency to shrink from thinking things out to their finality and to leave ideas and beliefs tentatively and half-heartedly expressed. Such an attitude was abhorrent to Wesley. He knew how true it is that writing helps thought, and that without words it is impossible for the mind to grapple adequately and finally with any subject, least of all with religion. So in the Sermons we have an outstanding example of the co-operation between thought and word, which makes so clear the way of the would-be Christian, of the Christian disciple and of the matured saint, that the wayfaring man, though a fool, cannot, if he be an honest fool, err therein. Let it be said, however, that there are opinions and expressions in the sermons which would find general acceptance on the part of Christian people in Wesley's day, but would find little, if any, in ours.

That so many translations of the Sermons should have been made is particularly impressive and significant. It is very unlikely that the buoyant optimism of the reviewer who believed that 'the time will come when they will be read in all the languages of the world' will ever be justified, but that they should have been rendered into so many tongues, including those most widely spoken, is outstanding testimony to their peculiar excellence. Wesley seems to have been particularly fortunate in his translators and in the fact that the versions were made at times congenial to their reception. Translation is not the mere substitution of words in one language for their equivalents in another. The art of it lies in the power to transmit, often by a change of idiom, those ideas and emotions which moved the writer and his readers, to people who can only approach the work through another tongue. Those faithful translators of Wesley's sermons open up to us an astonishing vista of successful evangelism and religious influence, as we reflect upon those tracts and volumes each going forth as a missionary into a foreign land. Through their agency, to the many thousands of his fellow-countrymen who heard and saw Wesley face to face and who, through his ministry, entered into newness of life in Christ Jesus, must be added an incalculable host of men and women of many nationalities, some of whom became, in their turn, the ministers of God for good to their fellows. In a sense neither intended nor dreamed of by Charles Wesley, and making due allowance for numerical symbolism, the translations of his brother's sermons helped to answer the ardent longing of his soul:

> O, for a thousand tongues, to sing
> My great Redeemer's praise!

Of the volume of Forty-four Standard Sermons, as of many of the others, we say, with James Everett, that 'we pity the Methodist who has not thumbed its pages'.[9] But 'thumbing' will not content

[9] *Wesleyan Takings*, II.17.

the reader whose interest has once been aroused and on whom its pages have cast their fascination, and he will discover that, while the voice in his ears is so often that of a gentleman, a scholar and a Christian of the Eighteenth Century, the truths expressed are those that live on through all centuries, because they have eternity in their hearts.

CHAPTER XVI

EARLY MORNING PREACHING

ONE OF THE most distinctive features of John Wesley's ministry was his early morning preaching. In his *Journal* for Monday, 5th April 1784, he tells us how he came to institute it.

I was surprised when I came to Chester to find that there also morning preaching was quite left off, for this worthy reason: 'because the people will not come, or, at least, not in the winter'. If so, the Methodists are a fallen people. They have 'lost their first love', and they never will or can recover it, till they 'do the first works'. . . . As soon as I set foot in Georgia I began preaching at five in the morning, and every communicant, that is, every serious person in the town, constantly attended throughout the year; I mean, came every morning, winter and summer, unless in the case of sickness. They did so till I left the province. In the year 1738, when God began his great work in England, I began preaching at the same hour, winter and summer, and never wanted a congregation. If they will not attend now, they have lost their zeal, and then, it cannot be denied, they are a fallen people. . . . Let all the preachers that are still alive to God join together as one man, fast and pray, lift up their voice as a trumpet, to convince them that are fallen, and exhort them instantly to 'repent and do the first works'; this in particular—rising in the morning, without which neither their souls nor bodies can long remain in health.

On his arrival in England Wesley was soon assailed by the advocates of Stillness and the Doctrine of Election. To meet the attack, he commenced in June 1740, at the Foundery, a series of early morning expositions of the basic doctrines of evangelical Christianity and recorded their outlines in his *Journal*. Curnock sums up the *Diary* entries, showing how seriously he addressed himself to this work. He rose, prayed and then robed. Usually he spoke fasting. After the exposition he returned to his rooms, where he drank chocolate or tea, and then wrote out the substance of what he had just been saying.

As the years passed Wesley became increasingly convinced of the importance of the practice, and regarded it as conducive to the physical health of both preacher and hearer. At the Conference of 1768 inquiry was made: 'What can be done to revive and enlarge the work of God?'. The answer was:

> Let the preaching at five in the morning be constantly kept up, wherever you can have twenty hearers. This is the glory of the Methodists. Whenever this is dropped they will dwindle away into nothing. Rising early is equally good for soul and body. It helps the nerves better than a thousand medicines, and, in particular, preserves the sight and prevents lowness of spirits, more than can well be imagined.

In his correspondence Wesley frequently referred to early morning preaching as 'the glory of the Methodists', and foretold its departure should the practice ever cease. On 15th March 1784, he was at Stroud and wrote:

> To my surprise I found the morning preaching was given up, as also in the neighbouring places. If this be the case while I am alive, what must it be when I am gone? Give up this, and Methodism too will degenerate into a mere sect, only distinguished by some opinions and modes of worship.

Wesley's personal success in drawing congregations at this early hour is very impressive and testifies abundantly to his power as a preacher. On 30th March 1787, there was an unusual prologue to the service, which seems greatly to have pleased him. This was at Burslem.

> I had appointed to preach at five in the morning; but soon after four I was saluted by a concert of music, both vocal and instrumental, at our gate, making the air ring with a hymn to the tune of *Judas Maccabaeus*. It was a good prelude.

A notable instance of Wesley's insistence on this service occurred at City Road, on 9th September 1787. He had arrived in London on Friday, the 7th, and had joined the four preachers who were living in his house by the Chapel. Two of these were ordained clergymen, Dr Coke and James Creighton, and the others were Samuel Bradburn and John Atlay. The *Journal* reads:

> *Sun. 9th.* I went down at half-hour past five, but found no preacher in the chapel, though we had three or four in the house; so I preached myself. Afterwards, inquiring why none of my family attended the morning preaching, they said it was because they sat up too late. I resolved to put a stop to this: and therefore ordered that (1) every one under my roof should go to bed at nine: that (2) everyone might attend the morning preaching. And so they have done ever since.

Apparently nothing except physical disability ever prevented Wesley from engaging in this early morning exercise. It was in vain, for example, that Brother Williams of Philipstown, Ireland, tried to dissuade him from 'preaching so early as five o'clock, being sure none would rise so soon'. 'But', writes Wesley, 'I kept my hour, and had a large as well as serious congregation' (31st March 1748). He was eighty-six when Nature at last intervened and he wrote (16th November 1789):

After an intermission of many weeks, through the dryness of my mouth, I resolved to try if I could not preach at five in the morning, and I did so with not much difficulty; and I now hope to hold on a little longer.

But the old powers had waned too far, though a flickering hope remained, for he wrote to Henry Moore in the following June:

My sight is much as it was; but I doubt I shall not recover my strength till I use that noble medicine, preaching in the morning.

The story of those early morning services is an astonishing one to many modern readers of the *Journal*, but there are certain considerations which must be kept in mind.

Wesley's congregations were composed, for the most part, of working-class people. Their hours of labour were far longer than anything that would be tolerated today. Readers familiar with such books as those of the Hammonds, on Town and Country Labourers, will be well aware of the general conditions. When Wesley died the Industrial Revolution had barely begun, and throughout his century the condition of the rank and file of the people was hard. To attend a service at five in the morning would necessitate very little, if any, earlier rising than that to which many were accustomed. Ten, twelve, even fourteen hours of labour were common, and not till 1847 was the Ten Hour Act passed, and that applied only to textile workers. For the common people the day began early and they went to bed at a much earlier hour than we do today. Long hours of labour, with little help from machinery, induced great exhaustion. Oil lamps or tallow candles, which they were obliged to use on dark mornings, but could economize in at night, cost money which they could ill afford. Amusements were few and some expensive, and most of them were distasteful to Christian people. Literature in the homes was scanty, though Wesley did much to remedy that, and there was much illiteracy. When Wesley declared that the continued existence of Methodism depended upon the observance of this service, he did not envisage an eight-hour day; homes and churches well illuminated at night; a plentiful supply of literature and streets well-lighted and safe, to say nothing of the many and varied amusements of a later age.

There must have been many who took Wesley's advice to retire early and rise early, and who were able comfortably to attend the morning preaching in consequence. But most of his people did not need such exhortation; the conditions of their lives made early rising and retiring imperative. These were the people who helped to make life easy and luxurious for the leisured classes, and they were also the people who were Wesley's chief concern.

How wise he was! He drew them, at no great hardship to themselves, at a time when their minds were most fresh and alert, and before they had become jaded by a day of long and heavy toil. Many were facing unattractive tasks, and with what strengthened and rejoicing hearts must those early morning worshippers have engaged in their wonted toil! How much lighter and more endurable must all have seemed! So we behold them in retrospect, walking, often before sunrise, the cobbled streets of the town, the rough country roads and the slag-strewn paths of industrial and mining districts, and singing on their way the hymns that Charles Wesley had written for them, in which his brother's words lived again:

> Forth in thy name, O Lord, I go
>   My daily labour to pursue;
> Thee, only Thee, resolved to know,
>   In all I think or speak or do.
>
> The task thy wisdom has assigned,
>   O, let me cheerfully fulfil!
> In all my works thy presence find,
>   And prove thy acceptable will.
>
> Thee may I set at my right hand,
>   Whose eyes my inmost substance see;
> And labour on at thy command,
>   And offer all my works to thee.

There are less desirable ways of starting a working day. We begin to understand how right John Wesley was, when he described the early morning preaching as 'the glory of the

Methodists'. If the conditions of his day had persisted, which, happily, they did not, there would have been force and reason in his judgement, delivered when he was eighty-six years of age: 'Whenever the morning preaching is given up, the glory of Methodism is departed from us.' One feels that those services were among the most effective of that great ministry.

CHAPTER XVII

GOSPEL SERMONS

JOHN WESLEY took strong exception to the term 'Gospel Sermons'. Simple, expressive and unexceptionable as it is in itself, it had been largely appropriated by people whose ideas lacked the breadth and vigour of New Testament teaching. His most trenchant condemnation of this type of sermon occurs in a letter written to Miss Bishop (18th October 1778).

I find more profit in sermons on either good temper or good works than in what are vulgarly called gospel sermons. That term has now become a mere *cant* word. I wish none of our society would use it. It has no determinate meaning. Let but a pert, self-sufficient animal, that has neither sense nor grace, bawl out something about Christ and his blood or justification by faith, and his hearers cry out, 'What a fine gospel sermon!' Surely the Methodists have not so learnt Christ! We know no gospel without salvation from sin.

Six years earlier, in a letter to his brother Charles (4th November 1772), he had said much the same thing.

If we *duly join* faith and works in all our preaching, we shall not fail of a blessing. But of all preaching, what is usually called gospel preaching is the most useless, if not the most mischievous; a dull, yea or lively, harangue on the sufferings of Christ or salvation by faith without strongly inculcating holiness. I see more and more that this naturally tends to drive holiness out of the world.

In the *Journal* for 14th November 1776, Wesley records how he showed 'what the gospel is, and what it is to preach the gospel'. He continues:

The next evening I explained, at large, the wrong and the right sense of 'Ye are saved by faith', and many saw how miserably they had been abused by those vulgarly called gospel preachers.

Wesley's was not the type of mind that can rest content in a negative conclusion. Having shaken a false conception, he regarded it as a duty to establish a true one in its place. Hence he was greatly concerned that men should know what really are both a 'gospel sermon' and a 'gospel minister'. He wrote an important letter, probably to Ebenezer Blackwell, on 20th December 1751, wherein he declares that:

I mean by 'preaching the gospel', preaching the love of God to sinners, preaching the life, death, resurrection and intercession of Christ, with all the blessings which in consequence thereof are freely given to true believers. By 'preaching the law' I mean explaining and enforcing the commands of Christ briefly comprised in the Sermon on the Mount.

Then occur these notable words:

I think the right method of preaching is this. At our first beginning to preach at any place, after a general declaration of the love of God to sinners and his willingness that they should be saved, to preach the law in the strongest, the closest, the most searching manner possible; only intermixing the gospel here and there, and showing it, as it were, afar off.

After more and more persons are convinced of sin, we may mix more and more of the gospel, in order to *beget faith* . . . but this is not to be done too hastily. Therefore it is not expedient wholly to omit the law; not only because we may well suppose that many of our hearers are still unconvinced, but because otherwise there is danger that many who are convinced will heal their own wounds slightly: therefore it is only in private converse with a thoroughly convinced sinner that we should preach nothing but the gospel.

If, indeed, we could suppose a whole congregation to be thus convinced, we should need to preach only the gospel. . . . But when these grow in grace and in the knowledge of Christ, a wise builder would preach the law to them again; only taking particular care to place every part of it in a gospel light, as not only a command but a privilege also, as a branch of the glorious liberty of the sons of God.

Toward the end of the letter Wesley returns to this 'new' type of 'gospel preaching' and contrasts it with the old. Because stress has been laid upon the *promises* and little said about the *commands*, he believes great harm has been done both to the preachers themselves and those who have accepted their presentation of the Gospel: 'all of whom are but shadows of what they were: most of them have exalted themselves above measure, as if they only "preached Christ, preached the gospel". And as highly as they have exalted themselves, so deeply have they despised their brethren. . . . I think it has likewise done great harm to their hearers, diffusing among them their own prejudice against the other preachers; ... against the scriptural, *Methodist* manner of preaching Christ, so that they could no longer bear sound doctrine—they could no longer hear the plain old truth with profit or pleasure, nay hardly with patience.'

Wesley then declares, as a result of his own observation in all parts of the country, that 'preachers of this kind spread death, not life, among their hearers'. From the beginning Methodists have been taught *both* the law and the gospel. 'God loves *you*: therefore love and obey *Him*. Christ died for *you*: therefore die to sin. Christ is risen: therefore rise in the image of God. Christ liveth evermore: therefore live to God, till you live with Him in glory.' He concludes: 'So *we* preached; and so *you* believed. This is the scriptural way, the *Methodist* way, the true way. God grant we may never turn therefrom, to the right hand or to the left.'

It amounts to this. Wesley knew that the only way of preaching effectively to a miscellaneous crowd of human beings is, first of all, to make men conscious of sin, by convincing them that their manner of life contravenes God's law of righteousness. By expounding this law and opposing it to their own lawlessness, the preacher establishes the need for 'good works'. But how shall these people, with their awakened consciences, have power wholly to forsake their old, evil ways, and do the works of God? At that point the preacher proclaims the essential gospel of salvation from sin through the power that comes through faith in the redeeming work of Christ. Wesley dreaded lest, having declared their faith in Christ for the forgiveness of sin, they should elect to remain at that stage and regard it as the whole demand of God. He had no respect for a mere gospel of Salvation by Faith, which ended there, having seen too much of the evil resulting therefrom and the inevitable tendency to Antinomianism. True to New Testament teaching, Wesley urged, again and again and in one form of words after another, 'Faith, if it have not works, is dead', and challenged his hearers, like the Apostle James of old, 'Shew me thy faith apart from thy works, and I, by my works, will shew thee my faith'.

To us, today, it seems so simple and so obvious, that it is difficult to see it as a truth about the Gospel for which Wesley had strenuously to contend in certain quarters. Hence the wisdom of his advice to 'mix' the 'gospel' and the 'law', continuously and at every stage of the Christian progress. The quickened soul must never be allowed to forget that God demands of him that he shall work the works of righteousness while it is yet day, through the divine strength and wisdom granted through his faith.

So men and women, and Wesley's Methodists in particular, listened to these things and then they sang Charles Wesley's hymns:

> Your faith by holy tempers prove.
>   By actions show your sins forgiven,
> And seek the glorious things above,
>   And follow Christ, your Head, to heaven.

> Whilst Thou didst on earth appear,
> Servant to Thy servants here,
> Mindful of Thy place above,
> All Thy life was prayer and love.
> Such our whole employment be,
> Works of faith and charity;
> Works of love on man bestowed,
> Secret intercourse with God;

swelling to the moving and uplifting strain of

> Ready for all Thy perfect will,
>   My acts of faith and love repeat,
> Till death Thy endless mercies seal,
>   And make the sacrifice complete;

and how 'ready' many of them were, and how triumphantly they 'made the sacrifice complete', is one of the brightest stories in the annals of the Christian Church.

CHAPTER XVIII

(a) LONG SERMONS, (b) ITINERANCY, (c) FREQUENCY

JOHN WESLEY was no lover of long sermons. He knew the dangers attendant upon them, and cautioned offending preachers both directly and indirectly. For example, when a lady in Ireland had complained to him about the length of services he replied (16th February 1777):

If any other of the preachers exceed their time (about an hour in the whole service), I hope you will always put them in mind what is the Methodist rule. People imagine the longer a sermon is, the more good it will do. This is a grand mistake. The help done on earth, God doth it Himself; and He doth not need that we should use many words.

Against two offending preachers he went so far as to say: 'Unless you can and will leave off preaching long, I shall think it my duty to prevent your preaching at all among the Methodists.'[1]

Great as was Wesley's concern for long-suffering congregations, there are more indications of his concern for the physical and mental health of the transgressors themselves. Sometimes he rebuked them gently, as in a letter to one of his most valued friends, Robert Carr Brackenbury, of Raithby Hall, Lincolnshire (19th November 1781):

I rejoice to hear that your health is so well re-established, and am in hopes it will continue. Your preaching frequently will be no hindrance, but rather a furtherance to it, provided you have the resolution always to observe the Methodist rule of concluding the service within the hour. The want of observing this has many times hurt you; and we must not offer murder for sacrifice. We are not at liberty to impair our own health, in hopes of doing good to others.

Writing to other guilty preachers he stigmatized the practice as 'a mere trick of the devil's to make you murder yourselves'.

Brevity must, then, have been one feature of Wesley's own sermons. This is borne out by the *Journal*, in which he mentions a quarter of an hour as his normal practice. There were times, however, when he transgressed his own rule, but these were so

[1] *Letters*, VII.70.

rare that he makes special reference to and gives good reason for them. He seems to have been conscious of a kind of dispensation from God, giving him, occasionally, a larger freedom. Wesley knew that common sense should be exercised in relation to all his rules, and that in their flexibility lay much of their value. They were for general guidance, rather than rigid, mechanical observance. Thus, at Birstall (23rd April 1745): 'I was constrained to continue my discourse... near an hour longer than usual, God pouring out such a blessing that I knew not how to leave off.' Sometimes he describes this divine impression as an 'enlarging of the heart', as at Cardiff (19th October 1739), when 'my heart was so enlarged, I knew not how to give over, so we continued three hours'. There is a specially interesting entry describing a visit to Sheffield (25th July 1770):

My heart was so enlarged that I knew not how to leave off. Do some say: 'I preach longer than usual when I am barren'? It is quite the contrary with me. I never exceed but when I am full of matter; and still I consider it may not be with my audience as with me. So that it is strange if I exceed my time above a quarter of an hour.

Wesley's 'long' sermons afford one evidence of his extraordinary power over his hearers. At Stanley, near Gloucester, unusual weather conditions assisted him (7th October 1739).

I was strengthened to speak as I never did before, and continued speaking near two hours; the darkness of the night and a little lightning, not lessening the number, but increasing the seriousness of the hearers.

Wesley was also concerned about the *Frequency* of preaching. He himself observed no rule in this respect other than expediency, opportunity and physical ability. He was in Cornwall, for example (7th September 1768) and wrote:

This and the three following days I preached at as many places as I could, though I was at first in doubt whether I could preach eight days together, mostly in the open air, three or four times a day. But my strength was as my work; I hardly felt any weariness, first or last.

But Wesley knew that, with many of his preachers, zeal was apt to outrun prudence, and he therefore insisted that his helpers should not preach more than twice a day and three times on Sundays. This advice was embodied in a ruling of his last Conference, in 1790. Impressed by the evils of excessive preaching, at any rate on the part of others, Wesley became more emphatic in

(a) LONG SERMONS, (b) ITINERANCY, (c) FREQUENCY 179

its condemnation with the passage of the years. He was at Bath (5th September 1790), where the Methodist rule had been ignored, and he wrote in his *Journal*:

This day I cut off that vile custom, I know not when or how it began, of preaching three times a day by the same preacher to the same congregation; enough to weary out both the bodies and minds of the speaker as well as his hearers.

These directions as to frequency have an obvious bearing upon the *Itinerant System*, on whose value Wesley continually insisted and which has been recognized by the Christian Church from earliest times. Apparently those Apostles of whose travels we have any record remained but a few days in any one place and then passed on to preach elsewhere and to create new societies or churches. Even after these had been established, 'some Christians felt impelled to travel much through the churches, and must have promoted a constant circulation of ideas and of sentiments'.[2] This is what, in a modified form, occurred in the case of the Methodist Societies, and it helped greatly to weld them into that unity or 'connexion' that ultimately became the Methodist Church. Wesley himself remained, at most, but a few days in any place at one time. He was an itinerant in the fullest sense. His preachers, however, whilst also being itinerants, moved around for longer periods in those limited areas which in time became circuits.

Wesley knew the value of vigorous preaching, and that only such could be with power. He also knew that only men of almost superhuman ability could preach twice a day and three times on Sundays, for more than twelve months and in the same locality, and yet retain all their verve and freshness. In 1756 the Rev. Samuel Walker, of Truro, who sympathized largely with Wesley's teaching but was critical of some of his methods, had been urging him to seek episcopal ordination for some of his outstanding preachers and get them settled in parishes, there to carry on their work in a more regular way. In his reply Wesley points out that:

be their talents ever so great, they will ere long grow dead themselves, and so will most of those that hear them. I know, were I myself to preach one whole year in one place, I should preach both myself and most of my congregation asleep. Nor can I believe it was ever the will

[2] R. Rainy, *The Ancient Catholic Church*, p. 28.

of our Lord that any congregation should have one teacher only. We have found by long and constant experience that a frequent change of teachers is best. This teacher has one talent, that another. No one whom I ever yet knew has all the talents which are needful for beginning, continuing and perfecting the work of grace in a whole congregation.[3]

Wesley himself remains an outstanding example of an itinerant preacher. It has been estimated that during fifty years he travelled 250,000 miles, an annual average of 5,000. This is an astonishing figure for the eighteenth century, when roads were bad and people had to travel on foot or horseback or in horse-drawn vehicles.

In all his far-reaching schemes Wesley never overlooked the importance of details nor ever lost his grip upon them. The length of a sermon and the reaction of the congregation; whether or not Brother A—— had accepted his advice thereon; the effect of his preaching upon the health of each individual helper; the frequency of his preaching—these were among the matters that came up for review. He dealt personally with the difficulties and with those who disregarded his advice. In the school of stern experience many of them learned how wise and far-seeing was the man who, in so many ways, was their Father-in God.

[3] *Letters*, III.194; see also Edwin Sidney, *Life of Samuel Walker of Truro*, Ch. 8.

CHAPTER XIX

OLD SERMONS

THERE IS A passage in the *Journal* (1st November 1778) which surprises many who read it for the first time, especially young ministers who have been warned during their college days against preaching old sermons.

I went to Tiverton. I was musing here on what I heard a good man say long since: 'Once in seven years I burn all my sermons; for it is a shame if I cannot write better sermons now than I could seven years ago.' Whatever others can do, I really cannot. I cannot write a better sermon on the Good Steward than I did seven years ago; I cannot write a better on the Great Assize than I did twenty years ago; I cannot write a better on the Use of Money than I did nearly thirty years ago; nay, I know not that I can write a better on the Circumcision of the Heart than I did five-and-forty years ago. Perhaps, indeed, I may have read five or six hundred books more than I had then, and may know a little more history or natural philosophy than I did; but I am not sensible that this has made any essential addition to my knowledge in divinity. Forty years ago I knew and preached every Christian doctrine which I preach now.

We must be careful not to read too much into these words, but to look at them reasonably and dispassionately. Clearly Wesley is thinking, not of ephemeral subjects, but of those whose character and importance continue unchanged from age to age; that is, the basic doctrines of the Christian Faith and such practical matters as those referred to in the foregoing quotation. Because of the kind of men and women who mainly formed his congregations, particularly in the early days, his preaching had in it a large element of instruction. People had to be told, simply and exactly, what are the tenets of Christianity and what the duties, in a general way, obligatory upon a Christian. Now these remain essentially the same from one generation to another, though the forms of the duties may change with changing social conditions. But the 'Gospel' today is what it was when the New Testament books were written. There is no transition in Christianity corresponding to that from Astrology to Astronomy or from Phrenology to Psychology. There were vital matters that had to be stated and explained to the men and women of the eighteenth century, as to those of the first. Wesley made their verbal presentation a matter of serious thought and prayer, seeking for the best word, the most fitting phrase, the most telling argument. Hence there is a certain artistry in these sermons. The essential truths of Christianity are expressed in the language and thought forms of the time, with a lucidity and a directness upon which Wesley felt himself unable to improve; and, let us remember, he was a master of clarity in the English tongue. The whole ground of the subject was covered, and the sermon itself, according to Wesley's ability, was a perfect whole; so much so, that he felt it to be right and wise thus to present it repeatedly to his ever-changing congregations. To his hearers, except such as followed him from place to place, the sermon would be new.

Because of his passionate yearning over the souls of men and his own living faith, we can hardly conceive that these carefully prepared presentations of vital truths ever became stale to John Wesley. He was no human gramophone. His message lived and glowed in his heart, when preaching on these themes, and found expression in studied words that had become so familiar that any radical alteration of them would have lessened their power of appeal.

Given, then, the right spirit, a deep yearning for the souls of men, there appears to be no valid reason why the Spirit of God should not use the word-perfect and oft-repeated discourse of the preacher. If he is incapable of presenting his message in a better and more persuasive form, it would surely be foolish to change to something inferior for the mere sake of change. The crucial consideration is the preacher's mental relation to the words which he is uttering. With this type of subject it does not appear that life, vigour, convincing power, necessarily diminish with repetition. It was certainly not so in the case of many outstanding preachers of the middle period of Methodism. They had certain sermons which people looked for, asked for and went to hear again and again, and they seem to have achieved results far beyond the power of mere eloquence.

We do not expect changes in our great hymns and liturgical prayers, and we should resent them if made. Next Sunday we may stand and sing, perhaps for the thousandth time,

> When I survey the wondrous cross, . . .

or kneel and pray:

Almighty God, unto whom all hearts be open, all desires known, and from whom no secrets are hid: cleanse the thoughts of our hearts by the inspiration of Thy Holy Spirit, that we may perfectly love Thee, and worthily magnify Thy Holy Name; through Christ our Lord—

and if we are truly worshipping, the familiar words will be as fresh and eloquently expressive of our feelings and desires as if we had never heard them before. We would not have a word altered. We should shudder if we were asked to sing:

When I look at the astounding cross. . . .

and yet the meaning is the same. But the hymn would be shorn of a felicity of word and phrase, whose beauty and familiarity make it a perennial medium of blessing and exaltation.

Change for the sake of change is folly, especially if it be from what is good to what is inferior. We should regard it as impudent sacrilege to alter a word of Shakespeare's impassioned diction; to rewrite a musical phrase in one of Handel's choruses, or to repaint, in part, one of the world's great pictures, even were it only to wash out the wart on the nose of the old man, in Ghirlandaio's *Old Man and Boy*.

These things being so, we can understand Wesley's love for and adherence to this particular type of sermon in the form which he had given to it. We know that thought forms change with the passing years and the phraseology of one generation is not wholly that of the next. This is true in the realms of Science and Philosophy. Electricity is no longer thought and spoken of as a 'fluid', and we do not talk about the 'ether'. These are days of Space-Time, Quanta, Atomic Physics, and who dares to say what will be the catch-words of Science tomorrow? But the natural phenomena themselves, the familiar things with which such words are concerned, remain unchanged. Light, as men experience it, is what it was to Israel in Egypt and to the Shepherds of Bethlehem; and a molecule of water is the same as that of the water which Rebekah drew for the camels of Abraham; which valiant men fetched for David from the well of Bethlehem; and which the widow of Zarephath gave to slake the thirst of Elijah.

It is similar with the language, the verbal expression, the thought-forms of Christianity. During Wesley's life-time these varied little. It was an 'even' century, in which, so far as the popular mind was concerned, there was little progressive thought, and the general outlook and understanding of those who lived near its close were little different from those of their grandsires at the beginning. In consequence, there was no such pressing necessity for Wesley to alter his verbal presentation of Christian truth as there would have been if his life had been extended to the middle of the following century.

This 'apology' for John Wesley must not be regarded as a plea for, or a justification of the preaching of old sermons as a regular practice. It is both dangerous and foolish for a preacher to regard even his 'best' sermon, if he possesses such a document, as a masterpiece whose modification would be an act of sacrilege. Most preachers feel that, so far as they themselves are concerned, there is always room for improvement in the presentation of even such themes as we have been considering, and they are right. We live in days of unceasing change, both in the world of action and of thought, and the effective sermon, whilst proclaiming the eternal and unchanging truth of God, must do so in words that the hearers use and understand. That John Wesley, in his regard for some old sermons, should have been unmindful of this elementary truth, is unthinkable. Had he spoken in a tongue that was becoming outworn and archaic, divorced from the life around him, he could never have become a mighty instrument in the hands of God for the spiritual re-awakening of his fellow-countrymen.

CHAPTER XX

THE SERMON REGISTER

ALTHOUGH WE know so little about the craftsmanship and phraseology of Wesley's ordinary preaching, we know much about his subjects and more about his texts. In respect of the latter, we are fortunate in having a register of those which he used during a period of fifteen years: from 14th January 1747, to 25th December 1761. Nehemiah Curnock studied this document closely, comparing it with the *Journal*, and came to the conclusion that Wesley took a number of sermons and expository notes with him on his journeys. Some of these were 'useful as manifestos, as expositions of doctrine or as means of effectual appeal', and they were employed frequently; but he also preached many sermons that were new or re-made. To the last days of his life the *Diary* records, 'writ sermon'.

The comparison also shows that Wesley preached on every possible occasion and always expounded a text when meeting the Society and the Bands. Where the *Journal* simply notes that he preached, the Register often has three or more texts. This means that, on reaching his destination, Wesley preached in the evening and then expounded in a Society Meeting; spent the night in that place; preached at five o'clock the next morning and again before his departure.

The Register is arranged in the alphabetical order of the towns and villages visited, but Nehemiah Curnock undertook the laborious task of re-writing it in chronological order. In this much more useful form it is presented at the end of the Standard Edition of the *Journal*, where it runs to eighty-two pages. On many occasions it supplements the *Journal* and it mentions nearly 400 visits to which the latter makes no reference.

Let us now select one of the texts and trace its fortunes through these fifteen years, with the *Journal* and the Register to guide us. St Mark's Gospel, 1[15] is an easy one for the eye to detect as we make our way through the eighty-two pages of Scripture references: *The Kingdom of God is at hand: repent ye and believe the Gospel*. That the passage should read, *believe in the Gospel*, is not relevant to our purpose here.

We notice, first of all, that it is the text of the important Standard Sermon entitled *The Way to the Kingdom*. Now in the opening of this discourse Wesley insists that 'the Kingdom of God is not meat and drink', but the 'substance' of it lies in 'righteousness, peace and joy in the Holy Ghost'. This declaration was frequently upon his lips and it was the burden of his message on that memorable Sunday in June 1742, when he preached standing upon his father's tombstone in Epworth churchyard. It is generally believed that this was the sermon whose substance he then delivered. If so, it must have been a part of his *repertoire* before the date on which the Register begins; nor is it likely that his first use of it was on this occasion.

The text is registered 132 times: an average of nine times a year, but the intervals between its occurrences are very irregular. The first entry is under date Monday, 23rd February 1747, at Laceby, near Grimsby. From then to 11th September of the same year, Wesley employed it sixteen times: in Yorkshire, Northumberland, Cheshire, Devonshire, Cornwall, and Berkshire. Thereafter he allowed it to rest for eight months, when it resumed duty in Ireland. As we follow its fortunes we notice that Wesley would preach from it a number of times in quick succession and often in the same neighbourhood. Then we meet it on odd occasions, only to lose sight of it for months at a stretch, as from 10th July 1750, to 22nd May 1751. After that date it only appears twice until 27th May 1752. 10th September 1753, to 15th April 1755, is another long interval. On 27th June 1756, it takes on a new lease of life, and thereafter occurs, at short, varying intervals, till we meet it for the last time in the Register, when Wesley preached from it in Bradford, on 15th July 1761. During those fifteen years it did duty in every part of England, in Wales and Ireland and as far north in Scotland as Aberdeen. But it never passed entirely out of use, and it can be traced in the *Journal* and *Diary* to the last weeks of Wesley's life, and this was his text when, under an oak tree at Winchelsea, he preached for the last time in the open-air.

So our text has a long record of distinguished service, from, at the latest, June 1742 to October 1790: forty-eight years.

We further learn from the Register that there were seven places where Wesley preached from this text on two separate occasions and at one place on three. This happened at Brentford, for the first time on 16th November 1748, and again on 24th January

1760. He took the text twice at Limerick within nine years; at Canterbury within seven; at Longford (Ireland) within six; at Bristol within four; at Penryn (Cornwall) within two, and at the Bull-and-Mouth, once a Quaker meeting-house near St. Martin's-le-Grand, twice in the same month. He also used the text again at Epworth, when he opened the 'new house' there on 10th April 1759, nearly seventeen years after preaching for the first time from his father's tombstone. Norwich came in for exceptional treatment. He preached there from the text on 1st July 1755, and again on 30th August 1759. There had been much trouble in the Society, and Wesley describes the congregation on this second occasion as 'large, rude and noisy'. Four months later he visited the city again: delivered twenty sermons during his stay, and for the third time took St Mark 1^{15} as his text. Perhaps he felt that it was specially apposite. He tells us that they had 'a time of refreshing'.

We close our brief survey of the Register by noting the significance of certain figures. Taking eighty-five as the average number of texts entered upon each of the eighty-two pages, we have evidence for these fifteen years of about 7,000 sermons and expositions: a yearly average of, let us say, 470. A note, pencilled on the Register, states that 266 of the texts are from the Old Testament and 1,088 from the New, none, we assume, being counted more than once. These texts, totalling 1,354, were used on some 7,000 occasions, an average of five times each. But this text alone, whose fortunes we have traced, was used on 132 occasions, and as we glance down the columns of the Register we observe others that, by their constant reappearance, enter into competition with St Mark 1^{15} for popularity. It is an obvious inference that the great majority of the 1,354 texts were but rarely used, and many of them only once. We therefore conclude that, in spite of the extensive use of such favourites as the one we have traced, Wesley's discourses, in respect of his texts, covered a wide and varied field.

The *Standard Journal* has a prefatory note to the Register, to which, after our rapid survey, we give unfeigned assent:

It is an amazing record, which throws new light on the fertility and the unbounded zeal of the great evangelist.

CHAPTER XXI

SIDELIGHTS ON WESLEY'S PREACHING

IN VARIOUS connections we have noted references which Wesley made to his own preaching: its nature, its aims, its subjects and its immediate reactions upon individuals, congregations and himself. It is clear that much of his advice on preaching was based on personal trial and result. For the most part, he was conscious of his power and confident as to its ultimate outcome, but always very humbly so. He has his own striking way of describing the salutary effects of his preaching, which he never ascribes to himself; they are always by the power and grace of God, whose servant he is, as when in Bristol, on 20th May 1739, 'He (God) spoke to three whose souls were all storm and tempest, and immediately there was a great calm.'

The *Journal* reveals a man responding to what he is assured is a divine call, and, after his grand spiritual awakening, conscious of being guided and used by the God from whom the call had come. But he does not ostentatiously advertise these matters nor insist upon them. Rarely does he indulge in pious ejaculations. The few that occur are of an unusual kind and neither lengthy nor fulsome, as, for example, after preaching in Moorfields (12th August 1764), when he records: 'Thousands heard with deep and calm attention. *This also hath God wrought!*' Far more characteristic is the brief account of a service in Sheffield (17th June 1742): 'I began preaching about five, on *The Righteousness of Faith*; but I had not half finished my discourse when I was constrained to break off in the midst, our hearts so filled with a sense of the love of God, and our mouths with prayer and thanksgiving. When we were somewhat satisfied herewith, I went on to call sinners to the salvation ready to be revealed.' We note how again and again, in his short descriptions of services, and especially those which were most manifestly blessed to his congregations, Wesley naturally uses Scripture words and phrases, and often in such a way as to illuminate and illustrate their spiritual significance, as during a visit to York (13th May 1753), when the people had been profoundly stirred: 'God, as it were, bowed the heavens and came down. The flame of love went before Him; the rocks were broken in pieces and the mountains flowed down at His presence.'

Like all preachers, however, Wesley had his moments of depression and discouragement, but they were remarkably few. This may have been due, in part, to his constant change of scene and congregation. The depression caused by a 'dead' audience would be counteracted and relieved, a few hours later, by facing one that was eager and responsive. This latter type became increasingly common with the passage of time. A *Journal* entry for 22nd June 1739 runs: 'In the afternoon I preached at the Fishponds, but had no life or spirit in me, and I was much in doubt whether God would not lay me aside and send other labourers into his harvest. I came to the society full of this thought; and began, in much weakness, to explain, *Beloved, believe not every spirit, but try the spirits, whether they be of God.*' Wesley's doubts were soon dispelled in the exhilarating experiences which followed. He was too busy a man to have time to pander to his feelings or to nurse a temporarily wounded spirit.

Wesley always insisted on the sacredness of appointments and the duty of keeping them, and faced his preachers with the questions, 'Do you see the great sin and fatal consequences of it? (viz., disappointing a congregation). Will you break a limb rather than wilfully break your word herein?'[1] In the *Large Minutes* we read: 'Be sure never to disappoint a congregation, unless in case of life or death.'[2] Wesley always acted in the spirit of these words. He tells how, when at Sandwich (16th December 1789), he was so hoarse that he could neither sing nor speak. 'However', he continues, 'I determined to *show* myself, at least, where I had appointed to preach'. He 'trusted in God and began to speak', his voice strengthening as he went on, so that 'in a few minutes I think all could hear; and many, I believe, took knowledge that what they heard was not the word of man, but of God'. When the parish minister of Sligo (29th June 1760) urged him to continue his work in that town for another day, Wesley refused, for, 'as my journeys were fixed, I could not do that without disappointing several congregations'. On Thursday, 9th March 1758, he arrived in Bedford, having promised to preach the Assize sermon, but found the service was to take place the following day. Had he known this, he would have declined the invitation, as he was due to preach at Epworth on the Saturday. However,

[1] *Mins.*, p. 562. [2] ibid., 685.

he remained to preach in St Paul's Church, Bedford, on *We shall all stand before the judgement seat of Christ*, after which the judge invited him to dine with him. 'But', wrote Wesley, 'having no time I was obliged to send my excuse, and set out between one and two.' Epworth was expecting him, and even a judge's invitation must give way.

When Wesley tells us that he preached in such or such a place, he frequently does so in words that arrest and charm by their direct simplicity. 'I endeavoured to explain the way of salvation'; 'I declared the gospel of peace to a small company'; 'I offered the grace of God'; 'I offered Christ to about a thousand people'; 'I offered the redemption which is in Jesus'; 'I quietly declared the whole counsel of God'. These and similar expressions suggest that Wesley saw himself as God's ambassador, proclaiming a divine message, offering a divine gift, and thereby imposing upon his hearers the onus of choosing between Darkness and Light: between Death and Life.

Wesley was much helped by knowing the immediate needs of his congregation. Sometimes he was able to ascertain these beforehand and sometimes he became aware of them as the service proceeded. He found, on occasion, that people had been subjected to a type of sermon unsuited to them and detrimental to their spiritual health, and this he straightway sought to remedy. He was a true physician of the soul, skilful to diagnose the morbid conditions of those who gathered about him, and to speak words of hope and healing and life to them. He tells how, at Edinburgh (2nd August 1767), 'I was sorry to find both the society and congregations smaller than when I was here last. I impute this chiefly to the manner of preaching which has been generally used. The people have been told, frequently and strongly, of their coldness, deadness, heaviness and littleness of faith, but very rarely of anything that would move thankfulness. Hereby many were drawn away, and those that remained were kept cold and dead. . . . I encouraged them strongly at eight in the morning; and about noon preached on Castle Hill on *There is joy in heaven over one sinner that repenteth.*' Arriving in Canterbury (1st December 1768), he notes that the people here 'have been so often reproved (and frequently without a cause) for being dead and cold, that it has utterly discouraged them, and made them cold as stones. How delicate a thing is it to reprove! To do it will require more than human wisdom.'

Sometimes it was only when he was in the pulpit that Wesley saw clearly what his subject ought to be. Thus (20th May 1739), 'seeing many of the rich at Clifton Church, my heart was much pained for them, and I was earnestly desirous that some, even of them, might enter into the kingdom of heaven. But full as I was, I knew not where to begin in warning them to flee from the wrath to come, till my Testament opened on these words: *I came not to call the righteous, but sinners to repentance*, in applying which my soul was so enlarged that methought I could have cried out (in another sense than poor, vain Archimedes), "Give me where to stand, and I will shake the earth".' Nor did he hesitate to discard a predetermined subject in favour of one more suited to the needs of his congregation. Thus, at Horncastle (4th July 1788), 'My design was to have preached seriously; for which purpose I chose that text: *The harvest is past, the summer is ended, and we are not saved*; but I was turned, I know not how, quite the other way, and could preach scarce anything but consolation. I believe this was the very thing the people needed, although I knew it not.'

Nor were the needs of children forgotten when occasionally Wesley preached to them. It was probably when he visited Bolton, in 1786, and when 'such an army of children got about me when I came out of the chapel, that I could scarce disengage myself from them', that he fulfilled a promise which he had made, and preached to them 'in a simple, plain, familiar style', using no word of more than two syllables.[3]

At times, in order to drive home his message to a certain type of hearer, he would use ironical expressions, in which he sometimes surprised himself. At Kelso (10th June 1757) he faced 'a pretty large congregation. I suppose the chief men of the town were there, and I spared neither rich nor poor. I almost wondered at myself, it not being usual with me to use so keen and cutting expressions, and I believe that many felt, for all their form, they were but heathens still.' He could also employ humour, as in his sermon on *Dress*, in which he quotes an unnamed Dean as having said to his congregation at Whitehall, 'If you do not repent, you will go to a place which I have too much manners to name before this good company.'

Wesley was always suspicious of what are called 'popular sermons', as he was, indeed, of popularity in general. In a letter to Thomas Wride, one of his preachers (22nd January 1774) he

[3] *Journal*, VII.155; Tyerman, *Life of Wesley*, III.472; W.H.S., IV. 119.

makes a caustic reference to another preacher: 'John Hilton is a pleasing preacher, but perhaps not so deep as some others. Yet I suppose he is and will be a popular one. He has a good person and an agreeable utterance.' Wesley strove, however, to be fair in his judgements and recognized that the ways of God are not always what men expect. He wrote to Joseph Benson (28th June 1774): 'Your congregations in Edinburgh are large: Hugh Saunderson's are larger still. Your preaching, and perhaps mine, has stirred up a sleepy people: his preaching has stirred them up still more.' Benson had evidently asked Wesley, 'Why does God work more by him that has far less sense than we?, and Wesley replies: 'To stain the pride of our wisdom.' He continues: 'The generality of the congregation prefer his preaching to either yours or mine. They feel therein more of the power of God, though it has less of the wisdom of man. Now, I see more than any single preacher can see (because of his itinerancy) which of the preachers do most good, who have most fruit: and according to this I form my estimate of them.'

To a charge that Methodists, including himself, preached only 'dry morality', Wesley replied with vigour and recalled how, when preaching at Witney on Gal. 6^{14}, 'with uncommon freedom of spirit', an 'honest Predestinarian' had remarked that it was 'a pretty *moral* discourse'. On this he comments, concerning the Methodists, 'I think we likewise have the Spirit of God', and continues: 'I think even I, to speak as a fool, can judge a little of preaching the gospel.'[4]

But there was one aim in his preaching which transcended every casual or temporary one, and that was 'to save souls'. It is a recurrent theme in all his writings. In a letter to Charles Wesley (26th April 1772) he put it quite plainly: 'Your business as well as mine is to save souls. When we took priests' orders, we undertook to make it our *one business*. I think every day lost which is not (mainly, at least) employed in this thing. *Sum totus in illo*.' [To this I am wholly committed.]

This 'saving of souls' demanded more than preaching a 'good sermon', considered as a work of art. This 'extra' Wesley enforced both upon his preachers and himself. Weighty words of his on this subject are recorded in the *Large Minutes*: 'It is far easier to preach a good sermon than to instruct the ignorant in the principles of religion. And as much as this work is despised by

[4] *Letters*, V.58.

some, I doubt not but it will try the parts and spirits of us all.'
He quotes Archbishop Usher:

Great scholars may think it beneath them to spend their time in teaching the first principles of the doctrine of Christ. But they should consider that the laying the foundation skilfully, as it is the matter of greatest importance in the whole building, so it is the masterpiece of the wisest builder. . . . And let the wisest of us all try whenever we please, we shall find, that to lay this groundwork rightly, to make an ignorant man understand the grounds of religion, will put us to the trial of all our skill.[5]

As to results, Wesley was no light-hearted optimist, hailing a golden summer with every swallow which flew zigzag across his sky. He believed in the searching test of time. Had not our Lord Himself spoken of seed falling upon rocky places as symbolic of the man who 'heareth the word and straightway with joy receiveth it; yet hath he not root in himself, but endureth for a while'? Wesley knew this type and reserved his judgement. When he paid his first visit to Wallingford (17th October 1769) he noted how the people 'received the word with joy', and commented: 'How pleasant it is to see the dawn of a work of grace! But we must not lay too much stress upon it. Abundance of blossoms! But when the sun is up, how many of these will wither away!' He showed similar caution at Gravesend (14th December 1772): 'The stream here spreads wide, but it is not deep. Many are drawn, but none converted, or even awakened. Such is the general method of God's providence: where all approve, few profit.' From time to time he noted in his *Journal* both his disappointments and his hopes. He wrote of Shaftesbury (30th September 1771): 'I scarce know a town in England where so much preaching has been to so very little purpose.'

But the seasons of abundant blessing far outnumbered those of seeming failure or flickering hope. In *An Earnest Appeal to Men of Reason and Religion* Wesley gives a simple account of the type of preaching which yielded him the greatest satisfaction. He begins by relating an encounter which he had with a man who once was rich but had become poor; who was sick and wretched and a confessed atheist. He said to Wesley: 'I hear you preach to a great number of people every night and morning. Pray, what would you do with them? Whither would you lead them? What religion

[5] *Mins.*, pp. 470-3.

do you preach? What is it good for?' To this Wesley replied:

I do preach to as many as desire to hear, every night and morning. You ask, what I would do with them: I would make them virtuous and happy, easy in themselves and useful to others. Whither would I lead them? To heaven; to God the Judge, the lover of all, and to Jesus the Mediator of the new covenant. What religion do I preach? The religion of love; the law of kindness brought to light by the gospel. What is this good for? To make all who receive it enjoy God and themselves: to make them like God; lovers of all; contented in their lives; and crying out at their death, in calm assurance, 'O grave, where is thy victory! Thanks be unto God, who giveth me the victory, through my Lord Jesus Christ'.[6]

In June 1755, Wesley wrote in his *Journal* a short review of the way in which God had blessed him and all associated with him, in the results of the Methodist preaching. He records reaching London on the nineteenth and continues:

From a deep sense of the amazing work which God has of late years wrought in England, I preached in the evening on those words (Ps. cxlvii.20), '*He hath not dealt so with any nation*'; no, not even with Scotland or New England. In both these God has indeed made bare His arm, yet not in so astonishing a manner as among us. This must appear to all who impartially consider (1) the numbers of persons on whom God has wrought; (2) the swiftness of His work in many, both convinced and truly converted in a few days; (3) the depth of it in most of these, changing the heart as well as the whole conversation; (4) the clearness of it, enabling them boldly to say, 'Thou hast loved me; Thou hast given Thyself for me'; (5) the continuance of it. God has wrought in Scotland and New England, at several times, for some weeks or months together; but among us He has wrought for near eighteen years together, without any observable intermission.

Through all the varied fortunes of his ministry, in times of success and of seeming failure, the great themes of his preaching remained unchanged. To the end of his life he continued faithful to those doctrines whose publication in the highways and byways had helped to transform society and create a new national conscience. Rather touchingly he affirms his loyalty in a letter written to John Mason about a year before his death (13th January 1790): 'I have been uniform both in doctrine and discipline for above these fifty years; and it is a little too late for me to turn into a new path, now I am grey-headed.'

[6] *Works*, VIII.8.

CHAPTER XXII

EVENSONG

As, IN THOUGHT, we accompany John Wesley along the highways and byways of our land, imagination re-creates that indomitable, entrancing little figure, clad, for preaching, in cassock, gown and bands, and reproduces that clear, ringing, cultured voice, 'offering salvation' in words that won men by their simplicity, sincerity, and loving constraint. For over fifty years he wrought that amazing ministry. Others faltered and some failed and dropped out; *he never*. There seems to have been no moment in his life when he was tempted to play the traitor to the spirit of his brother's hymn:

> I would the precious time redeem,
>   And longer live for this alone,
> To spend and to be spent for them
>   Who have not yet my Saviour known;
> Fully on these my mission prove,
> And only breathe, to breathe Thy love.[1]

This faithfulness to his call to preach is one of the outstanding wonders in a wonderful life. It has aroused the admiration of many understanding minds, like that of William Cowper, who, having praised Wesley for his many and varied excellencies, concludes:

> Yet, above all, his luxury supreme
> And his chief glory was the Gospel-theme:
> There he was copious as old Greece or Rome,
> His happy eloquence seemed there at home.
> Ambitious not to shine or to excel,
> But to treat justly what he loved so well.[2]

At last came the closing years, when John Wesley had become established as a part of the British scene. Even people well beyond middle age could not recall an England in which, whether in evil or in good report, he was not a conspicuous figure. Now, like such of his great predecessors as John Wycliffe and

[1] *M.H.B.*, No. 390.   [2] *Conversation*, pp. 619ff.

Hugh Latimer, he belonged to the common people. Even numbers of the clergy were welcoming him as an honoured guest in their pulpits and their homes, and mansions of 'the gentry' had wide-open doors for him. What reverent affection breathes in this little note, and how many such must Wesley have received during those later years of victory!

> Ramsbury Park, Oct. 30. 1774.
> If dear Mr Wesley has any time for retirement this winter, we shall be exceeding glad if he will please to come to Ramsbury Park, where we shall think it an honour to furnish him, as the Shunamite did the Prophet Elisha, with a bed, a stool and a candlestick.

The writer was Sally, wife of James Nind, a local preacher and well-to-do farmer, living four miles from Marlborough. Wesley had warm admiration for the family.[3]

There is the same reverential regard in the Diary entry of Mrs Dobinson of Derby.

> *July 1782.* Last week dear Mr Wesley was here. . . . On Monday a letter came to hand, informing us that he would be with us on Thursday and continue with us two nights. I could not help saying, 'It is the Lord's doing', and, I trust, it has been for the good of many souls. He preached from the Lawyer's answer to our Lord, in Luke x, on Thursday evening; and on Friday evening, from James iii.17, he shewed us what fruit the Wisdom that is from above will produce.[4]

In 1789 Wesley paid his last visit to Ireland, reaching Dublin on Sunday morning, 29th March. Crookshank tells us that

> during this visit to the metropolis Mr Wesley met with very great respect and attention from several persons of rank in Dublin and its vicinity, including the Earl of Moira. Mr Myles (who was then the junior preacher in the circuit) says he never saw the venerable evangelist more honoured by those who were not members of the Society than at this time. They seemed to think it a blessing to have him under their roof: and such a sacred influence attended his words that it was no ordinary privilege to have the opportunity of listening to his conversation.[5]

But above all he belonged more and more to his Methodists and he belongs to them still. Modern Methodists are not blind to his defects nor do they embrace all his opinions. Upon that,

---

[3] *W.M.M.* (1787), p. 217; see also *Journal*, VI.57, 289; *Letters*, VI.179–80, 183.
[4] ibid. (1803), p. 560; see also *Journal*, VI.360.
[5] C. H. Crookshank, *History of Methodism in Ireland*, I.451.

he would never have insisted; but they make sensible allowance for what, in his theological outlook, is untenable today, as being natural to the religious and intellectual climate of his age. He belongs to them, in that they return again and again to the presence of that John Wesley, minister of Jesus Christ, whose calling it was, above all else, 'to publish abroad His wonderful Name'; who, with his brother Charles, declared the power of that Name in hymns that men will sing with thrilling joy while the Christian Church endures; who lived out the vital doctrines of the Christian Faith and exemplified its graces: and they come out from his presence with strength renewed and re-inspired to do their Lord's will while it is day.

Wesley's popularity during these years is impressive. He himself marvelled at the great change which had occurred, especially among the more influential classes and those in official positions. In a letter to Elizabeth Ritchie he contrasts the popularity which George Whitefield achieved so early in his career with his own. He had never sought it, but it had appeared at the end of a long and toilsome road. The letter was written in Dublin in 1785.

Many years ago I was saying, 'I cannot imagine how Mr Whitefield can keep his soul alive, as he is not now going through honour and dishonour, evil report and good report, having nothing but honour and good report attending him wherever he goes'. It is now my own case: I am just in the condition now that he was in then. I am become, I know not how, an honourable man (viz., held in honour). The scandal of the Cross is ceased; and all the kingdom, rich and poor, Papists and Protestants, behave with courtesy—nay, and seeming goodwill! It seems as if I had wellnigh finished my course, and our Lord was giving me an honourable discharge.[6]

Honour! Courtesy! Goodwill! These were unlooked-for favours, for Wesley had made no such demands on his own account. Once, like Zion of old, he had been 'forsaken'; now he was 'sought out'. His astonishment at this change is repeatedly expressed in the *Journal*. He preached twice at Allhallows Church on Sunday, 26th January 1777, and remarks:

I found great liberty of spirit; and the congregation seemed to be much affected. How is this? Do I yet please men? Is the offence of the Cross ceased? It seems, after being scandalous near fifty years, I am at length grown into an honourable man!

[6] *Letters*, VII.277.

On 18th June 1786, at the invitation of the Vicar, he preached twice in the beautiful old Church of the Holy Trinity in Hull, which, in the afternoon, 'was, if possible, more crowded than before'. 'Who would have expected, a few years since, to see me preaching in the High Church at Hull?', is his comment. When visiting Falmouth (18th August 1789), he recalls how, forty years before, he had been 'taken prisoner by an immense mob, gaping and roaring like lions', and continues:

But how is the tide turned! High and low now lined the street from one end of the town to the other, out of stark love and kindness, gaping and staring as if the King were going by.

Some of the references to Wesley's preaching during the last years are unusually interesting. It seems that everywhere great congregations attended his ministry and people both distinguished and destined for distinction sat at his feet. Sir Walter Scott, during his boyhood, heard him and recorded his impressions. Wesley was then eighty-one years of age.

When I was about twelve years old I heard Wesley preach more than once, standing on a chair in Kelso churchyard. He was a most venerable figure, but his sermons were vastly too colloquial for the taste of Saunders. He told many excellent stories. One I remember which he said had happened to him in Edinburgh. 'A drunken dragoon', said Wesley, 'was commencing an assertion in military fashion, "God eternally damn me", just as I was passing. I touched the poor man on the shoulder, and when he turned round fiercely, said calmly, "You mean, *God bless me*".' In the mode of telling the story he failed not to make us sensible how much his patriarchal appearance and mild, yet bold rebuke, overawed the soldier, who touched his hat, thanked him and, I think, came to chapel that evening.[7]

1790 was the last complete year of Wesley's life and reminiscences of him are plentiful, but we should bear in mind that these are rarely by people who knew him in the heyday of his powers. On Saturday, 1st May, he arrived in York, where, the same evening, 'Dicky' Burdsall heard him preach and later had supper with him.[8] Burdsall's daughter, aged nine, was greatly impressed by Wesley, who placed his hands upon her head as he left the pulpit and blessed her. She became the mother of John

---
[7] Lockhart, *Life of Sir Walter Scott*, VI.45–6.
[8] *Memoirs of Richard Burdsall* (Edn 1838), pp. 156–7.

Lyth, who wrote the *History of Methodism in York*. The *York Courant* of the 4th of that month refers to this visit.

On Saturday last the Rev. Mr Wesley arrived in this city, where he preached that evening and twice on Sunday. When it is considered that he is now near his ninetieth year, who can withold their surprise that at such an age this truly venerable man should be capable of the exertions he now uses?[9]

On that journey northward Wesley got at least as far as Aberdeen, and on his return called at Lincoln, which he reached on the 1st July. He was still able to astonish people who only knew him by repute, for after hearing him preach for the first time, a lady of the city exclaimed, 'Is this the great Mr Wesley of whom we hear so much in the present day? Why, the poorest person in the chapel might have understood him!' We are told that the gentleman to whom the remark was made replied, 'In this, madam, he displays his greatness: that, whilst the poorest can understand him, the most learned are edified and cannot be offended.'[10]

The middle of October found him in East Anglia. On Monday, the 11th, he reached Colchester and preached in the evening. In his congregation was Henry Crabb Robinson, who later moved in the same literary circles as Wordsworth, Coleridge, Lamb, and Hazlitt. Though he was only fifteen at the time, he wrote a letter in which he described this experience, dated 18th October 1790.

I felt great satisfaction last week in hearing that veteran in the service of God, the Rev. John Wesley. At another time, and not knowing the man, I should almost have ridiculed his figure. Far from it now. I looked upon him with a respect bordering upon enthusiasm. After the people had sung one verse of a hymn he arose and said: 'It gives me a great pleasure to find that you have not lost your singing; neither men nor women. You have not forgotten a single note. And I hope, by the assistance of God, which enables you to sing well, you may do all other things well.' A universal 'Amen' followed. At the end of every head or division of his discourse, he finished by a kind of prayer, a momentary wish as it were, not consisting of more than three or four words, which was always followed by a universal buzz. After the last prayer he rose up and addressed the people on liberality of sentiment, and spoke much against refusing to join with any congregation on account of difference in opinion.

[9] See *Journal*, VIII.63n. [10] *Journal*, VIII.77.

Later in life Crabb Robinson looked back upon that day and gave a further account of it.

He stood in a wide pulpit (in the 'great, round meeting-house') and on each side of him stood a minister, and the two held him up, having their hands under his armpits. His feeble voice was barely audible; but his reverend countenance, especially his long, white locks, formed a picture never to be forgotten. There was a vast crowd of lovers and admirers. It was for the most part a pantomime, but the pantomime went to the heart. Of the kind, I never saw anything comparable to it in after life.[11]

On the 15th of that month Wesley preached in Lowestoft. In his audience was George Crabbe, clergyman and poet. It was not the first time that Crabbe had heard him preach. About the year 1781 he had attended a service conducted by Wesley in the City Road Chapel, where, the crowd being so great, he had been obliged to stand on the pulpit steps. In his *Life* of his father, Crabbe's son tells how, on this later occasion, the poet and some of his friends

adjourned to a dissenting chapel to hear the venerable John Wesley on one of the last of his peregrinations. He was exceedingly old and infirm, and was attended, almost supported in the pulpit, by a younger minister on each side. The chapel was crowded to suffocation. In the course of the sermon he repeated, though with an application of his own, the lines from Anacreon—

> Oft am I by women told,
> Poor Anacreon! thou grow'st old;
> See. Thine hairs are falling all,
> Poor Anacreon! how they fall!
> Whether I grow old or no,
> By these signs I do not know;
> But this I need not to be told,
> 'Tis time to *live* if I grow old.

My father was much struck by his reverend appearance and his cheerful air, and the beautiful cadence he gave to these lines; and after the service introduced himself to the patriarch, who received him with benevolent politeness.[12]

Deeply stirred as Wesley was by some of the events of these years, he yet, for the most part, kept an iron hand upon himself

---

[11] Quoted by Tyerman in his *John Wesley*, III.627–8.
[12] *Life of George Crabbe*, by his Son, Ch. 6.

and held his emotions in check. He was no 'weeping prophet', but during this period there were occasions when his feelings passed beyond control. They were very rare. Thomas Taylor, one of his preachers, heard him preach in Bingley Church on 27th April 1776, and wrote in his private diary: 'I never saw him weep while preaching before now. He spoke awfully, and the congregation heard him attentively.'[13] Taylor's astonishment is evident. On 21st June 1778, he preached in Armagh. One of his auditors, William Black, has left on record that

Wesley preached from Luke xx.36: 'For neither can they die any more; for they are equal unto the angels, for they are sons of God, being sons of the resurrection'; and when he came to speak on the second clause he repeated it several times—'for they are equal unto the angels'—and his soul being so filled with rapture that he could not proceed, he burst into tears, saying, 'Let us pray'. An overwhelming influence fell upon the assembly.[14]

There was a moving scene in Bolton when Wesley preached there on 19th April 1788. Charles Wesley had died a fortnight before, and the second hymn of the service was one that many people, including Isaac Watts, regard as his sublimest composition —'Come, O Thou traveller unknown'. The thought of his brother must have been overwhelmingly in John's mind, for, in reading out the lines,

> My company before is gone,
> And I am left alone with Thee,

he could not restrain his tears and sat down with his face hidden in his hands. Such a wave of emotion swept over the congregation that singing ceased and many wept. Presently the preacher, then eighty-five years of age, mastered his feelings and continued an unforgettable service.[15]

It was probably on Sunday, 10th October 1790, that an impressive incident occurred in City Road Chapel, where, after reading the liturgy,

Mr Wesley ascended the pulpit to conduct the remaining part of the service. A rush of holy thought poured into his soul, and, instead of announcing the hymn, he stood for ten minutes in perfect silence; his eyes were closed, his countenance devoutly lifted up to heaven, and

---

[13] *Journal*, VI.103.
[14] ibid., p. 200. Also Crookshank's *Methodism in Ireland*, I.323.
[15] *Journal*, VII.377. Also Tyerman, *supra*, III.527.

his hands clasped together on the pulpit Bible. Like Hannah in the tabernacle at Shiloh, 'he spake in his heart; only his lips moved, but his voice was not heard'. The congregation gazed in silent wonder as they saw him thus holding communion alone with God among a crowd of worshippers. . . . Then, opening the hymn-book with his accustomed seriousness, he gave out with more than ordinary tenderness, accompanied by holy unction, his brother's hymn of exultation:

> Come, let us join our friends above,
>   That have obtained the prize;
> And on the eagle wings of love,
>   To joys celestial rise.
>
> One family we dwell in Him,
>   One Church, above, beneath,
> Though now divided by the stream—
>   The narrow stream of death.

Never, perhaps, before or since, were earthly singers nearer to heaven than on that day.[16]

The time arrived when Wesley himself became conscious of failing physical power and his friends sorrowfully noted his increasing need for support in the pulpit. His memory also became less reliable. When he preached at Haworth (18th April 1790),

> he was accompanied by Joseph Bradford, who had the leading thoughts of his discourse written on slips of paper. When he found the memory of the venerable preacher at fault, he put before him the slip containing the thought he intended to express, which was at once taken up and the discourse continued in its appointed order.

We note the sense of urgency in many of Wesley's last *Journal* entries and letters. The hour of his departure was at hand and there was no time to be lost. More instant than ever, he must be about his Father's business. Henry Moore records how, when over eighty, Wesley said to him, in respect of the journey they were making together, 'We should lose no time—we have not, like the patriarchs, 700 or 800 years to play with.' This careful use of time was rather amusingly illustrated during Wesley's last visit to Hull, in June 1790. Proceeding from Bridlington, he reached Beverley on Friday, 25th. Mr Joseph Gee, an ardent Methodist of Hull, and about forty others,

> having received intimation of his intended visit, proceeded, some in chaises and others on horseback, to meet him at Beverley. After

---

[16] G. J. Stevenson, *History of City Road Chapel*, p. 105.

hearing him preach at noon, to a congregation whom he characterizes as 'serious and well behaved', most of the party, by arrangement, dined with him at his inn. As usual, his discourse was edifying and enlivening in a high degree; but it was characteristically brief. For just when the conversation had reached the climax of interest, and the delighted company had forgotten home and the way which led to it, he pulled out his watch, started on his feet, said his time was up, bade them good-day, and, his coach being ready, no entreaties could detain him for another moment. The party harnessed and followed as fast as they could; but it was with no small difficulty that some of them succeeded in joining the line of procession by the time it reached the suburbs of Hull. Mr Wesley felt much amused when he learned the particulars of the hurry into which his punctuality had put his youthful friends. . . .[17]

Though his bodily powers were failing and the silver cord of life being loosened, Wesley did not make this an excuse for withdrawing from those activities, especially preaching, which had long been dearer to him than life itself. He was not prepared, in Juvenal's famous words,

propter vitam vivendi perdere causas.[18]

After all, these symptoms of decay might be deceptive and God might have further use for John Wesley before calling him hence. Therefore it behoved him to make his plans for the future as though that future were fully assured. 'Give everything the last touch', is one of his epigrams. It is a mistake to imagine him wandering about the country, guided only by the fancy of the moment. He carefully planned his journeys and his Methodists were advised where and when to meet him. Method had marked his whole life, including his preaching; it had canalized his activities and put a check upon all that was wasteful or irrelevant, and to it much of his success was due. Whilst life lasted he felt the urge to methodical activity, and sought in direct action what anchorites sought in seclusion and quiescence. So he continued, to the very end, to compose his sermons and to make plans for his preaching journeys, even while sometimes expressing doubt of his ability to carry them through.

At Winchelsea, on 7th October 1790, Wesley preached for the last time in the open air. 'I stood under a large tree . . . and called to most of the inhabitants of the town, "The kingdom of heaven

---

[17] *W.M.M.* (1836), p. 494.
[18] Juvenal, *Satires*, VIII.84. 'For the sake of life, to lose the very reasons for living.'

is at hand; repent, and believe the gospel." It seemed as if all that heard were, for the present, almost persuaded to be Christians.'

His last sermon in his beloved City Road Chapel was preached in the evening of Tuesday, 22nd February 1791. The text was, 'We through the Spirit wait for the hope of righteousness by faith'. After preaching he gave out his favourite psalm, 'I'll praise my Maker while I've breath'. Mr Rogers notes: 'An excellent sermon!' The following day he preached for the last time. This was at Leatherhead and we have two accounts of what occurred. The service was held at the request of a magistrate who lent his house for the purpose and invited his neighbours to attend. James Rogers tells us that

a considerable number assembled and were ordered upstairs into a spacious dining-room, set round with fine mahogany chairs and covered with a beautiful carpet. The plain country people, who had come plodding through the mire, seemed rather out of their element; however, they all appeared to hear with deep attention, while Mr Wesley gave them a most solemn warning from Isaiah lv.6, 7: 'Seek ye', which was the last sermon this eminent minister of God ever delivered.[19]

Inevitably John Wesley looked backward over the way by which he had come and round him at the contemporary scene, and tried to estimate the gains and losses. During the half-century he had travelled 250,000 miles and preached more than 40,000 sermons, an average of over fifteen *per* week. It was in 1765 that he informed John Newton, 'I preach about eight hundred sermons in a year.'[20] What had all this preaching accomplished? There was the concurrent testimony of the *Journals*, with their references to many hundreds of services and his comments made on them at the time, either of pleasure or disappointment or both. In the pages of those little duodecimo volumes was recorded many an incident that made the enterprise of John Wesley's life well worth while, but they could not tell all. There were men and women in the pageantry of Methodism, who, under God, owed their 'soul's new creation', directly or indirectly, to his preaching, and whose presence there was indisputable proof of the Divine acceptance of and blessing upon his life's work; those whose names were written in the Lamb's

[19] *Journal*, VIII.134.   [20] *Letters*, IV.297.

Book of Life, because John Wesley's love for needy men had never faltered. 'One soul', he once wrote to William Black, 'is worth all the merchandise in the world.'[21]

What had been accomplished? Only on the day when all things shall be revealed will the answer be known. In his heart of hearts Wesley knew that he had not wholly failed, whatever casualties there might have been by the wayside to distress his soul: and casualties there had been, particularly those backsliders over whom his spirit yearned, and those Methodists who were unfaithful stewards of the opulence that had come to them. Those years of faithful preaching had brought forth rich and abundant fruit. Did he not tell Sophie v. la Roche, the German novelist, when, in September 1786, he and she crossed in the same vessel from Holland to Harwich, that he had 70,000 'disciples'? And did not the buoyancy of his spirit make her forget that she was fifty-four?[22] There is a touch of pardonable pride in his words, but no exaggeration, for the Bristol Conference of that year reported a world membership of 79,506. These 70,000 people of whom he was thinking were not his failures, but the men and women who crowned his life's endeavour and gave him joy and hope at the last.

On 24th March 1785, Wesley entered in his *Journal* a retrospective account of the way by which he had travelled.

I was now considering how strangely the grain of mustard-seed, planted about fifty years ago, has grown up. It has spread through all Great Britain and Ireland; the Isle of Wight and the Isle of Man; then to America from the Leeward Islands, through the whole continent, into Canada and Newfoundland. And the societies, in all these parts, walk by one rule, knowing religion is holy tempers; and striving to worship God, not in form only, but likewise 'in spirit and in truth'.

We know that five years later, when he had entered upon the last year of his earthly life, Wesley could have soliloquized in precisely the same strain. These are not the words of a man whose House of Dreams is crumbling about him. As Wesley looked back there must have risen to his lips words which Charles had written— How long ago? Nearly thirty years—and during those years the Divine harvesting had never ceased and *he*, in the providence of God, had been a labourer in the field:

[21] *Letters*, VIII.222.
[22] *Sophie in London* (1786). 'The Diary of Sophie', v. la Roche (Cape).

Father of everlasting grace,
  Thou hast in us Thy arm revealed,
Hast multiplied the faithful race
  Who, conscious of their pardon sealed,
Of joy unspeakable possessed,
Anticipate their heavenly rest.[23]

[23] *P.W.*, IX.381; *M.H.B.* (1779), No. 480.

CHAPTER XXIII

AVE ATQUE VALE

JOHN WESLEY'S extraordinary versatility is apparent to every reader of the *Journal*. He had talents and natural interests which, suitably directed, would have assured him of a distinguished and lucrative position in several walks of life: Scholarship, Literature, Medicine, Law, and Politics. Had he accepted a living in the Established Church, eschewed all distinctively 'Methodist' emphasis in doctrine and thus obtained episcopal approval, he might have become a Bishop. He was keenly interested in the Science of his day and kept well abreast of new discoveries, theories, and inventions. Abundant evidence of the truth of these statements could be given, but considerations of space forbid their inclusion.

Confronted by these possibilities, what did John Wesley choose? The answer is astonishing as we contrast it with what might have been. He chose to be an itinerant preacher of Christ's Gospel in a parish that knew neither Bishop nor boundary. To the casual observer, this might have seemed the erratic decision of an incompletely balanced mind; a closer acquaintance with John Wesley would have convinced him how beautifully balanced that mind was. Assured that 'it were better for me to die than not to preach the gospel of Christ',[1] he made a choice which for self-abnegation, heroism and far-reaching consequences has few parallels in the history of human excellence.

Wesley's choice cannot be accurately dated, but he set his seal to it on 2nd May 1739, when he preached for the first time in the open air, and stood publicly committed to what he was sure was the will of God. It was a supreme act of faith in a God who had been working hitherto—who shall say from how remote a past! Behind John Wesley were centuries of Christian history; hereditary influences; family tradition; his own early training and events in his life subsequent to his return from Georgia. All these aided in intensifying the yearning of his soul to be wholly what God wanted him to be, and ever more clearly it was being revealed to him what that was.

[1] *Letters*, II.77.

But the power of the Past was directive, rather than compelling. In respect of his choice Wesley was a free man; it was a *real* choice. True, the way before him lay in deep shadow, but he was sure of the Divine will, expressed in certain outward events and in the compulsions of his own logical mind. At almost any point thereafter he could have given up all and returned to the Oxford that he loved. There can be no true estimate of his greatness where that fact is obscured or ignored. He did not drift thoughtlessly into a life of preaching, only to find later that he had committed himself irrevocably and that henceforth every other avenue of useful activity was closed to him. It was a gigantic and, in the eyes of some, a preposterous venture of faith, but let us not for a moment imagine that Wesley's choice meant the deliberate wastage of any talent that he possessed. In varying degrees he made all those interests which we have already noted subservient to and adjuncts to his ministry and his preaching. In his use of them, they were 'baptized into Christ'.

'I here proclaim my firm belief', writes George Sampson, 'that John Wesley was the greatest Englishman of the eighteenth century.'[2] He died on the 2nd March 1791, at the age of eighty-eight, and, thanks to Mrs Ritchie,[3] we know much about those closing hours, when it seemed to Mrs Rogers that 'a cloud of the Divine presence rested on all'. His passing was that of a great man and a distinguished soldier of Jesus Christ.

> The tongues of dying men
> Enforce attention like deep harmony,[4]

and we read special significance not only in what they say, but also in what they do not say. Frequently it is in those moments, when a man's past lives with compelling vividness in his mind; when his active life is ended and stands complete; when nothing can be added to it and nothing taken away, that the great choices of his life muster their forces about him, for weal or woe, and in the court of his judgement stand approved or condemned. John Wesley's judgement was that of an untroubled soul: *All is well.* There were few regrets, in spite of those disappointing Methodists who persisted in stumbling on their road to Heaven by way of Lombard Street and Vanity Fair. After all, there were not many

---
[2] *The Century of Divine Songs* (Wharton Lecture, 1943), 9.
[3] See *Journal*, VIII.131ff. and notes for what follows.
[4] Spoken by John of Gaunt: Shakespeare, *Richard II*, Act II. Sc. 1.

of them, and in the providence of God they might find the right way at last. As he lay there Wesley's mind was still running on sermons and his beloved preaching. The great choice of his life was still the nearest to his heart and mind. On Sunday, 20th February, two of his own discourses on the *Sermon on the Mount* were read to him. On the following Sunday 'the fever was very high, and at times affected his head; but even then he was generally either meeting classes, going to preach, or something that proved that, though his head was subject to a temporary derangement, his heart was wholly engaged in his Master's work.' On the next day (Monday), he enquired

what the words were on which he preached at Hampstead a short time before. He was told they were these: 'Ye know the grace of our Lord Jesus Christ, that, though he was rich, yet for your sakes he became poor, that ye through his poverty might be rich.' He replied, 'That is the foundation, the only foundation; there is no other'.

On the Tuesday he had difficulty in expressing himself and asked for pen and paper, but was unable to write. When one of his friends offered to act for him and asked what he should write, the reply was, 'Nothing, but that *God is with us*'. It was clear that something else lay on his mind, and after a struggle he asked, 'Where is my sermon on the Love of God? Take it and spread it abroad.'

This appears to have been John Wesley's last reference to preaching, and it reveals his longing not only to 'preach Him in death', as he had so often desired in song, but to continue preaching Him when death was passed; to preach the one thing that had come to matter—'my sermon on *the Love of God*'. It can still be read.[5] The actual title is *God's Love to Fallen Man*, and in obedience to the author's dying desire 10,000 copies were later printed and given away.

The Love of God! Of all his preaching, all his texts, this it was that stood out at the end, alone and glorious. All those other subjects on which he had so often discoursed—Riches, Education, Health, Sleep, Dress, Marriage—even the great doctrines of orthodox faith and 'our Doctrines', yielded at last to what matters above them all—the Love of God. Refuse or deny that Love, and all else becomes of little account. It is not by the *beliefs* but by the *acceptances* of religion that men are 'saved'.

[5] *Works*, VI.231.

Accept, then, this Love of God; take this free gift into your heart in all its richness, its beauty, its power to raise the dead to life, and all else follows; all else will take its rightful place. There could have been no Wesley hymns with immortality in the heart of them, had not the Love of God been their prevailing theme. How often had John's heart been moved by those old German hymns, that somehow make that Love so real, and how superbly he had translated them to enrich both the singing and the experience of his Methodists!

> O Love, how cheering is thy ray;
>   All pain before thy presence flies,
> Care, anguish, sorrow, melt away,
>   Where'er thy healing beams arise:
> O Jesu, nothing may I see,
> Nothing desire, or seek, but Thee.[6]

And there was that hymn by Brother Charles, that Isaac Watts held to be superior to anything he himself had written:

> 'Tis Love! 'tis Love! Thou diedst for me!
>   I hear thy whisper in my heart:
> The morning breaks, the shadows flee,
>   Pure, universal Love Thou art;
> To me, to all, Thy mercies move;
> Thy Nature and Thy name is Love.[7]

But it was not a Love to be absorbed and expended in a cloistered, self-regarding mysticism; that was alien to all he had ever preached. '*Take it and spread it abroad*', for

> The Love of Christ doth me constrain
> To seek the wandering souls of men.[8]

> Outcasts of men, to you I call.[9]

It was all there in the *Choice*; that Choice sealed in the open air where the 'outcasts of men' were to be found, and adhered to right to that October afternoon under the oak tree at Winchelsea. It was a fair summary of his life's work, as pictures out of the long past emerged and dissolved before him; and as he passed 'to where beyond these voices there is peace', the exquisite beauty of the Benediction was radiant in his soul: The *Grace* of our Lord Jesus Christ, and the *Love* of God, and the *Fellowship* of the Holy Spirit! Yes! The choice made in diffidence had issued in almost

[6] *M.H.B.*, No. 430.   [7] ibid., No. 339.   [8] ibid., No. 783.   [9] ibid., No. 361.

unbelievable achievement, and, triumphant above all, there was *Methodism*, bearing the sign-manual of God's approval and big with a promise that the years were to fulfil. So, at the end, the oft-expressed desire of his heart was granted to him:

> Happy, if with my latest breath
> I may but gasp his name!,[10]

and, praising his Maker, John Wesley passed to prove the truth that he had so often preached:

> Stands our City on a Rock,
> On the Rock of Heavenly Love.[11]

[10] *M.H.B.*, No. 92.   [11] *P.W.*, VI.44; *M.H.B.* (1779), No. 65.

INDEX OF NAMES

ANNESLEY, DR SAMUEL, 5
Arnold, Matthew, 139-40
Atlay, John, 169

BENNET, JOHN, 43
Benson, Joseph, 192
Berridge, John, 132
Bishop, Mary, 173
Black, William, 201, 205
Blackstone, William, 108
Blackwell, Ebenezer, 64, 174
Blake, William, 94
Böhler, Peter, 20ff., 28
Brackenbury, R. C., 177
Bradburn, Samuel, 169
Bradford, Joseph, 202
Buckley, Thomas, 110
Buffon, G. de, 140
Bunyan, John, 156
Burdsall, Richard, 198
Burton, Dr, 14f.
Butler, Joseph, 40
Butler, Samuel, 45
Butts, Thomas, 135

CARVER, ROBERT, 162
Chapman, Mrs, 16
Chesterfield, Lord, 93
Church, Thomas, 128
Cicero, 151
Clay, Sarah, 111
Coke, Thomas, 169
Cole and Postgate, 99
Combe, William, 98
Cordeux, Rev., 113
Cowper, William, 124, 195
Crabbe, George, 200
Creighton, James, 169
Curnock, Nehemiah, 17, 63, 168, 185

DEMOSTHENES, 151
Dimond, S. G., 131
Dobinson, Mrs, 196
Dobrée, Bonamy, 80

ENTWISLE, JOSEPH, 163
Epicurus, 88
Everett, James, 166

FIELDING, HENRY, 93, 99
Furly, Samuel, 141ff.

GAMBOLD, JOHN, 24
Gee, Joseph, 202
Gibson, Bishop Edmund, 32
Goethe, 140
Goldsmith, Oliver, 93
Green, Richard, 12, 88
Griffiths, Robin, 10
Grimshaw, William, 53, 132, 152
Gwynne Stephen, 126

HAIME, JOHN, 70
Hampson, John, 145, 153
Harris, Howell, 66, 121
Herbert, George, 6, 150
Hervey, James, 48
Heylyn, Dr, 12
Hill, Richard, 97
Hilton, John, 192
Hogarth, William, 30, 58
Homer, 148
Hopper, Christopher, 43
Hotham, Sir Charles, 73
Hunter, William, 117
Hutton, James, 16, 23, 26, 39, 66

IGNATIUS, 81
Ingham, Benjamin, 13, 26, 31
Inman, Rev., 5f.
Ironside, Bishop Gilbert, 2

JEFFRIES, DAVID, 120
Johnson, Dr Samuel, 140
Junius, 103

KENNICOTT, DR, 107
Kinchin, Charles, 21, 22
King, John, 148
Koker, Dr, 33

LA ROCHE, SOPHIE V., 205
Law, William, 24
Letts, Thomas, 12
Liden, Professor J. H., 112f.
Lyth, John, 198-9

MACAULAY, LORD, 126
Mallet, Sarah, 148
Marzials, Thomas, 163

INDEX OF NAMES

Mason, John, 194
Mason, Rebecca, 121
Mather, Alexander, 117
Maxfield, Thomas, 7
Moira, Earl of, 196
Moore, Henry, 170, 202
Mort, James, 111f.
Moss, Richard, 119
Moss, Robert, 113f.

NELSON, JOHN, 42-3, 115ff.
Newton, John, 124, 204
Nind, Sally, 196

OGLETHORPE, GENERAL, 14
Osborn, George, 112

PATER, WALTER, 139
Paul, St, 36
Pope, Alexander, 99
Potter, Bishop John, 9, 10, 32

RALEIGH, SIR WALTER, 140
Rankin, Thomas, 118
Rattenbury, J. E., 21
Rea, James, 52
Ritchie, Elizabeth, 130, 197, 208
Robinson, Henry Crabb, 199-200
Rogers, James, 204
Rogers, Mrs, 208
Rogers, Dr, 17
Rutherford, Dr Thomas, 133
Rutherford, Thomas, 117

SACK, MESSRS, OF BERLIN, 162
Sampson, George, 208
Sassoon, Siegfried, 70
Saunderson, Hugh, 192
Scott, Sir Walter, 198
Sharp, Archdeacon, 49
Sharpe, Archbishop of York, 4

Shent, William, 43
Shepherd, Mary Freeman, 124
Shepherd, T. B., 75
'Smith, John', 50
Smollett, Tobias, 74
Staniforth, Sampson, 70
Steel, Richard, 90
Summerhill, Dame, 110

TAYLOR, ISAAC, 41
Taylor, Thomas, 152, 201
Tennant, Thomas, 118
Tholuck, Dr, 163
Told, Silas, 122
Tripp, Thomas, 76
Tyerman, Luke, 11, 43

USHER, ARCHBISHOP, 193

VIRGIL, 159
Vulliamy, C. E., 70

WALKER, GEORGE, 110
Walker, Samuel, 136, 179
Walpole, Horace, 74, 125
Webb, William, 109
Wesley, Bartholomew, 1, 37
  Charles, *passim*.
  Hetty, 10
  John (Senr), 1, 2, 37
  John, *passim*.
  Samuel (Senr), 3, 37, 66, 85
  Samuel (Jr), 5, 30
  Susanna, 5, 26, 38
White, John, 3
Whitefield, George, 12, 33-4, 44, 57, 132
  197
Wilkes, John, 103
Williams, Ethel C., 9
Williams, Thomas, 43
Winter, Robert, 120
Wood, Charles, 112
Wride, Thomas, 149, 191
Wycliffe, 36

GENERAL INDEX

ANACREON, 200
Arminianism, 3, 32

BAPTISMAL REGENERATION, 102
Book of Common Prayer, 136
Business, 101

CALVINISM, 101
Canon Law, 49
Chapels, Methodist, 53
Children, 191
Cleanliness, 53
Common people, the 72-3, 79
Conference, Methodist, 29, 49, 50, 68, 89, 168-9, 205
Congregations, 57ff.
Controversy (religious), 61, 101
Conversation, 101
Courtesy, 96f.
Crime, 67

DECEIT, 100
Deism, 102
Dreams, 123
Dress, 90
Drunkards, 100

ELECTIONS, 104
Executions, 67ff.

FIELD-PREACHING, 45ff.
Fits, 131ff.
Flattery, 100
Food, 100-1

GESTURE, 149ff.
Gordon Riots, 74

HEALTH, 89
Hell, 106
Holy Club, 11, 21, 24
Homilies, the, 17
Hooligans, 74ff.

ILLUSTRATIONS, SERMON, 153ff.
Indians, American, 15, 19, 27
Itinerancy, 179

LEISURE, 101
Lollards, 36
Lots, 34

Luxury, 100
Lying, 100

MARRIAGE, 92
Methodists, 58
Mobs, 74ff.
Money, 94
Moravians, 13, 20, 22, 24, 26, 28, 30, 33, 102
Music, 101
Mythology, 155

NATURAL SCENERY, 54

PARABLES, 155
Pastimes, 101
Politics, 102ff.
Poor, the, 72-3
Prayer, 21, 101
Preaching, early morning, 168ff.
 frequency, 178
Prisoners, 66ff.
Profanity, 101
Pulpits, 52f.
Punishment, 106

QUOTATIONS IN SERMONS, 158

READING, 101
Roman Catholicism, 64, 74, 77, 80, 120

SERMONS, 84ff., 138f.
 Gospel, 173ff.
 long, 177
 old, 181
 published, 160ff.
Services (religious), 136
Sleep, 89
Sloth, 100-1
Slovenliness, 90
Smuggling, 98
Soldiers, 69ff.
Stillness, 102
Style, 139ff.

TEMPERANCE, 99f.

VOICE, 146ff.
Voting, 104

WILL, MAKING A, 96
Workhouses, 69

www.ingramcontent.com/pod-product-compliance
Lightning Source LLC
Chambersburg PA
CBHW070315230426
43663CB00011B/2141